The Baker's Dozen

The Cole Foundation Collection: Volume III

Dr. Harris "Cole" Vernick

Special thanks to Margaret and Team Pearl of Author House
for the last minute arrangements prior to publication, allowing for the
special dedication to those effected by the ecological catastrophe currently
being experienced in the waters of the Gulf of Mexico – 2010.

authorHOUSE®

AuthorHouse™
1663 Liberty Drive
Bloomington, IN 47403
www.authorhouse.com
Phone: 1-800-839-8640

First published by AuthorHouse 10/21/2010

ISBN: 978-1-4490-9748-6 (sc)

Library of Congress Control Number: 2007909106

Printed in the United States of America
Bloomington, Indiana

This book is printed on acid-free paper.

THE COLE FOUNDATION
FOR THE ARTS

The Publication of this book is
Supported by a grant from the
Cole Foundation for the Arts

Logo Designed By: Joshua A. Bohm

As this poetic trilogy closes, a new chapter in human history unfolds. Man-made disaster in the waters of the Gulf of Mexico, threatens all life along its coasts, and if an answer is not soon found, the world and its oceans will be forever changed in ways which stagger the imagination This event has already cost innocent lives; impacted many livelihoods; human health is compromised; sea creatures are suffering and dying. At and beyond ground zero, the only thing we can do is hope and pray that mankind will find a way to correct that which has come about through faulty human planning. Tracking reports may be observed at: oilspill.skytruth.org Current estimated gallons spilled can be found at PBS.org

One of our poets in this volume, Professor Christopher Rhodes who has earned the distinction of becoming the youngest professor of physical chemistry in the UK, and who has worked in the aftermath of the Chernobyl nuclear disaster, wrote prophetically, about such ecological catastrophe as we are now experiencing, in a poem titled *The Oil of Progress* (page 229).

In closing this final Volume III, is dedicated to the people and wildlife who live near and depend upon the waters of the Gulf of Mexico, and beyond, in the years to come - the only way a poet knows how: by sharing heart felt thoughts, from pen in hand, to paper – on July 9th, 2010. Also, to those involved in finding the needed answers to this tragedy, a heart felt wished, God's speed.

A Fragile Planet Deeply Sighs
Maxene A. Alexander – Executive Editor
(Free Verse)

Silently, watches our world
as the waters of the Gulf of Mexico
struggle beneath, a burden deep
caused by those upon the land

In the home of the brave and the free
J.L. Seagull, the first to be
Trapped in a dying world
born of man's greed

Let us pray, and may our prayers be heard
each to God, as we each know - our God to be

May we find the peace that poets seek
and come to understand the harmony
of the earth beneath our humble feet
and may a wisdom reign, our earth to keep

In the name of all that is good and holy
a fragile planet deeply sighs … Amen

The Death Throes of J.L. Seagull
Dr. Harris "Cole" Vernick – Cole Foundation Editor
(Tanka)

seagull, my seagull
dying of man's greed disease
I mourn you J.L.
What shall I tell my children?
I knew you once wild and free!

Defining The Bakers Dozen Trilogy

As this trilogy closes with Volume III, some concluding ponderings emerge: With the Internet and the World Wide Web having become an every day occurrence for many worldwide, the early twenty-first century becomes the first time in history that poets from around the world may gather together and share their artistry through various multi and genre-specific website workshops. It was while participating in such workshops that Dr. Harris "Cole" Vernick; poet, art appreciator, patron of the arts, and retired physician, discovered talented poets from all walks of life in various geographical locations throughout the world. Recognizing many were deserving of being published, he created the Baker's Dozen Trilogy and gifted 38 poets with merit-based scholarship publication. This has resulted in the first publication of its kind where each book in the trilogy represents 13 authors through individually formatted books of their poetry as they each envisioned their individual publication, under one collective cover, through merit-based scholarship. In this final volume, Dr. Vernick gifts his fellow poets and others who enjoy poetry, with a sampling of his own work which is appropriately titled: *Eclecticism*.

While the series has been completed with the help of three talented self-made editors who assisted in the complex electronic documentation and final polishing required of such a manuscript for publication; the poetry of each author remains pristine, none have had their poetic expressions altered in any way, resulting in a true reflection of individual talents. Additionally, each author's book is illustrated using caricature through commissioned artwork done by a professional graphic artist from South Africa.

This trilogy becomes unique for all the above stated reasons, as well as for the fact that other than through electronic correspondence, the majority of the 39 poets involved in this project - have never actually met. Present day technology allows our trilogy to become a historical first in the world of publishing and also well demonstrates what may be done in the arts beyond the challenges of any one single artist's geographical, social and communication boundaries. It has been said that a good book may place the world at one's feet and take the imagination far and away from the beaten path. Today's technology literally places worldwide; information, people, and inspiration at one's fingertips, making such a trilogy as this possible.

Gifted by a patron of the arts, The Baker's Dozen Trilogy is the first and only merit based scholarship publication of its kind, offering multi-genre poetry in illustrated individual mini-book format, and representing contemporary poets from around the world. Such a work serves to help define the productive use of modern technology in the world of literary arts - in a world where artists are no longer separated by geographical and social boundaries.

In addition to serving as Executive Editor for this trilogy, I was also one of the merit-based scholarship poets in Volume One. It has been my pleasure to know through correspondence, and to bring together, all thirty-nine very talented poets and assist them in their literary goals. Having never envisioned such an accomplishment, I will always have deepest gratitude for having had the opportunity to work with Dr. Vernick in completing his artistic vision through this first of its kind publication. For his past and continuing altruistic efforts in the arts, he remains, the most amazing man, and arts benefactor, I have never met,

Maxene A. Alexander, Executive Editor

INTRODUCTION

By Dr. Harris "Cole" Vernick

Perhaps the hardest task for me, as a Writer, has been and is, putting together this last introduction for Volume Three of the Baker's Dozen Trilogy. From the vaults of my mind where I imagine my explosions of thought interact with blockers and erasers - finally, phrases are created, and left to stand, stored in those vaults according to the emotion stirred, along with the importance of what I want to say ... only then, are the vaults unsealed and brought to paper.

I have to say that this last introduction finds me experiencing both happiness as well as some sadness because while I introduce the work of the of another thirty-nine excellent poets, I also finish and come to the end of years of work. This final volume of poetry represents the end of a dream conceived by me. A dream that became shared, carried, and nursed along to fruition by the greatest of editors in my estimation. My editors, Maxene Alexander, Yvonne Crain and Vivienne Harding are also people I consider as my most unusual, and important, friends. We are four friends who met on the Internet, we communicate quite often, and yet uniquely – we have never met. Our friendship, and our work is truly the product of Internet-technology as it was known in the early twenty first century. The World Wide Web brought together this dreamer from New Jersey with fellow dreamers, Maxene Alexander from Florida, Yvonne Crain from California and Vivienne Harding from South Africa. The four of us shared a need to gift the poetic art and beauty of poets from around the world- to readers, and art appreciators around the world.

Volume Three, like the previous two, reflects the hearts and minds of its authors in this art called poetry. The thirteen poets in this, and all three volumes, were discovered on the Internet over time and through various web sites. I have personally observed, read, critiqued, and finally approached each one, asking them to be part of this dream through merit-based scholarship. Each poet has contributed an individual mini-book representing some of the best of their work, and these final works have been selected and presented in a trilogy which now represents poets from around the world - from all walks of life.

While there is some sadness for me in this dream ending, there is also healing as a new dream begins. One of my Volume One poets, Sue DuBois, has gifted all of us with a new Internet poetry site called poetsview.com - it is a site where poets can come to introduce their work to our world at no charge, and join with other artists, movie producers, photographers, painters, prose writers in a place truly designed to meet all our wishes and needs. It is international in aspect and brings together every style of writing from almost every country of the world. Many of the poets of the Baker's Dozen Trilogy are actively involved in this newest dream.

I do have to admit that I hold all these poets in my heart, and especially my editors because in accomplishing this dream through merit based awards from the Cole Foundation given to these selected few, I have found out it was really a gift to myself. It enabled me to accomplish something that years ago, seemed my impossible dream.

Without further ado - as our genius mentor Shakespeare would have said: let me re-introduce the wonderful poets of Volumes One and Two and tell you something about these final thirteen poets in Volume Three.

Trilogy Editors

Maxene A. Alexander - Executive Editor
Yvonne Marie Crain - Senior Editor
Vivienne L. Harding - Managing Editor

Volume One Poets (2006)

Vivienne Lorraine Harding - EXPRESSIONS OF MY SOUL
Maxene A. Alexander - THE ART OF JAPANESE POETRY
Levan Tatishvili - VIGOR OF PEGASUS OR PATH TO HELICON
Sheila R. Weber - FROM THE HEART
Sheryl Anne Bright - STORM-TOSSED MUSINGS AND SUN-KISSED WHIMSIES
Connie Minshew - COME ON IN --THE WATER'S FINE!
Rachel C. Nicholson - LULLABY MY REQUIEM
Barbara V. Fidler - TREASURES FROM MY HEART ~ ROMANTIC POETRY
Robert Allen Burd – SENSATIONS
Mattie Sue Dubois - JOURNEY THROUGH THE MYSTICAL WORLDS OF POETRY
Lauren E. Kammerer - FOR THE LOVE OF LIFE
Yvonne Marie Crain - YVONNE'S WORLD OF POETRY
Elaine Duffy Ashley - PERCEPTIONS IN POETRY

Volume Two Poets (2007)

Thomas Teti - THUNDER IN THE SUNRISE
Thelma Maxwell - IN BETWEEN TIMES
Lil Mac Dermott - IRISH LIFE LOVE LAUGHTER & TEARS
Suzanne S. Walker - NIGHT'S CATCH OF DREAMS
Christopher William Cianci - POETIC VERDIGRIS
Jenny Buzzard - SHADOWS OF THOUGHT
Ginger Erickson-Johnsen - A GLIMPSE INTO A TORMENTED MIND
Darell V. Hine - SILHOUETTES WET FROM CREATION
Charmaine Elizabeth Lloyd - CHARMAINE'S SONG
Deborah D. Cashwell - REFLECTIVE PONDERINGS
Robert Crockett - PEBBLES OF THOUGHT
Helen Michele McManus - ECHOES ON THE WIND
Robert Joseph Hughes - MY SOUL AND ME ALONE

VOLUME THREE POETS

Kuniharu Shimizu - THE EGG-SHAPED STONE

Volume three opens with the poetry of Kuniharu Shimizu. In my estimation, Kuni-San is a true haiku master. At the time of this publication, he serves as Advisor to the World Haiku Association and Judge of their monthly Haiga Contests. I am very proud to have Kuniharu Shimizu join the poets of Volume Three.

Special thanks is given to Professor Shirane, Shincho Professor of Japanese Literature at Columbia University for his gifting of this mini-book's conclusion, *Basho, Buson & Modern Haiku Myths* - an award-winning essay offered here with kind permission from Professor Shirane, for those seeking knowledge of (and inspiration from) the art of Japanese poetry

Donna Leviash Al-Mahadin - VEILED TRANSPARENCIES

Donna Leviash Al-Mahadin has been writing on many of the poetry web sites that I have also participated in over a number of years. She writes under the pen name of Karima Hassan. Donna brings us several cultures in her writing. There is American, Jordanian and Costo-Rican experience in her magical writing. She is the author of two published books that bring us her tri-nationality.

Trenton T. Battle - THE PERCEPTIONS OF A POET

Trenton Battle, is a warrior, or what he describes as a humble soldier for God. His life and work is based on the goodness of peace, and on love. Trenton writes most definitely from his soul and we are delighted to have this published poet with us.

Billie Beck - BILLIE'S BOOK OF POETIC MEMORIES

Billie Beck brings the experience of the Midwest into her poetry. She is accomplished in a number of styles, and here we will experience and enjoy her observations and reflections which span many years from the Great Depression through today's modern world.

Allen Gail Brady - OF GRACE AND GRATITUDE

Alan Brady passed from this world prior to publication. Many of us were fortunate enough to experience his exuberance for life while we wrote with him and we are grateful that he prepared this manuscript for Volume Three. Alan's strength and courage, makes him a role model for all of us.

Amanda Dawn Vanessa Cianci - POETRY RAQS!

In addition to being an excellent poetess - Amanda Cianci is also our trilogy's love story. In the course of publication, she met and married fellow poet Christopher William Cianci from Volume Two. A Canadian by birth, Amanda brings us the love, and art, of Bellydance into her writings. It is a true pleasure to share her artistry.

Joy Ann C. Lara - ROOTS AND WINGS
Joy Ann Laura writes under the name JJG Cabanos. I actually found Joy when she read her work at a poetry reading in Fanwood, New Jersey. She is an accomplished artist in both painting and poetry and often brings both talents together into her work.

Mary Merryweather Travis - WALKING WITH WORDS
Maryanne Merryweather-Travis comes to us from the UK. Her interest in writing was interrupted by her role as mother and now this previously published author is back to work bringing us poetry that is a pleasure to read.

Christopher James Rhodes - FRESH LANDS
Professor Christopher James Rhodes is a physical chemist with many published scientific articles. He has a strong interest in environmental issues. His interest in poetry is of long experience and we can now enjoy the art of this scientist. Professor Rhodes also recently has published a novel titled University Shambles (2009).

Sarah True - COME WALK WITH ME AWHILE
Sarah True brings us her combined experience drawn from both motherhood, and professional Nursing. She has lived in Texas, Virginia, and Pennsylvania and she offers a number of styles she favors, including an interest in the dark-side. Sarah True is a real pleasure to read.

Barbara Truncellito - AFFAIRS OF THE HEART
Barbara Truncellito is one of the few poets I have actually met more then once. We share an island for our summer home and I attend her readings there with much joy at her skill. She very readily shares with us her feelings about family and friends and is an amazing reader of her work.

Joree Williams - TAPESTRY OF LIFE
Joree Williams has literally been with me on every poetry site where I have critiqued or submitted my own work. Joree brings us poetry inspired by many of her experiences in life, even those that were extremely painful.

Dr. Harris "Cole" Vernick – ECLECTICISM
Dr. Vernick has asked me, his Executive Editor, to say a few words of introduction on his behalf. Cole, as he prefers to be addressed, has been an art collector/appreciator for over fifty years and so the title of his work, Eclecticism, is well suited. The poetry of our benefactor reflects many life experiences from the perspective of a well-respected physician, as well as a devoted husband, father, and grandfather. He is poet in truest sense of the word and serves well as mentor for those seeking to refine their literary talents. His poetry – speaks for itself.

When Cole began this project so many years ago, it was with the hopes of elevating poetry to its rightful status. I believe we have collectively discovered that poetry is - alive and well in the hearts and minds of people everywhere.

TABLE OF CONTENTS

The Egg-Shaped Stone

by
Kuniharu Shimizu

Mountain Poet ~ Touching the Sea ~ On a Postcard

Kuniharu Shimizu

山の詩人ポストカードの海に触れ

About the Author

Born in Tenri, Nara, Japan in 1949, Kuniharu Shimizu moved to Hawaii at the age of 15. He returned to Japan in 1972 upon receiving his Bachelor of Fine Arts in painting from the University of Hawaii. Kuniharu continues to successfully pursue his creative efforts in the fine arts, which include graphic, editorial, and monument design as well as exhibition planning.

- Artistic Awards include: The Purchase Award at Artist of Hawaii Exhibition (Purchased for the permanent collection of the Academy of Art in Honolulu); 1st Place in Ichiretu-kai Scholarship Foundation Logo Mark Contest; and 1st Place in Japan Toy Association Logo Mark Contest.

- Haiku Awards include: Valentine Awards (2003 and 2004; Special Mention (Heron's Nest); Second Prize in "Best of 2003"(Mainichi Daily News); Special Prize at the Mongolian Spring Festival Haiku Contest in Tokyo, April 2007; and Merit Based Scholarship Publishing through the Cole Foundation for The Arts in *The Baker's Dozen – Volume III*.

In 2000, Kuniharu Shimizu designed and continues to operate the website project *See Haiku Here* (link provided below). This is a world wide exhibition of Haiga (illustrated haiku) accomplished through the collaborative efforts of over 250 international haijin (haiku poets). By the end of 2006 the collections in this exhibition numbered a total of one thousand.

Kuniharu Shimizu is currently the well-respected advisor to The World Haiku Association and Judge of the WHA Monthly Haiga Contest. Just prior to the publication of the Baker's Dozen Volume III, Kuniharu has completed four electronic books in which he offers Japanese poetry written by several haijin artists. The titles are: Wind, Water, Light, and Life. He is currently working on a publication of Basho's Narrow Road to the Deep North.

Websites:

- *See Haiku* http://www.seehaikuhere.blogspot.com/
- *The World Haiku Association* http://www.worldhaiku.net/

Editorial Note:

Both artist and poet, Kuniharu Shimizu is well schooled in the art of Japanese poetry bringing the ancient art of haiku, haiga, and haibun into present day while retaining the elements found in the many works of masters past. A master in his own right, Kuniharu is also known for being the most beloved Judge of the monthly haiga contest sponsored through the World Haiku Association based in Japan. For those students and poets seeking a deeper education and understanding of Japanese poetry the above listed web sites, along with the poetry of Kuniharu Shimizu, will provide a most valuable offering – one which embraces the art of Japanese poetry from the perspective of the land in which it was born, gifting us with further definition of these beautiful art forms which now find the passions of poets worldwide.

Maxene A. Alexander, Executive Editor - The Baker's Dozen, Volume III

Contents

The Conclusion, Basho, Buson & Modern Haiku Myths is an award-winning essay written by Haruo Shirane - Shincho Professor of Japanese Literature, Columbia University. Offered here with kindest permission from Professor Shirane, for those seeking knowledge of (and inspiration from) the art of Japanese poetry

Definition of Terms (offered by Maxene Alexander):

Haiku may be defined as a short Japanese poem (in the neighborhood of 17 syllables spanning one to three lines) that may embrace humankind, which is part of, rather than separate from, nature. Written outside of Japan, haiku may also utilize the language tools accepted in the country of origin. The term haiku is both singular and plural.

Haibun is an ancient Japanese poetic form of journaling, which may include waka/tanka, hokku/ haiku, or senryu along with narrative either before, after, or framing inner verse. This is a newly resurrected form that currently holds no strict rules regarding length or structure of narrative. As with haiku, the term haibun is both singular and plural.

Haijin is the term used for Japanese poet, or one who writes Japanese poetry (either singular or plural and either male or female).

Haiku

Winter sun
a last ray flares
from behind clouds

Wintry shore,
setting sun takes with it
blue of the sky

Stone garden —
this morning the islands
float on snow

Snow on snow,
between the layers are
buried sounds

Snowflakes...
frail lines of my pencil
dissolve into the paper

On black eyes
of a baby,
a field of virgin snow

One year older,
a boy tackles mochi (rice cake)
with long chopsticks

Oolong tea
in such a small cup
so much warmth

Mountain flowers,
still shy to face
the spring sun

Ukrainian haijin puffs...
I know what flower
he means to tell

Drawing spring breeze,
pencil lines tangle
and untangle

Morning haze…
unfocused gaze of a hundred souls
drifts in the train

Wetting my color-faded
aloha shirts,
April waves

May Day —
bees collecting nectar
from wilted azaleas

A family of carp streamers
all swimming
in the same direction

Commencement day
wind not strong enough
to flutter the flag

All day rain —
she detects
a stolen puff

Flood subsiding,
pieces of paper and vinyl
decorate tree branches

Downpour,
pickpocket and I are
under the same roof

Summer breeze
across the rice paddies,
a hint of cow feces

Left unplanted —
young rice plants
still so green

Coming to the thicket,
summer wind
suddenly audible

Summer afternoon,
nuns giggle
in a dim corridor

Studio window,
a fly walks
from cloud to cloud

A lone child—
hundreds of soap bubbles
befriend her

Cityscape—
almost unnoticed reflection
of a pristine sky

Kenyan stars glitter
in the sky
in children's eyes

Country road,
I quietly cross
the Equator

Holidays over,
dry roses
on the secretary's desk

Morning cool …
silhouettes of the faithful
murmuring chants

Cool chapel,
icon silently receives
kissing and hugging

Misty morning,
tips of pine needles
round with dew

The three-year-old child
in you and me,
chasing the dragonflies again

Much chirping —
sparrows settle on the wire
evenly spaced

Grasshoppers jump
and crickets sing—
bankrupt amusement park

Kyoto temple
and yet, tourists admire
the setting sun

Waiting for a night train,
a long platform
all to myself

Drawing circles,
finally one deformed enough
to be the earth

Black smoke
billows up into
God's eye

September night
dust and smoke
hide so many stars

Distant stars
calmly watching
earthly turmoil

Late night chill—
gazing at the distant stars
I think of NY friends

His life, and then
her life gone ...
distant fireworks

Funeral bouquet,
her monochrome photo
amid pink and purple

Funeral over,
traces of tears wiped
from my spectacles

Sunflowers wither
leaving seeds
embedded with hope

Blue sky…
always there
to fill in the loss

Manhattan skyline—
I gather egg-shaped stones
by the river

Security check —
a lady without shoes
waits for her turn
(LA Airport)

Even seagulls
assume eagle-like stare —
water's edge of this land

Hollywood pavement,
I pick up city dust
from stars' handprints

Little Tokyo,
a throng of people lines up
for fallen leaf-like meat
(shabu-shabu restaurant)

Almost admirable —
sprayed graffiti high above
at an impossible place

Neatly lined teeth
and tanned faces,
sun-kissed people grin

Haibun

Travelers' Treat
Published: Frogpond & American Haibun & Haiga (2003)

A mountain haijin has come to the seaside. I am at a hot spring along the coast of the Japan Sea (a twelve hour train ride from my town). The spring is located in the open, right by the beach. A few steps away is the wide, wide expanse of the Japan Sea. I watch the huge sunset as I warm myself in the hot water.

> *Calm sea...*
> *a boat's wake*
> *leads to the setting sun*

Basho walked along this beach on his "Narrow Road of Oku" and wrote the following haiku:

> *The rough sea —*
> *flowing toward Sado Island*
> *the river of Heaven*

Sado is too far to see from where I am. And I do not stay outside to observe the river of heaven, the Milky Way. I have a party to attend and, having been in the hot spring too long, I am more attracted to cold beer and sake.

> *A treat for travelers,*
> *milk for Basho*
> *and sake for me*

Ending

Published: American Haibun & Haiga (2004)

Matsumoto-san is a sweet old man. He sends me some haiku every three months or so and I make one or two haiga from the batch. He likes to frame the haiga so I send him printouts with my hanko and signature. In return, he sends me a gift, a box of English tea one time and of some expensive European chocolate another.

Occasionally, he calls me on the phone. He has some kind of lung disease so he cannot speak for too long. He speaks little by little but with a clear and crisp typical Tokyo dialect. Our conversation is almost entirely one way--he talks about his haiku and I listen. Then ~

> *Year's end phone call —*
> *the aged haijin clicks off*
> *at my "so, how is...?"*

I am used to such conversation. My father, who is the same age as Matsumoto-san, does the same. Usually we "talk" over sake. I just keep on drinking sake, ending up more drunken than my father, and usually pretty badly hung over next morning.

> *Year ending —*
> *with a long stream of clouds*
> *Mt. Fuji runs*

At the beginning of last autumn, Matsumoto-san sent me a new batch. I picked one and made a haiga. I edited his haiku, switching a few words and providing an English translation:

> *June rain passing...*
> *baking scent of*
> *doll cookies lingers*

As usual, I made a printout and sent it to him. As usual, he sent me a gift. As usual, he called me, confirming that the gift had arrived OK and expressing gratitude for the correction. And then, as usual, he was gone.

A few months passed. One December day, I received a letter. It was from Matsumoto-san's wife. Only then I learned that Matsumoto-san had passed away the month before. I decided to add my own haiku to his doll haiga:

> Passing November rain...
> something departs from an un-owned doll

The Egg-Shaped Stone

Published in *Ginyu*
An International Haiku Magazine (No. 22, April 2004)

Quiet morning. Snow still fresh on the park ground. A group of youngsters, probably members of a school track team, jogs nearby. Their joyful chatting comes and goes. I am at the west bank of Hudson River. For a while I stand still, my gaze fixed on the lone spire of the Empire State Building.

> *Clear day —*
> *loud unheard voices*
> *still hang in the air*

> *Freezing park -*
> *my urine reminds me*
> *how warm I am*

Another cold day in NYC. I'm traveling with a cameraman on a magazine assignment. We pick a spot by the Brooklyn Bridge, one of the oldest landmarks in the city. Stones weathered round by the centuries roll beneath my feet. I pick some up to take home.

> *Twin grandchildren gone —*
> *old Brooklyn Bridge bears up*
> *in the wind chill*

> *Manhattan skyline —*
> *I gather egg-shaped stones*
> *by the river*

We walk the streets of Lower Manhattan down to Chinatown. Suddenly, we are in a whole new world. Let's have lunch here. Let's eat like the locals. Our guide leads us through narrow side streets to a restaurant packed with hungry Chinese. We try the guide's recommendation -- steamed rice topped with minced meat of beef and salted fish. The smell hits us hard. Shit-like smell of the salted fish. Our high expectations quickly wane, and after a few bites we give up.

> *Street performance —*
> *a red creature waits*
> *for its turn*

One of our assignments is to photograph notable examples of store renovation. We walk around the SOHO district, looking for possibilities, like The Apple Store. Originally a post office, then a hardware shop, the building now houses a flashy computer store. No photograph, the storekeeper says, for security reasons. We move on and try Prada. Talk to the head office first, says the manager. No time, we leave early next morning.

SOHO show window,
the sunlit ass
of a naked mannequin

Mannequins are the best dressers in town. They enjoy the latest fashions, always one or two steps ahead of city folks. We are still in SOHO. The sun is a little warmer today. For our enjoyment: colorful spring collections for the eyes, and a bit of sunshine for the cold bodies.

Cityscape,
almost unnoticed reflection
of a pristine sky

There's a student show at the art gallery. One of the exhibits is a telephone sculpture, made up of scores of handsets connected with wire, resembling tangled spaghetti. The same space houses concerts and other kinds of exhibits. Each time an event is held, the sculpture which dominates the limited space is pushed into a corner to make room, then put back once the event is over. This expansion and contraction occurs almost everyday, like a kind of organism. That is probably not the intended conception of the artwork, but it is that aspect which intrigues me.

Midnight gallery,
a telephone sculpture
comes alive again

I am home with the egg-shaped stones of New York. When I pocketed them, they held their icy cold for a long time. The air is a lot warmer here at home. Life in them seems to be getting ready to come forth.

Hatching from
egg-shaped stones...
NY haiku, and more

A Spring Day

Three cold days, four warm. That's how March is around here -- a bit warm, a bit cold, gathering spring in small steps.

Today is warm, and a holiday. I wake early. As I walk up to my studio, I notice Ume flowers are blooming. A pair of bush warblers are busily sucking the nectar, not minding me. I watch for a long while, also knowing the joy of a fresh breakfast.

> *Decorated by flowers*
> *and visited by birds,*
> *this aged ume branch*

I check my e-mail. The daughter of a recently deceased haijin has sent permission to use the haijin's haiku for my haiga. I upload the haiga on my website, and in a while some ideas begin to form. Three haiga materialize, two don't. All the while my radio is tuned to my usual FM station.

> *A mega-hit song*
> *after so many springs*
> *still stings my heart*

Suddenly, light falls on my working desk, almost spotlighting me in a dim room. It's the early evening sunlight reflected from a neighbor's window. Time to go home. The air is different -- looks like tomorrow will be one of the cold days.

Worldman

Web-Published: Contemporary Haibun Online
(September 2007, Vol. 3 No. 3)

At an obscure corner of my large bookshelf, I find my high school yearbook. Picking it up, I puffed a few times to blow dust off the cover. It's been almost 40 years since I graduated from McKinley High School in Honolulu, the class of 1968.

Flipping through the pages, looking at smiling faces of boys and girls, and reading brief well-wishing messages written by my school friends, I become interested in finding out how they are doing now. I have long lost contact with them so I begin to do web searching.

I do not bother with girls, for they probably no longer go by their maiden names, and besides I knew so few, having been a shy boy then. Though very few, I find a message written by the homecoming queen. How I got it, I cannot remember now. Good looking girl like her surely have married and go by different name now. So, I decide to pick only boys names like Richard Nagatomo, Russell Higa, Edmond Ching, Dickson Lau, William Torabio, Leo Keone, Leslie Kuebitz, Dexter Puluti, Jerry Fitzgerald (no relation to F. Scott Fitzgerald, obviously), and Howard Palmerton.

None hits.

Well, to be exact, there are some hits, like Howard Palmerton, but the search result is something about Dr. Howard Palmerton, and that Palmerton, who ridiculed me for not knowing the local slang for masturbation, whom I helped gotten through his pre-algebra class, and who had trouble disassembling and reassembling the ROTC rifle, could never have made a doctor. No, this is a different guy.

Howard was the kind of guys I hanged around. I was, then, like just off the boat (I actually took a ship to come to Hawaii from Yokohama, a seven-day ocean trip), going through miserable high school life: I was struggling with English, was under constant puzzlements about school life in America. Howard and the likes made fun of me but were also helpful in my getting used to the foreign environment.

Back on the yearbook, I come to the page about the student council. Yes, I know one more guy, the president of McKinley Student Council. His name is Worldman Kimm, and we were in the same physics class in our senior year. We did some experiments together and at times, he asked for my help in clarifying some concepts. He was the president, a member of National Honor Society, and only senior moving on to the Harvard University. Imagine a prospective Harvard guy asking for help from a nobody, a miserable off-the-boat student from rural Japan. I was honored and flattered. I liked him and we began to chat time to time.

A person like him must be very successful in some respectable field, with all his leadership and education, I reckon. Expecting something exciting to turn out, I do the web-search under his name. There must be many hits, line after line of related links to *Worldman*. To my surprise, however, Google provides only one link. Something about Harvard Radcliff Class of 1972 Reunion.

How come only this?

I click the link. A single webpage appears. On the left side are menu bars, and on the right is a chart of names.

What is this? It says, *In Memoriam*. Memoriam, that's impossible!

But I cannot find his name in any other part of the page so I go down the list of names until I come to *Mr. Worldman Young Ha Kimm* and next to the name is Death Date *04/27/78*.

What! He is dead already!

And he died so young, at 27 or 28. Six years after graduation with bright future ahead, and the chart tells that his life has already ended.

This finding shocks me. My expectation was to see wonderful findings, to see his name listed like, Dr. Worldman Kimm gives a lecture ... or CEO Worldman Kimm announces the merger of ... or Chairman Worldman Kimm presides over the annual convention held at ... or CNN Special world report by Worldman Kim.

 I was expecting to see something befitting his name, Worldman. A person with such a name must have made some dent in the society. Instead, in the Internet world, he has only one line: *Worldman Young Ha Kimm / Death Date 04/27/78*.

Too many years have passed already and there is no way for me to find out what happened to him. Or, maybe I do not want to know what happened and how he died. We all die some time in one way or another.

My knowing will make no difference for a man who died thirty years ago. And I cannot say I was so close to him as to miss him now. What bugs me is the old, old question as to why a good-natured, promising guy like Worldman had to die so young.

There is no easy answer, I know. After a while I come to settle on the only comfortable notion - that he has been reborn and is leading a new life somewhere.

I look at the yearbook again. On his photograph, Worldman wrote:

Kuniharu,

Good luck and best wishes
To a great physicist and person

Aloha,

Worldman

I did not turn out to be a great physicist, but at least I am trying to be a good person, good to my wife, children, grandchildren, neighbors and friends. I am positive Worldman would have been the same, too.

Even though there is only one mention of him on web, this haibun page, when picked up by a Google search engine, becomes his second link.

The second Worldman in the World Wide Web.

That is the best I can do for him.

Hope Worldman would be happy to have another presence in the Web.

Sunflowers wither
leaving seeds
embedded with dreams

Wetting my color-faded
aloha shirts,
April waves

An ox after all

"If you lie down like that, you're gonna become an ox for sure", my nanny so cautioned me again after the meal. I was three or four years old then, and I had a habit of lay down on the tatami mat soon after the meal, flipping through a children's picture book or two. My nanny was raised in a strict samurai family, thus knew all the refined manners. I guess that was what my parents thought and asked her to look after me.

Every time I heard her caution, I got scared and sat up right away. I had seen how the animal lived: in a near-by farm, there was an ox, always smelling badly, always munching something with saliva dripping from the mouth, never minding sleeping next to the dung. Yuck! I never want to become an ox.

With its swaying tail.
an ox shoos away
flies and a boy

As I got older, I learned that I had been born in the year of the ox, and became interested in my disposition, comparing with that of the ox. I learned also that the ox is a ruminant, which explains the constant munching. I came to like the dairy products, and longed for the treat of sukiyaki meal with juicy beef. The ox seems slow in motion and maybe in head as well. However, as in bullfighting, the animal makes quick but wise, and challenging moves. I made the similar move when I met a wife-to-be girl, though I am still unsure if I was as wise as the ox.

2009 is the year of the ox again, and is my fifth ox year, meaning I will be sixty when my birthday comes (12 zodiac signs x 5 = 60). I am thankful that I have made it through all these years. I contemplate my life thus far and my coming old age, just as the ox seems to do, standing still in a meadow, munching slowly. I am, however, still young enough to meet the new challenge, and I know I will make a quick and wise move 'cause I am an ox after all.

The year of oxen -
I wonder where
the red muerte is[1]

---

1   muerte is the bullfighter's red cape

Conclusion

Beyond The Haiku Moment
Basho, Buson & Modern Haiku Myths

Written by Haruo Shirane
(Shincho Professor of Japanese Literature, Columbia University)

What does North American haiku look like when observed from Japan? What kind of advice might haiku masters such as Basho and Buson give to English haiku poets? What would Basho and Buson say if they were alive today and could read English and could read haiku done by North American poets?

I think that they would be delighted to find that haiku had managed to cross the Pacific and thrive so far from its place of origin. They would be impressed with the wide variety of haiku composed by North American haiku poets and find their work most innovative. At the same time, however, they would also be struck, as I have been, by the narrow definitions of haiku found in haiku handbooks, magazines, and anthologies. I was once told that Ezra Pound's famous metro poem first published in 1913, was not haiku.

> *The apparition of these faces in the crowd:*
> *Petals on a wet, black bough.*

If I remember correctly, the reason for disqualification was that the metro poem was not about nature as we know it and that the poem was fictional or imaginary. Pound's poem may also have been ruled out since it uses an obvious metaphor: the petals are a metaphor for the apparition of the faces, or vice versa. This view of the metro poem was based on the three key definitions of haiku - haiku is about direct observation, haiku eschews metaphor, and haiku is about nature - which poets such as Basho and Buson would have seriously disputed.

Haiku as Direct Personal Experience or Observation

One of the widespread beliefs in North America is that haiku should be based upon one's own direct experience, that it must derive from one's own observations, particularly of nature. But it is important to remember that this is basically a modern view of haiku, the result, in part, of nineteenth century European realism, which had an impact on modern Japanese haiku and then was re-imported back to the West as something very Japanese. Basho, who wrote in the seventeenth century, would have not made such a distinction between direct personal experience and the imaginary, nor would he have placed higher value on fact over fiction.

Basho was first and foremost a master of haikai, or comic linked poetry. In haikai lined verse, the seventeen syllable hokku, or opening verse, is followed by a 14 syllable wakiku, or added verse, which in turn is followed by the seventeen syllable third verse, and so forth. Except for the first verse, which stood alone, each additional verse was read together with the previous verse and pushed away from the penultimate verse, or the verse prior to the previous verse. Thus, the first and second verse, the second and third verse, third and fourth verse formed independent units, each of which pushed off from the previous unit.

The joy and pleasure of haikai was that it was imaginary literature, that the poets who participated in linked verse moved from one world to the next, across time, and across space. The basic idea of linked verse was to create a new and unexpected world out of the world of the previous verse. Once could compose about one's daily life, about being an official in China, about being a warrior in the medieval period, or an aristocrat in the ancient period. The other participants in the haikai sequence joined you in that imaginary world or took you to places that you could reach on with your imagination.

One of the reasons that linked verse became so popular in the late medieval period, in the fifteenth and sixteenth centuries, when it first blossomed as a genre, was because it was a form of escape from the terrible wars that ravaged the country at the time. For samurai in the era of constant war, linked verse was like the tea ceremony; it allowed one to escape, if only for a brief time, from the world at large, from all the bloodshed. The joy of it was that one could do that in the close company of friends and companions. When the verse sequence was over, one came back to earth, to reality. The same occurred in the tea ceremony as developed by Sen no Rikyu. The tea hut took one away from the cares of this world, together with one's friends and companions.

In short, linked verse, both orthodox linked verse (renga) and its comic or casual version (haikai), was fundamentally imaginary. The hokku, or opening verse of the haikai sequence, which later became haiku, required a seasonal word, which marked the time and place of the gathering, but it too had no restrictions with regard to the question of fiction. Indeed, poets often composed on fixed topics (dai), which were established in advance. Buson, one of the great poets of haiku of the late eighteenth century, was in fact very much a studio or desk poet. He composed his poetry at home, in his study, and he often wrote about other worlds, particularly the tenth and eleventh century Heian aristocratic world and the subsequent medieval period. One of his most famous historical poems is: *Tobadono e gorokki isogu mowaki kana*, probably composed in 1776. (All translations are my own.)

> *To Toba palace*
> *5 or 6 horsemen hurry*
> *autumn tempest*

Toba palace, which immediately sets this in the Heian or early medieval period, was an imperial villa that the Cloistered Emperor Shirakawa (1053 - 1129) constructed near Kyoto in the eleventh century and that subsequently became the location of a number of political and military conspiracies. The galloping horsemen are probably warriors on some emergency mission - a sense of turmoil and urgency embodied in the season word of autumn tempest (nowaki). An American equivalent might be something like the Confederate cavalry at Gettysburg during the Civil War or the militia at Lexington during the American Revolution. The hokku creates a powerful atmosphere and a larger sense of narrative, like a scene from a medieval military epic or from a picture scroll. Another noted historical poem by Buson is: *Komabune no yorade sugiyuku kasumi kana*, composed in 1777.

> *the Korean ship*
> *not stopping passes back*
> *into the mist*

Komabune were the large Korean ships that sailed to Japan during the ancient period, bringing cargo and precious goods from the continent, a practice that had long since been discontinued by Buson's time. The Korean ship, which is offshore, appears to be heading for port but then gradually disappears into the mist (kasumi), a seasonal word for spring and one associated with dream-like atmosphere. The Korean ship passing into the spring mist creates a sense of mystery, of a romantic other, making the viewer wonder if this scene is nothing but a dream. Another example from Buson is: *inazuma ya nami moteyueru akitsushima*, composed in 1776.

lightning --
girdled by waves
islands of Japan

In this hokku, the light from the lightning (inazuma), a seasonal word for autumn associated in the ancient period with the rice harvest (ina), enables the viewer to see the waves surrounding all the islands of Akitsushima (an ancient name for Japan that originally meant the islands where rice grows richly). This is not the result of direct experience. It is a spectacular aerial view - a kind of paean to the fertility and beauty of the country - that would only be possible from far above the earth. Even the personal poems can be imaginary.

piercingly cold
stepping on my dead wife's comb
in the bedroom

The opening phrase, *mini ni shimu* (literally, to penetrate the body), is an autumn phrase that suggests the chill and sense of loneliness that sinks into the body with the arrival of the autumn cold and that here also functions as a metaphor of the poet's feelings following the death of his wife. The poem generates a novelistic scene of the widower, some time after his wife's funeral, accidentally stepping on a comb in the autumn dark, as he is about to go to bed alone. The standard interpretation is that the snapping of the comb in the bedroom brings back memories of their relationship and has erotic overtones. But this is not about direct or personal experience. The fact is that Buson (1706-83) composed this while his wife was alive. Indeed Buson's wife Tomo outlived him by 31 years.

Why then the constant emphasis by North American haiku poets on direct personal experience? The answer to this is historically complex, but it should be noted that the haikai that preceded Basho was almost entirely imaginary or fictionally haikai. Much of it was so imaginary that it was absurd, and as a result it was criticized by some as "nonsense" haikai. A typical example is the following hokku found in Indoshu (Teaching collection, 1684), a Danrin school haikai handbook: *mine no hana no nami ni ashika kujira o oyogase.*

making sea lions and whales
swim in the cherry blossom waves
at the hill top

The hokku links cherry blossoms, which were closely associated with waves and hill tops in classical Japanese poetry, to sea lions and whales, two non-classical, vernacular words, thereby comically deconstructing the poetic cliché of "waves of cherry blossoms". Basho was one of the critics of this kind of "nonsense" haikai. He believed that haikai should describe the world "as it is". He was in fact part of a larger movement that was a throwback to earlier orthodox linked verse or renga. However, to describe the world as it is did not mean denying fiction. Fiction can be very realistic and even more real than life itself. For Basho, it was necessary to experience everyday life, to travel, to expose oneself to the world as much as possible, so that the poet could reveal the world as it was. But it could also be fictional, something born of the imagination. In fact, you had to use your imagination to compose haikai, since it was very much about the ability to move from one world to another. Basho himself often rewrote his poetry: he would change the gender, the place, the time, the situation.

The only thing that mattered was the effectiveness of the poetry, not whether it was faithful to the original experience.

One of the chief reasons for the emphasis in modern Japan on direct personal observations was Masaoka Shiki (1867-1902), the late nineteenth century pioneer of modern haiku, who stressed the sketch (shasei) based on direct observation of the subject as the key to the composition of the modern haiku. This led to the ginko, the trips to places to compose haiku. Shiki denounced linked verse as an intellectual game and saw the haiku as an expression of the individual. In this regard Shiki was deeply influenced by Western notions of literature and poetry; first, that literature should be realistic, and second, that literature should be an expression of the individual. By contrast, haikai as Basho had known it had been largely imaginary, and had been a communal activity, the product of group composition or exchange. Shiki condemned traditional haikai on both counts. Even if Shiki had not existed, the effect would have been similar since Western influence on Japan from the late 19th century has been massive. Early American and British pioneers of English-language haiku - such as Basil Chamberlain, Harold Henderson, R.H. Blyth - had limited interest in modern Japanese haiku, but shared many of Shiki's assumptions. The influence of Ezra Pound and the (Anglo-American) Modernist poetry movement was also significant in shaping modern notions of haiku. In short, what many North American haiku poets have thought to be uniquely Japanese had in fact its roots in Western literary thought.

We are often told, particularly by the pioneers of English language haiku (such as D.T. Suzuki, Alan Watts, and the Beats) who mistakenly emphasized Zen Buddhism in Japanese haiku, that haiku should be about the "here and now". This is an extension of the notion that haiku must derive from direct observation and personal experience. Haiku is extremely short, and therefore it can concentrate on only a few details. It is thus suitable for focusing on the here and now. But there is no reason why these moments have to be only in the present, contemporary world or why haiku can't deal with other kinds of time. This noted haiku appears in Basho's Narrow Road: *samidare no furinokoshite ya hikarido.*

> *Have the summer rains*
> *come and gone, sparing*
> *the Hall of Light*

The summer rains (samidare) refers both to the rains falling now and to past summer rains, which have spared the Hall of Light over the centuries. Perhaps Basho's most famous poem in Narrow Road is: *natsukusa ya tsuwamonodomo ga yume no ato* in which the "dreams" and the "summer grasses" are both those of the contemporary poet and of the warriors of the distant past.

> *Summer grasses --*
> *traces of dreams*
> *of ancient warriors*

As we can see from these examples, haiku moments can occur in the distant past or in distant, imaginary places. In fact, one of Buson's great accomplishments was his ability to create other worlds.

Basho traveled to explore the present, the contemporary world, to meet new poets, and to compose linked verse together. Equally important, travel was a means of entering into the past, of meeting the spirits of the dead, of experiencing what his poetic and spiritual predecessors had experienced. In other words, there were two key axes: one horizontal, the present, the contemporary world; and the other vertical, leading back into the past, to history, to other poems. As I have shown in my book Traces of Dreams: Landscape, Cultural Memory, and the Poetry of Basho, Basho believed that the poet had to work along both axes. To work only in the present would result in poetry that was fleeting. To work just in the past, on the other hand, would be to fall out of touch with the fundamental nature of haikai, which was rooted in the everyday world. Haikai was, by definition, anti- traditional, anti-classical, anti-establishment, but that did not mean that it rejected the past. Rather, it depended upon the past and on earlier texts and associations for its richness.

If Basho and Buson were to look at North American haiku today, they would see the horizontal axis, the focus on the present, on the contemporary world, but they would probably feel that the vertical axis, the movement across time, was largely missing. There is no problem with the English language haiku handbooks that stress personal experience. They should. This is a good way to practice, and it is an effective and simple way of getting many people involved in haiku. I believe, as Basho did, that direct experience and direct observation is absolutely critical; it is the base from which we must work and which allows us to mature into interesting poets. However, as the examples of Basho and Buson suggest, it should not dictate either the direction or value of haiku. It is the beginning, not the end. Those haiku that are fictional or imaginary are just as valid as those that are based on personal experience. I would in fact urge the composition of what might be called historical haiku or science fiction haiku.

Haiku as Non-metaphorical

Another rule of North American haiku that Basho would probably find discomforting is the idea that haiku eschews metaphor and allegory. North American haiku handbooks and magazines stress that haiku should be concrete, that it should be about the thing itself. The poet does not use one object or idea to describe another, using A to understand B, as in simile or metaphor; instead the poet concentrates on the object itself. Allegory, in which a set of signs or symbols draw a parallel between one world and the next, is equally shunned. All three of these techniques - metaphor, simile, and allegory - are generally considered to be taboo in English-language haiku, and beginners are taught not to use them.

However, many of Basho's haiku use metaphor and allegory, and in fact this is probably one of the most important aspects of his poetry. In Basho's time, one of the most important functions of the hokku, or opening verse, which was customarily composed by the guest, was to greet the host of the session or party. The hokku had to include a seasonal word, to indicate the time, but it also had to compliment the host. This was often done allegorically or symbolically, by describing some aspect of nature, which implicitly resembled the host. A good example is: *shiragiku no me ni tatete miru chiri mo nashi*:

gazing intently
at the white chrysanthemums --
not a speck of dust

Here Basho is complementing the host (Sonome), represented by the white chrysanthemums, by stressing the flower's and, by implication, Sonome's purity. Another example is: *botan shibe fukaku wakeizuru hachi no nagori kana*, which appears in Basho's travel diary Skeleton in the Fields (Nozarashi kiko).

Having stayed once more at the residence of Master Toyo, I
was about to leave for the Eastern Provinces.

from deep within
the peony pistils -- withdrawing
regretfully the bee

In this parting poem the bee represents Basho and the peony pistils the host (Master Toyo). The bee leaves the flower only with the greatest reluctance, thus expressing the visitor's deep gratitude to the host. This form of symbolism or simple allegory was standard for poets at this time, as it was for the entire poetic tradition. In classical Japanese poetry, object of nature inevitably serve as symbols or signs for specific individuals or situations in the human world, and Japanese haikai is no exception. Furthermore, poets like Basho and Buson repeatedly used the same images (such as the rose for Buson or the beggar for Basho) to create complex metaphors and symbols.

It is no doubt a good idea for the beginner to avoid overt metaphor or allegory or symbolism, but this should not be the rule for more advanced poets. In fact, I think this rule prevents many good poets from becoming great poets. Without the use of metaphor, allegory and symbolism, haiku will have a hard time achieving the complexity and depth necessary to become the object of serious study and commentary. The fundamental difference between the use of metaphor in haiku and that in other poetry is that in haiku it tends to be extremely subtle and indirect, to the point of not being readily apparent. The metaphor in good haiku is often buried deep within the poem. For example, the seasonal word in Japanese haiku tends often to be inherently metaphorical, since it bears very specific literary and cultural associations, but the first and foremost function of the seasonal word is descriptive, leaving the metaphorical dimension implied.

Allusion, Poetry about Poetry

The emphasis on the "haiku moment" in North American haiku has meant that most of the poetry does not have another major characteristic of Japanese haikai and haiku: its allusive character, the ability of the poem to speak to other literary or poetic texts. I believe that it was Shelley who said that poetry is ultimately about poetry. Great poets are constantly in dialogue with each other. This was particularly true of haikai, which began as a parodic form, by twisting the associations and conventions of classical literature and poetry.

One of Basho's innovations was that he went beyond parody and used literary and historical allusions as a means of elevating haikai, which had hitherto been considered a low form of amusement. Many of Basho and Buson's haikai in fact depend for their depth on reference or allusion to earlier poetry, from either the Japanese tradition or the Chinese tradition. For example, one of Buson's best known hokku (1742) is: *yanagi chiri shimizu kare ishi tokoro dokoro.*

> *fallen willow leaves --*
> *the clear stream gone dry,*
> *stones here and there*

The hokku is a description of a natural scene, of "here and now", but it is simultaneously an allusion to and a haikai variation on a famous waka, or classical poem, by Saigyo (1118-1190), a 12th century poet: *michinobe ni shimizu nagaruru yanagi kage shibashi tote koso tachitomaritsure* (Shinkokinshu, Summer, No. 262).

> *by the side of the road*
> *alongside a stream of clear water*
> *in the shade of a willow tree*
> *I paused for what I thought*
> *would be just a moment*

Basho (1644-94) had earlier written the following poem (*ta ichimai uete tachisaru yanagi kana*) in Narrow Road to the Interior (*Oku no hosomichi*), in which the traveler (Basho), having come to the place where Saigyo had written this poem, relives those emotions: Basho pauses beneath the same willow tree and before he knows it, a whole field of rice has been planted.

> *a whole field of*
> *rice seedlings planted - I part*
> *from the willow*

In contrast to Basho's poem, which recaptures the past, Buson's poem is about loss and the irrevocable passage of time, about the contrast between the situation now, in autumn, when the stream has dried up and the willow leaves have fallen, and the past, in summer, when the clear stream beckoned to Saigyo and the willow tree gave him shelter from the hot summer sun. Like many of Basho and Buson's poems, the poem is both about the present and the past, about the landscape and about other poems and poetic associations.

The point here is that much of Japanese poetry works off the vertical axis mentioned earlier. There are a few, rare examples of this in English haiku. I give one example, by Bernard Einbond, a New York City poet who recently passed away, which alludes to Basho's famous frog poem: *furuike ya kawazy tobikomu mozu no oto* (an old pond, a frog jumps in, the sound of water).

> *frog pond...*
> *a leaf falls in*
> *without a sound*

24

This haiku deservedly won the Japan Airlines First Prize, in which there were something like 40,000 entries. This poem has a haikai quality that Basho would have admired. In typical haikai fashion, it operates on two fundamental levels. On the scenic level, the horizontal axis, it is a description of a scene from nature, it captures the sense of quiet, eremitic loneliness that is characteristic of Basho's poetry. On the vertical axis, it is an allusive variation, a haikai twist on Basho's famous frog poem, wittily replacing the frog with the leaf and the sound of the frog jumping in with no sound. Einbond's haiku has a sense of immediacy, but at the same time it speaks to the past; it enters into dialogue with Basho's poem. In other words, this haiku goes beyond "the haiku moment", beyond the here and now, to speak across time. To compose such haiku is difficult. But it is the kind of poetry that can break into the mainstream and can become part of a poetic heritage.

The vertical axis does not always have to be a connection to another poem. It can be what I call cultural memory, a larger body of associations that the larger community can identify with. It could be about a past crisis (such as the Vietnam War or the loss of a leader) that the poet of a community is trying to come to terms with. The key here is the larger frame, the larger body of associations that carries from one generation to the next and that goes beyond the here and now, beyond the so-called haiku moment. The key point is that for the horizontal (contemporary) axis to survive, to transcend time and place, it needs at some point to cross the vertical (historical) axis; the present moment has to engage with the past or with a broader sense of time and community (such as family, national or literary history).

Nature and Seasonal Words

One of the major differences between English-language haiku and Japanese haiku is the use of the seasonal word (kigo). There are two formal requirements of the hokku, now called haiku: the cutting word, which cuts the 17 syllable hokku in two, and the seasonal word. English-language haiku poets do not use cutting words per se, but they use the equivalent, either in the punctuation (such as a dash), with nouns, or syntax. The effect is very similar to the cutting word, and there have been many good poems that depend on the cutting. However, there is no equivalent to the seasonal word. In fact, the use of a seasonal word is not a formal requirement in English-language haiku, as it is for most of Japanese haiku.

In Japan, the seasonal word triggers a series of cultural associations which have been developed, refined and carefully transmitted for over a thousand years and which are preserved, transformed and passed on from generation to generation through seasonal handbooks, which remain in wide use today. In Basho's day, seasonal words stood in the shape of a huge pyramid. At the top were the big five, which had been at the core of classical poetry (the 31-syllable waka): the cuckoo (hototogisu) for summer, the cherry blossoms for spring, the snow for winter, the bright autumn leaves and the moon for autumn. Spreading out from this narrow peak were the other topics from classical poetry - spring rain (harusame), orange blossoms (hanatachibana), bush warbler (uguisu), willow tree (yanagi), etc. Occupying the base and the widest area were the vernacular seasonal words that had been added recently by haikai poets. In contrast to the elegant images at the top of the pyramid, the seasonal words at the bottom were taken from everyday, contemporary, commoner life. Examples from spring include dandelion (tanpopo), garlic (ninniku), horseradish (wasabi) and cat's love (neko no koi).

From as early as the eleventh century, the poet of classical poetry was expected to compose on the poetic essence (honi) of a set topic. The poetic essence was the established associations at the core of the seasonal word. In the case of the warbler (uguisu), for example, the poet had to compose on the warbler in regard to the arrival and departure of spring, about the emergence of the warbler from the mountain glen, or about the relationship of the warbler to the plum blossoms. This poetic essence, the cluster of associations at the core of the seasonal topic, was thought to represent the culmination and experience of generations of poets over many years. By composing on the poetic essence, the poet could partake of this communal experience, inherit it, and carry it on. (This phenomenon is true of most of the traditional arts. The beginner must first learn the fundamental forms, or kata, which represent the accumulated experience of generations of previous masters.) Poets studied Japanese classics such as The Tale of Genji and the Kokinshu, the first imperial anthology of Japanese waka poetry, because these texts were thought to preserver the poetic essence of nature and the seasons as well as of famous places.

Famous places (meisho) in Japanese poetry have a function similar to the seasonal word. Each famous place in Japanese poetry had a core of poetic associations on which the poet was obliged to compose. Tatsutagawa (Tatsuta River), for example, meant momiji, or bright autumn leaves. Poets such as Saigyo and Basho traveled to famous poetic places - such as Tatsutagawa, Yoshino, Matsushima, Shirakawa - in order to partake of this communal experience, to be inspired by poetic places that had been the fountainhead of the great poems of the past. These famous poetic places provided an opportunity to commune across time with earlier poets. Like seasonal words, famous places functioned as a direct pipeline to the communal poetic body. By contrast, there are very few, if any places, in North America that have a core of established poetic associations of the kind found in famous places in Japan. And accordingly there are relatively few English haiku on noted places.

The point here is that the seasonal word, like the famous place name in Japanese poetry, anchors the poem in not only some aspect of nature but in the vertical axis, in a larger communal body of poetic and cultural associations. The seasonal word allows something that is small to gain a life of its own. The seasonal word, like the famous place name, also links the poem to other poems. In fact, each haiku is in effect part of one gigantic seasonal poem.

People have often wondered about the brevity of the Japanese poem. The seventeen syllable haiku is the shortest form in world literature, and the thirty-one syllable waka or tanka, as it is called today, is probably the second shortest. How then is it possible for poetry to be so short and yet still be poetry? How can there be complexity or high value in such a simple, brief form? First, the brevity and the overt simplicity allow everyone to participate, making it a communal, social medium. Second, the poem can be short and still complex since it is actually part of a larger, more complex poetic body. When the poet takes up one of the topics at the top of the seasonal pyramid or visits a famous place, he or she enters into an imaginary world that he or she shares with the audience and that connects to the dead, the ancients. To compose on the poetic essence of a topic is, as we saw, to participate in the larger accumulated experience of past poets. It is for this reason that the audience takes pleasure in very subtle variations on familiar themes.

This communal body, the vertical axis, however, is in constant need of infusion, of new life. The haikai poet needs the horizontal axis to seek out the new experience, new language, new topics, new poetic partners. The seasonal pyramid can be seen as concentric circles of a tree trunk, with the classical topics at the center, followed by classical linked verse topics, the haikai topics, and finally modern haiku words on the periphery. The innermost circles bear the longest history and are essentially fictional worlds and the least likely to change. The outer circles, by contrast, are rooted in everyday life and in the contemporary, ever-changing world. Many of those on the circumference will come and go, never to be seen again. Without the constant addition of new rings, however, the tree will die or turn into a fossil. One of the ideals that Basho espoused toward the end of his life was that of the "unchanging and the ever-changing" (fueki ryuko). The "unchanging" implied the need to seek the "truth of poetic art" (fuga no makoto), particularly in the poetic and spiritual tradition, to engage in the vertical axis, while the "ever changing" referred to the need for constant change and renewal, the source of which was ultimately to be found in everyday life, in the horizontal axis.

Significantly, the Haiku Society of America definition of haiku does not mention the seasonal word, which would be mandatory in Japan for most schools. Maybe half of existing English-language haiku have seasonal words or some sense of the season, and even when the haiku do have a seasonal word the usually do not serve the function that they do in Japanese haiku. The reason for this is that the connotations of seasonal words differ greatly from region to region in North America, not to mention other parts of the world, and generally are not tied to specific literary or cultural associations that would immediately be recognized by the reader. In Japan, by contrast, for hundreds of years, the seasonal words have served as a crucial bridge between the poem and the tradition. English-language haiku therefore has to depend on other dimensions of haiku for its life.

In short, while haiku in English is inspired by Japanese haiku, it can not and should not try to duplicate the rules of Japanese haiku because of significant differences in language, culture and history. A definition of English-language haiku will thus, by nature, differ from that of Japanese haiku. If pressed to give a definition of English-language haiku that would encompass the points that I have made here, I would say, echoing the spirit of Basho's own poetry, that haiku in English is a short poem, usually written in one to three lines, that seeks out new and revealing perspectives on the human and physical condition, focusing on the immediate physical world around us, particularly that of nature, and on the workings of the human imagination, memory, literature and history. There are already a number of fine North American haiku poets working within this frame so this definition is intended both to encourage an existing trend and to affirm new space that goes beyond existing definitions of haiku.

Senryu and English-Language Haiku

Maybe close to half of English-language haiku, including many of the best ones, are in fact a form of senryu, seventeen syllable poems that do not require a seasonal word and that focus on human condition and social circumstances, often in a humorous or satirical fashion. I think that this is fine. English-language haiku should not try to imitate Japanese haiku, since it is working under very different circumstances. It must have a life and evolution of its own.

Senryu, as it evolved in Japan in the latter half of the eighteenth century, when it blossomed into an independent form, was heavily satirical, poking fun at contemporary manners and human foibles. English-language haiku magazines have established a distinction between the two forms, of haiku and senryu, in which those poems associated with nature are placed in the haiku category and those with non-natural subjects in the senryu category. According to the Haiku Society of America, haiku is the "essence of a movement keenly perceived in which nature is linked to human nature". Senryu, by contrast, is "primarily concerned with human nature; often humorous or satiric". While this definition of English-language senryu is appropriate, that for English-language haiku, which tends, by nature, to overlap with senryu, seems too limited.

One consequence of a narrower definition of haiku is that English-language anthologies of haiku are overwhelmingly set in country or natural settings even though ninety percent of the haiku poets actually live in urban environments. To exaggerate the situation, North American haiku poets are given the alternative of either writing serious poetry on nature (defined as haiku) or of writing humorous poetry on non-nature topics (defined as senryu). This would seem to discourage haiku poets from writing serious poetry on the immediate urban environment or broader social issues. Topics such as subways, commuter driving, movie theaters, shopping malls, etc., while falling outside of the traditional notion of nature, in fact provide some of the richest sources for modern haiku, as much recent English-language haiku has revealed, and should be considered part of nature in the broadest sense.

For this reason I am now editing a volume of New York or urban haiku, which, according to the narrow definition of haiku, would often be discouraged or disqualified, but which, in my mind, represents the original spirit of Japanese haikai in focusing on the immediate physical environment. Projects such as Dee Evett's "Haiku on 42nd Street", in which he presented urban haiku on empty movie theatre marquees in Times Square, are, in this regard, both innovative and inspiring.

Conclusion: Some Characteristics of Haikai

The dilemma is this: on the one hand, the great attraction of haiku is its democracy, its ability to reach out, to be available to everyone. There is no poetry like haiku when it comes to this. Haiku has a special meaning and function for everyone. It can be a form of therapy. It can be a way to tap into one's psyche. Haiku can do all these things. And it can do these things because it is short, because the rules are simple, because it can focus on the moment.

However, if haiku is to rise to the level of serious poetry, literature that is widely respected and admired, that is taught and studied, commentated on, that can have impact on other non-haiku poets, then it must have a complexity that gives it depth and that allows it to both focus on and rise above the specific moment or time. Basho, Buson and other masters achieved this through various forms of textual density, including metaphor, allegory, symbolism and allusion, as well as through the constant search for new topics. For North American poets, for whom the seasonal word cannot function in the fashion that it did for these Japanese masters, this becomes a more pressing issue, with the need to explore not only metaphorical and symbolic possibilities but new areas - such as history, urban life, social ills, death and war, cyberspace, Haiku need not and should not be confined to a narrow definition of nature poetry, particularly since the ground rules are completely different from those in Japan.

How then can haiku achieve that goal in the space of seventeen syllables? The answer is that it does not necessarily have to. One of the assumptions that Basho and others made about the hokku (haiku) was that it was unfinished. The hokku was only the beginning of a dialogue; it had to be answered by the reader or another poet or painter. Haikai in its most fundamental form, as linked verse, is about linking one verse to another, one person to another. Haikai is also about exchange, about sending and answering, greeting and bidding farewell, about celebrating and mourning. Haikai was also about mutual composition, about completing or complementing the work of others, adding poetry and calligraphy to someone's printing, adding a prose passage to a friend's poem, etc.

One consequence is that haikai and the hokku in particular is often best appreciated and read as part of a sequence, as part of an essay, a poetry collection, a diary or travel narrative, all forms that reveal the process of exchange, linkage, and that give haikai and haiku a larger context. Basho's best work was Narrow Road to the Interior (Oku no hosomichi), in which the haiku was embedded in a larger prose narrative and was part of a larger chaing of texts.

In Basho's day, haikai was two things: 1) performance and social act, and 2) literary text. As a social act, as an elegant form of conversation, haikai had to be easily accessible; it had to be spontaneous; it had to perform social and religious functions. Thus, half of Basho's haiku were greetings, parting poems, poetic prayers. They served very specific functions and were anchored in a specific place and time, in a dialogic exchange with other individuals. For Basho, however, haikai was also a literary text that had to transcend time and place, be understood by those who were not at the place of composition. To achieve this goal, Basho repeatedly rewrote his poetry, made it fictional, gave it new settings, added layers of meaning, emphasized the vertical axis (linking it to history and other literary texts), so that the poem would have an impact beyond its original circumstances. One hopes that more North American haiku poets can take inspiration from this complex work.

VEILED TRANSPARENCIES

By

Donna Leviash Al-Mahadin

Pen Names:
Karima Hassan
Grammy

Within this book you will find several Arabic words. As the Arabic language is not universally understood, many terms used here are annotated and defined by Senior Editor, Yvonne Marie Crain.

In many religions, it is a common practice to be given a new name. When Donna accepted and adopted Islam as her way and belief in life, she was given and accepted the Arabic name Karima (pronounced ka-REE-mah) defined as generous and giving.

I have found Karima to be a true joy to work with. The poetry of Karima is a shining glory, representative of the true meanings found in such words as humble, honor, share, and peace (Senior Editor, Yvonne Marie Crain).

When Life Opens a Door...

Don't Hesitate ~ Walk Through
Donna Leviash Al-Mahadin

About the Author

My name is Donna Leviash Al-Mahadin, my life began in the Midwestern Unites States. I am married to a Jordanian and adopted by his home, family, religion, and culture. I have two children, Poett and Julian. I am grandmother to Sebastian and James. My formal education concluded with high school graduation.

I began writing my first novel while living in Los Angeles, California. The setting for this book is in Costa Rica, my daughter and I moved to Dominical on the Southern Pacific Coast with the idea of completing this novel on location. This novel entitled *"The Three-Legged-Dog Bite"* was completed; our return to live in the United States was not.

Owning and working a cattle ranch, Poett and I lived for ten years without electricity. Our only entertainment was reading by candlelight. Books took on an incredible importance to us, and we became expert readers. I made up bedtime stories for Poett, and believe they were the catalyst that activated the creative part of my brain. Had television been available, I believe this would not have happened.

I enjoyed life as Vice-President with the Board of Directors for *El Municipal de Perez Zeledon*, a professional soccer team in Costa Rica. Soccer is more of a passion than a sport in Costa Rica. Also, I opened my home to care for last-stage cancer patients.

Being tri-national, I consider all three countries home, and I am fluent in English, Spanish, and Arabic. I now reside in San Isidro General, Costa Rica for six months and Karak, Jordan within the remaining six months.

Using the Spanish language I had a short story, *Que Dice La Gente,* and poetry published. Currently, I write using two pen-names, Karima Hassan and Grammy. I additionally have had two poetry books published entitled *Gliding Beauty* and book for young children titled *One Dozen Tales For James.* Hopefully, soon to be published, an already completed Volume II.

I extend my warmest thanks to Dr. Harris (Cole) Vernick with *The Cole Foundation for the Arts.* Your confidence in me, providing an opportunity for publication in this prestigious anthology of international poets leaves me humbled and eternally grateful. To Maxene Alexander, Executive Editor and Yvonne Marie Crain, Senior Edito*r,* I extend my thanks. Your dedication has made *The Baker's Dozen, Volume III* an artistic reality. I thank my family and friends from both Costa Rica and Jordan, and my on-line friends for your support. Your encouragement has helped to polish and inspire my poetic endeavors. Very special thanks I give to *Daniel Hug (Gino),* my lifetime friend. May you find peace and joy reading as much as I found writing poetry.

Table of Contents

Against Those Tides

For Umahmad[11]

Seas between us,
The pavement gobbled gone.
Voices whispered, "run-away ~ just run!"
But you cancelled all your flights;
Kept faithfully your daily prayers at dawn.

Oh, I had stopped believing
That I would ever see you again.
Erased your disconnected numbers;
Whispered to the bees about the birds
While hours flipped into second year's end.

Some things are just what they are;
There is no thing or one to take its place.
Tears and panic give way to resolution;
The heart groans and grows a cubit.
Still; no one has~ your voice~your walk~your face.

Muse of my latter quest,
Cold the waves that buried you from me.
Endless notebooks, filled with loving words
Were the tools I used for slaying
Those devils, trying to push you out to sea.

---

1   *Arabic word, umahmad, in English translates to mean women. However, in this case Umahmad is a personal name much as rose is a flower, but can be a personal name as well. As a person's name the literal translation is "mother (um) of Ahmad," or Ahmad's mother.*

In The Poetry
For Umahmad[22]

The difference was in the poetry.
All the hours in silence,
A cloistered life;
No chapel bells or vespers.
We listened to the call to prayer
On every street corner;
Every four hours.
You went crazy, while I went into Free-Verse
Cinquain, and cried it out in sonnets.
I walked into terror rooms of frightened eyes,
While you walked the street at night.
Your sainthood dragging on the ground,
Getting dirtier by the block.
My husband was sleeping the days away,
Catching his breath.
But yours was buried in an unmarked grave.
So; the difference was in the poetry.

I wrote in chunks of raw meat
Marinating in tears and fears,
While you just put yourself away
So as not to rot in the light.
I leaped over the water to bring you back
To me and to life.
I typed and typed, and
Feared for my life.
My chorus singing out:
"You knew what the play was about,
When you bought the ticket."
Ah! But you never had a clue,
Stoic victim of destiny with a martyr's courage.
All gleams in titanium perfection, here
In my room with no view.

My keyboard knows when it is dark, but you don't.
Your house is draped and brown.
Your days get confused, and every time a voice speaks;
It is a surprise proclamation that
You're unsure it's right to follow.
Those orders, that send you into the night again,
To walk them out of your mind.
Hollowed eyed, I stared into my own
Confused state of being, air-borne
Like a virus, and those too close got infected.
So sick, and yet I healed
The difference was in the poetry.

---

2   Ibid.

32

Karak Summer Night

For Umahmad[3]

I watched our shadows walk on castle's wall
A Karak[4] night of desert summer's call.
Our black abayas[5] flapping at our knees
Enchantment, once again on Karak breeze.

It was so much like memory had stored
The scene, returned to me as if reward.
I held your hand so gently inside mine,
Protecting you, from supple serpentines.

Your face tonight a blank with soul retired,
Captured profile, looking uninspired.
Too painful for my heart to glance and see,
Those eyes, a million miles away from me.

Your break-apart, psychotic episode
Keeps you from living, Karak's gift bestowed.
Oh, warm and secret wind of mystery
Fell Karak's spell tonight, only to me.

The saddest truth I bear my witness to,
I am, and yet; am not a part of you.

---

3   Ibid.

4   The name of a city in Jordon. Also, this is translated from Arabic to English as: temporary housing.

5   Head to toe clothing worn by Islamic women.

One Cup

For my family in Jordan

Harsh lands bring soft embraces,
Here we all drink from one cup.
Before we put our share to our mouths,
We make sure there is enough.

Oven winds bake a glaze on my face,
While dry eyes squint to the sky.
Two leathered hands sift Martian sands,
I can't pull away yet, and I know why.

Destiny's prisoner, I smile and submit,
While drying out my soul is refreshed.
The cool realization; I am where I should be
Makes me know I am doubly blessed.

I choose to stay, in an open doorway,
Trembling ~ indecisive, but I don't leave.
Feels like a premonition or a déjà vu,
On impulse I cancel my flight of reprieve.

Harsh lands bring soft embraces,
Here we all drink from one cup.
Before we put our share to our mouths,
We make sure there is enough.

Mated Beauty

For umahmad[66]

In your arms, my pain meets its master's call
To transform obediently tonight
Into a funny child with laughing eyes
Who glows over the room with gentle light.

The gifts we get are measured and beloved,
The Writer of our book knows just the time
To leave a present when we ache too much;
A healing salve to cure a soul sublime.

So lie beside me, hear the morning call.
Our prayers today beginning side by side,
Before we rise to give our thanks on knees,
Tell me you feel our destiny's still tied.

I kiss you, not with a lover's passion,
But from a deeper need that lies here, too.
The search for that one soul to bind entwined
My mated beauty, you and only you!

6   Ibid.

Ramadan Impressions 2007

First Day of Ramadan[7] Sept. 13

The naked eye sees new moon over the horizon peek,
Mouth-to-mouth the news is spread around the world.
Ears on buzzing phone lines, whole networks going down;
Millions jumping in their cars to buy last minute treats.
Dates and cookies;
Nuts and seeds,
Fruit and tea..
Don't forget the dried apricot drink,
Or sweet coffee.
Keep our bottled water at bedside,
Before dawn take our last drink.
Offer this time to cleansing our soul
For healing the world
While fasting one month,
We should think of those who starve all year

Time for us to read and reflect,
The Qur'an[8] helps our spirits prepare.
When we hear the adthan[9] being sung
We pray together, and it's a family affair.

---

7   Holy period of worship and meditation celebrated during the ninth month of the Islamic calendar in which fasting is practiced from sunrise to sunset.

8   The greatest literary work in classical Arabic. Representative of the Word of God (Allah) in the Islamic religion.

9   A sound that is used when being called to prayer.

At sunset we wait for the muezzin[1010] to chant,
Break our fast with dates, water and prayer,
Eat fatoosh[1111] lentil soup, "Pass the stuffed grape leaves please,"
Then walk to mosque in the cool evening air.

We visit our neighbors and relatives,
Talk and watch our favorite Ramadan fare,
Give alms to the poor and be kind to all.
Let our generosity show that we care.

We go to bed late after having sahour[1212],
A tasty 3 am lunch to help our bodies repair.
Then wake before dawn and wash ourselves well,
The fast is renewed with the next Morning-Prayer.

Even young children take part in the fast.
They feel grown-up and proudly aware
We decorate our homes in stars and crescent moons,
And feel festive when we go anywhere.

Nothing can describe after fasting, the taste
Of a sip of water, or a bite of date.
A deliciously humbling flavor of gratitude
That is totally beyond compare.

---

10 0 The Islamic call to prayer.

11 1 A variety of vegetables with pita bread as a common ingredient.

12 2 In a low populated area of Palestine, a house to sleep called Night Watch.

Howler

The shrieking wind blows the tent off the top of the hill.
I watch from my room while it splits in two,
Trying to comb my curtains into shreds below.
Howler, from the East, occupies the land, blasting
The battlement of my sandstone castle.
Banshee devil from Saturn's plains,
Trees gyrate to your convulsive bursts,
Then almost silence invades the olive groves,
While you go to gather forces, align with the malign,
To come back in whispered screams of invisible upgrading.
Plastic chair walks, scraping the cement floor, a zombie
Pushed by your quick anger unmanaged,
Gusts now tyrannically assault the door
Bang~ Bang~ weeeeeeeeeeee!
The goat-hide tent rolls over and over,
Somersaulting down the grazed-to- dust hill.
Silhouettes in flapping white pants like sea flags,
Look after it in immobility and silent gesturing
It was a home before it flew away,
In demonic howling arms of destructive force
Now it returns once more to assault my door
Bang~ Bang~ weeeeeeeeeeee!

Slaughter of the Lamb
For Ali

We all knew it was coming.
The women huddled with their morning tea,
The one who knew to slit a throat with mercy
Today was not available;
Another one showed up.
His head wrapped in a turban… red and white,
The women huddled closer,
Stopped drinking their tea,
I heard one say,
"May he take it far away, so as not to hear."

I went to get my ipod.
Yes, I was between
The time of Abraham and Apple,
Trapped within the group and could not leave.
The "Mummers Dance" droned as loud
As earphones allowed.
I heard nothing,
But saw a sad silent movie unfold.

Those listening with small children
Covered their ears and clutched them tight.
Buffered in my music, I just asked Allah inside,
Why did this custom, old as humankind arise?
Tradition says to celebrate the joy
Of a live and hearty birth,
Another small innocent creature of God
Must be condemned to die.

Editorial Comments:

To slaughter a lamb is a once a year custom and may also be a part of a celebration marking the birth of a child. This custom is done with respect for the lamb and love for Allah. A very specific method is followed, and if properly done, causes no unnecessary pain or torture to the animal (Yvonne Marie Crain, Senior Editor).

When It's Over

For O

Once upon a lifetime
Your chest was the safest place to lay my head,
And wherever I was, you called it home.
Now even my sighs are irritating,
My smile grates on your blackboard of grievances.
When it's over, we know it, don't we?

Provoking is the new word of the week,
Everything wears it that swirls too near me,
One sentence of mine, a provocation,
Each "Could we just talk?" a cry to raise arms.
This and that, all provoke you into raging attack.
When it's over, we know it, don't we?

I pack some things just in case,
Feeling the fall- out of our poor love gone plop!
I hit the street not like a ball but like an egg,
Raw, cracked, cooking on the sidewalk
Of your hot abuse.
I look into the mirror,
Someone has grown so sad and worn.
When it's over, we know it, don't we?

Silver Wedding Ring

For O

I took your silver wedding ring
And threw it out to sea,
My name engraved upon it,
Caused the waves to crash on me.

Your finger only holds one band
I found ours in a drawer,
Hers graces and adorns you now
Mine filed for evermore.

I felt a freedom when it flew
Believed it sailed away,
From so much heartache daily
Since your second wedding day

Although you hold a paper
That says I'm still your wife,
I looked out to seas horizon,
And glimpsed another life.

Big-Holed Sieve
For O

Each day passes right through without touching me,
Big-holed sieve ... nothing of any value stays,
An entire starry evening goes straight down the drain.
What is the purpose of pouring
Into the porous leftover of my life
One more day?
Yet I know not how to leave you,
Certainly not how to make it right.
Repeated cliffs so high with your disdain
Block out all the sunlight.
Afternoon sulfuric rains
Maintain your kingdom dry and cruel,
It all continues to flow into me.
When I grab the air for anything,
I realize something was there...
Before it washed through me,
And was gone.

Up

Let me rise away
Higher than the atmosphere,
The conic dome of black-arched stratosphere,
I leave it all behind
And up I rise and rise.

Down there are stagnant things,
Lines that resist and depress.
If I find my lightness I go tonight.
Unpacking everything is how I pack,
I don't look back as I leave it far below.

Can't take a thing if I want to go up
Gravity is denied only to the weightless.
I go this way, weightless,
Like in the womb before I came.
I leave the salty residue of one million tears,
You know, I could never get off the ground,
Not even with ten held inside.
I throw all the heavy things out over my edge
And up I rise and rise.

Strawberry Sands

Afternoon pink mountains, glazed strawberry sands,
Wadi Rum beds down for the night.
Valley of mystery, battles, last stands,
Blood mixed with tears, I take flight.

I leave painful bad dreams, may they all sift through,
Your dunes now contain my grains too,
I toss them behind me to haunt moonless nights
My wail, a breeze whispering, "untrue."

Crags of violet, peaks of the palest red wine,
Stand guard and bid me adieu,
Allah chose only pastels in His desert design,
Engraved within me, forever to view.

Last rays of your sun, last days, and then free
I will miss you, but that jungle does call,
All towering green with bright flowering trees,
It says, "Get off your knees and stand tall."

Coming Up From The Dead

Corcovado National Reserve Costa Rica

Coming up from the dead, I exhale back into life, Palm trees sway in the
building breeze.
They appear as a tight picket fence to contain the sea,
Even stripped of their nuts, they are still supple proud trees.

I have witnessed re-birth on these tropical shores
While macaws crack almonds perched high on tree-tops.
If the wheel stopped here, I'd be the first to disembark
For I've been buried too long, in my zombie-life plot.

Paired, colorful rainbow-flyers soar overhead;
Tears come so easily when I perceive freedom's call.
Like watching painted inserts in a sepia toned film
I fill my lungs with their oxygen, crawl out past death's wall.

I heard someone say, "Tomorrow we go back to reality."
But I say, they will only return to their graves.
Is there anything more real than living each precious moment
While tossing all troubled thoughts to the waves?

One more glorious gift I hold tight in my hand.
A return from the dead, my shroud, a colorful gown…
All vibrant n' green, with aqua-water sleek bows,
Red, yellow, blue streamers high on top like a crown.

21 Karat Gold

21 karat gold,
So easily bent
Malleable to the slightest touch,
Too rich in its softness,
Damaged by applied pressure,
Glorious in its orange hues of purity,
Yet so quickly twisted into
The grotesque and the shapeless.

I bend you around my finger
In an age-old dance,
But you close yourself
In the door jam,
Become flattened and unattractive.
Who can wear you like this?
Must I put you on a chain
That restricts us both?
Feel you clang against
My new found armor,
With every step we take?
You are beauty before my gaze,
Then I watch you melt down into ore.
Once such a worthy shape
Now you reverse all alchemy
And we become lead.
Pounding yourself into
A steaming hot key,
You have the power
To lock my door forever,
Before you run away.

Your Treasure
For lonely wolf

How I wanted to climb your high-walled soul
As I sensed you had something hidden inside,
Something brilliant and battered in gold;
Pounded to compassion in a priceless design.

There was barbwire and I had to be bold.
I so wanted to graze just the palm of your hand.
Your muscles flexed and I lost my hold,
But resolve grew bigger and helped me to stand.

I slid down the sides of your high-walled soul.
I was surrounded by a smoothness and light;
Your pressed pain had made diamonds glow,
This beauty inspired a poetic fire to ignite.

When treasures are hidden they can start to mold,
Yet what is worthless roams too freely outside.
You were right to lock up the untold,
Because only the truest will hang on the whole ride.

Like Glass
For my daughter Poett

Sometimes we can break through.
Our glass wall always allowed smiles, although
Communication had been muted and muffled.

It was not an abyss without a bridge,
More like a habit of keeping ourselves
Hidden from each other in our own lives.

Last night you reached out to me;
I saw the little girl who used to come
To share and find comfort in my bed.

I was profoundly moved.
Holding you in my arms again, I felt you
So sublimely, my daughter...my friend.

Least Resistance

For umahmad[1313]

Would it be lent to me once more,
I'd not return again what was not mine.
Each year I make some bad mistakes,
In spite of the good script I was assigned.

When we play to lose, we can win.
When we give up hope then we know defeat.
When we sell our souls for a sale,
We're like whores parading down easy street.

No one said this course was a cake,
But quitting in mid-term is forbidden.
I'd like to study notes with you,
And to possibly reach all that's hidden.

The road with rocks builds stronger legs.
When we console, rewards rain from above;
Our path of least resistance helps,
To pull us through the *needle's eye of love.*

---

13 Ibid.

On Ego-Soul Lane

Between the ego and soul
All of us build our nests.
Ego goes out to do and impress.
Soul stays home, cooks, sings and rests.

I am… I want… I do what I do, lucky me!
Ego's shrill horn blows its own melody.

I found a meal where even the bad taste good.
The soul hums invitingly to the neighborhood.

Ego grows flowers and lawns without weeds
It is important that all observe its large deeds.

Soul waters some seedlings hidden away deep within
Knows to wait for the moment the miracle will begin.

We can visit and bond with each now and then.
Ego has its moment of useful practicality,
But I like to pay a visit to the house with a soul,
Drink of its genuine warmth, its limitless hospitality.

If I Should Write A Love Poem
(With Threads of Gold)
For umahmad[1414]

If I should write one poem of my love
To you, it would be wrapped in threads of gold,
For you have been the treasure of my life,
Singular piece released from Allah's hold.

Words stammer not, but flow like sacred prayer.
In golden threads of spider's web I cling,
The intricacies of our lover's tale
Trap me above all lesser mundane things.

Your aura glows around your raven hair;
Our bodies glide, the straight path we do choose,
As evening light leaves golden threads behind
We bow, and pray our course to never lose.

You are for me my purest loving truth,
Golden threads tied to our souls do bind.
Our love affair, uncommon though it be,
Has lasted when all others fell behind.

How subtle and sublime this feels to me,
Love bound in threads of gold, eternally.

14   4 Ibid.

THE

PERCEPTIONS

OF A

POET

By

Trenton T. Battle

Poet's Persona

To all wonderful souls who grace the words and voices in the messages of my life, I bid you greetings.

I am a retired United States Air Force veteran of twenty-six years. My natural and spiritual educations have vastly shaped the content of my spirit and character.

Writing is a passion of my life, and I write the words that speak the voice of my spirit. Theoretical and empirical knowledge form the words of my poetry.

My inspiration for writing had little to do with an experience; moreover, with a constant voice echoing in my soul; longing to be expressed. The ever echoing voice is the breath of the Almighty proclaiming His unspeakable Love, Light and Life.

The words and voice of my poetry verbalizes what the Creator God purposed from eternities past.

HEAR THE CRY OF WISDOM

SHE IS ~ THE VOICE OF LOVE

Trenton T. Battle

POET'S PROFILE

I am Trenton T. Battle, a man who decided to follow my last name; *Battle*. I made the choice to combat and battle all forms of evil, hatred, and darkness found destroying worldwide peace; causing death to our soul. I am a humble soldier for *God* and a strong warrior for the goodness of peace and love. Greetings to all who embrace Love, Light, and Life!

Expressions of my inner thoughts, beliefs, and feelings are the resonating voice that rings forth my words. This originates from my eternal soul, and is my greatest interest. Making my home an expression and extension of what is found within my spirit, thrills my imagination. Poetry is certainly a part of my celestial make-up. It naturally flows from my mind to my pen, and has been that way since my youthful grade school years.

A burning desire to voice the words I hear within my spirit has always been my inspiration to write. Although my vocabulary had not developed and was limited during my youth, I still found ways to express the messages contained within the voice of my heart.

Life's experience, morality, and spiritual education motivate and compel me to continue writing today. Most of my poetic expressions and inspirations are influenced by my Christian/Biblical foundation and journey towards maturity.

As a poet, my goals in the present time are to continue motivating the hearts and minds of those who read and perceive my words and voice; to seek the wonders of *Love, Light and Life*. My future vision is to pen my life's journey in poetic highs and lows; that will ultimately bring me to level plains where light and dark are one and the same.

I have a few published works that I hope will continue to touch the life of each reader. However, thus far, most of my writings are expressions I pen and never send out to anyone.

My sincere gratitude to *Dr. Harris (Cole) Vernick* and the *Merit-Based Scholarship Grant* I received through *The Cole Foundation for the Arts;* for seeing and hearing within my humble writings a voice worth publication. *The Baker's Dozen: A Cole Foundation Collection: Volume III;* a trilogy will mark the first celebration and release of what is found within my soul.

Table of Contents

THOUGHTS

Thoughts are invisible waves upon a sea without waters
How they carry us, and toss us to and fro
Lifting us high and taking us low

How are your thoughts, are they a raging sea
Carrying you vehemently beyond rational degree?
Thoughts of pleasure...Thoughts of pain
Thoughts of sunshine...Thoughts of rain

Waves of thoughts rising high
Lift my fantasies and draw me nigh
My sea is swelling, a new high tide
Now my thoughts I no longer can hide

Night has fallen, and the moon is bright
My thoughts are drawn by the moon's humility light
Invisible waves of a drifting sea
Moon lit sky makes my thoughts run free

Idle time the waves will roll
Thoughts of everything flood my soul
When I beach on a desolate shore
All my thoughts shall be no more

A POEM PASSING THROUGH MY HEART

As the day progresses onward, so will thoughts of you;
Breaking the silence in my day, a cloudless sky so blue
I am here and you are there, no difference will it make
When your friendship is in my heart, nothing takes your place

Morning gives way to noonday; joy is running high,
Thinking of you all the morn, your spirit now draws nigh
Beautiful eyes, pretty hair, a heart wrenching smile;
Though you're far away, my affections span the miles

A friend as you...a lush as me...you've accepted as your friend
Not that I deserve it, but I pray it never ends
When one day I meet you, all radiant, bright and fair
You know I'll call you beautiful, as a priceless jewel is rare

SNOW

Looking out at the snow, while driving myself home

Every tiny flake sings a harmonious song
Little tiny rain drips frozen by the wind
Carried by a tempest, earth its final end

Blanketing the ugliness of a much forsaken land
God's frosty teardrops lends the earth His hand
All is now made beautiful, white with the snow
Death of the winter, in spring new life shall grow

A lovely coat of righteousness, the earth is now at rest
Purifying the land, life will spring from death
The snow of humility makes death a lovely thing
You see death is not the end, but the end to a means

Cover your heart in Snow, the Righteousness of God
With the driving Wind, the Spirit's correcting rod
With it will come death of all that is vile

When the snow is melted you'll have life undefiled

YOU ARE POETRY
(The Expressions of Life)

You are Poetry, the expressions of life
Expanding the imagination, joy so rife
You are Poetry, a musical key
Loosing emotions, the spirit set free

You are Poetry, formulating thought
An intangible substance you have wrought
A lovely tapestry wrought in the heart
Now made manifest, never to depart

You are Poetry, the expressions of life
You are sadness, passion and strife
You are Poetry, a perfectly strung harp
Resonates sounds that pierce the dark

You are Poetry, the stories of life
The books are open, revealing the light
You are Poetry, none can deny
The power of expression, none can defy

MORROW
(A Day We Search For; A Time Yet To Come)

Now is today leading toward the morrow
Will it bring sunshine...will it bring sorrow
When it arrives it then becomes now
The search will continue until morrow is found
Morrow means to seek and inquire
Laboring today for the morrow's desire
When the morrow arrives a new search begins
'Til time hereafter, never will it end
Morrow you are the breaking of the day
Rising early to start on your way
Morrow you bring the light of new hope
No longer in darkness will the sojourner now grope
Morrow your nature is to plough and to till
Breaking new ground, seeking God's will
Sowing new seed as you move through today
Believing the morrow will soon come your way
Morrow keeps searching...Because today will subside
When the new day comes...Morrow again will hide

THREE DRIVING SINS

Three driving sins propels all mankind
These three sins are ever on our mind
Sex, riches, and food... the lust of every man
For any of the three will destroy all who stand

Lust of sex is powerful, the downfall of many
The pleasure of it we love, and would share it with any
Its desire is ever burning in the members and the mind
Its passion will not rest until its fulfillment it doth find

Love of riches for the greedy whose palate never content
Pushing, shoving; stepping upon to gain every cent
Riches work with power to conquer in the world
Plundering, robbing, and deceiving to gain the costly pearls

Food to the surfeited, to stuff the belly of its glutton
Protruding from the stomach straining every button
Could it be a disease or evil spirit's driving force
From this endless glutton few will gain divorce

Which is it for you; we all have one or all
History has shown us either will bring our fall
Three driving sins depart from our lives
Break your wicked grip that truly we may thrive

IF I

If I could view forgiveness as simply as my Lord
My heart would not constrain me to close a ready shut door
The door of self-unforgiving remains yet open wide
The hurt, the pain, the sorrow...my emotions cannot hide

I cry aloud within my soul, but none would ever hear
The voice now sounds so loudly, and eyes now filled with tears
Wash away...Wash away...Sorrows deep inside
Set me free, O self in me, if only you would die

The hurt, the pain, the guilt, the shame...O ever would they be
If I could only forgive myself as my Lord's forgiven me
Forgiven me for my foolishness, which I have done so well
The foolish things of my dark soul, which points my way towards hell

A thousand years...a million tears...my sorrow cannot erase
The years of time, the salted lines of tears run down my face
The tracks of tears, increasing fears, ever will they race
My repentant soul, towards forgiveness-road, at an accelerating pace

If I would accept forgiveness, as my Lord does freely give
My soul would be delivered, and surely shall I live
A forgiven soul shall not grow cold by death's icy hand
The warmth of life, God's Sacrifice, has given me power to stand

Arise, O soul; you've been made whole, forgiveness of the Son
Accept His life, a Sacrifice, with Him your victory is won
Away my fears, self pity and tears; my heart no longer vexed
By His Blood; redeeming Love...I've learned to forgive and forget

YOUR HAZEL EYES
(How They Captivate The Soul)

Your hazel eyes how beautiful they appear
I can't help but stare into them, and chase away my fear
Your hazel eyes captivate my soul

My every emotion scarcely I can control
Surely God has planted them in your lovely face
A reflection of His beauty...His love...And His grace
Your hazel eyes till stare at me

Though not there before me, their glory I yet see
My heart still palpitates, and skips another beat
The eye of my soul, your hazel eyes do meet
If I could not behold them, where would love be

It is in your hazel eyes where love I do see
Your hazel eyes compliment your smile
Warm, soft and tender...Humble, meek and mild

Turning aside from them becomes a daunting task
Trying not to stare, my gaze I cannot mask
If you ever wonder why I gaze at you
...Look into a mirror, the answer will come through

THE LORD PAINTED US A RAINBOW

The LORD painted us a rainbow across a broken; cloudy sky
The message in its colors told of our love that will not die
We scaled the rainbow's heights in search of beginning and of end
Never could we find it for it is the love of eternal friends

A beautiful yellow shade of glory round about
In our hearts we feel the joy, causes us to shout
Standing under the rainbow beams of love; shining down
Though a bow far above me, you've become my crown

Trees stretching heavenward with arms stretched aloft
Sending up their praises with their leaves rustling soft
All at peace around us looking into each others eyes
A moment of love and romance...and passion tears we cry

SHE GAVE ME TWO WHITE ROSES

She gave me two white roses with one in full bloom
The other yet opening, for our love it gives more room
One fully open to our love that is no longer sealed
The other lies in waiting for the secrets to reveal

Manifested upon each soft petal is the love she's shared with me
With another still shrouded; longing to be set free
Open to receive the sunshine of a bright and shining love
Its petals reaching heavenward for romance high above

In darkness grows the second rose; concealing our passion
This one is intimately personal is our every erogenous action
Reserved for the one whom I am committed to for life
Scarce can I wait for our daylight to become our night

Both with pure white petals to show the sanctity of our union
No spot...No blemish...or, wrinkle to taint our love communion
With the open rose of day, and the closed one of the night
Love...Romance...And passion are both seen and hidden from sight

The warmth of our day rose, and the cool of our night
Both are one in the same, for in each other we delight
The sun of exaltation...and moon, and stars of humility
Will unite in total union to produce new brightness of tranquility

A Lover's Holiday approaches as two White Roses become one
We'll never cease to love each other even after this life is done

A COVENANT

A covenant ~ A covenant was made some years ago
Bonding two lives, body spirit and soul
How paradoxical that a covenant shall come to divide;
Yet with a Divine purpose to unite and unify

The Master of Covenants ordained it so,
Laying the way that we all should go
Enters the knife when we spike *I Do,*
Separate the old life, creating a new

Bone of my bones, and flesh of my flesh
Leaving the choice to God, He's given the Best
The sacrifice was made when we gave up our lives,
A woman for a husband, a man for a wife

The Master has taken our sacrifice,
And clave it asunder, arranged the pieces together,
One against another
Forming the Cross to separate other ties,
By the Power of His Sword, He has come to divide
Parted in pieces we felt love wouldn't survive,
But the smoke of His Spirit
And the Fire of His Light
Has passed between the pieces to bond a new life

A Covenant of Love invigorated this night,
Cherish your warmth, illuminated by God's Light
On a Lover's Holiday...it kindles new fire
Burning with love, passion and desire

Scarcely could I wait, my heart doth anticipate,
Loving the one who is my soul mate
This is my Covenant again unto you, to love and to cherish in the
words

I DO

THE STRENGTH OF THE MAN

Created from the dust without any form
Not of mortal parents were you born
Terrestrial dust with a celestial soul
Your strength to the heavenly Father you owe

A mist from the earth to water your soil
Formed of the clay without labor or toil
You arose with power, clothed in light
Everything about you was perfect and right

You are the height of all God's creation
Wisdom, understanding and knowledge to lead the nations
Given a command to dress and keep
A Garden Paradise, no tears to weep

Possessing the strength of an endless life
Yet, with it all for you; no wife
The strength of the man was found within
Drawn from your side, your most intimate friend

You looked upon her with much delight
Then said, **WO-MAN**, this one's just right
You've now discovered the strength of the man
Walk with her beside you, and take her by the hand

She gives you strength when your spirits are low
She is the one who is the might of your soul
The strength of the man was manifested from within
Choose to walk with her, until this life comes to its end

THE HEARTS OF SO MANY WOMEN CRY ALOUD

The hearts of so many women cry aloud
The secret pains and sorrow grip them with fury
The hands of angry and uncaring men tear them apart
Piercing words puncture like fiery darts

Lovely smiling faces hide the secret tears
A loving attitude to mask their fears
A cruel and vicious man in the shadows out of sight
Yet the aura of His presence always brings her fright

Hating her wholly though making love to her each night
Trying with her all to make it all seem so right
Abusive to her body, robbing it of its fruit
Pouring out her spirit as an unholy libation's juice

Year upon year of anguish shown upon her face
Crying and begging for one to show her grace
Trying to hold to the faith she has in God
While her life is being trampled as dung infested sod

Fearing every time he enters the door
Knowing his angry spirit as a lion will roar
Verbally, abusing her with the sleight of his mouth
The one he said he loved: the one he calls his spouse

Hatred, death, and darkness is the look upon his face
Leaving her with only tears of suffering she can't erase
When will one come to liberate her heart?
Give her true love, and with it a new start

You'll find such a one, you who are lovely and fair
There is such a man who will love you and care
When you feel you've stopped searching, then he'll appear
In him you will find a true and holy fear

He'll embrace you in love, binding your wounds
Through a fervent fiery love your heart he'll consume
Healing and restoration he'll bring to your life
Replacing all the pains…misery…and strife

A TEACHER
(A Disciple)

A teacher you are, one who would lead
Instructing the minds with enlightening seeds
A great profession have you chose
In wisdom, understanding, and knowledge you've rose

Accustomed to leading by your spoken word
Goading the hearts and mind by what they have heard
A disciplined leader who has gone on before
Diligently searching to open new doors

Doors that will lead to deeper levels of wisdom
Reflecting new light as the sun upon a prism
Well trained and eager to teach
A finger pointed upward to reach

A learned scholar through many a years
Some through laughter, many through tears
The tracks of your tears are the roads to follow
To fill hearts and minds those once were hollow

Now filled with instructions from the disciple along the way
Becoming a disciple growing stronger day-by-day
If I should encounter you, my teacher and my friend
I pray you show me wisdom to lead me to the end

THE CHIEF
(A Leader)

The Chief, A leader of mankind
He is the pinnacle of strength and perseverance
The overseer of vast horizons
One whose eyes are lit with discernment

He stands upon a foundation of wisdom
Wisdom gained following the leadership of his predecessors
His feet stand sure and tread a narrow path

His path is his legacy that others may follow
He has walked before those that he has led
Possessing new ground that his posterity may prosper

His legs are sturdy pillars that support his years of labors
Powerful and well refined, they've carried him through adversity
One a pillar of ebony that borne the weight of opposition
The other a pillar of ivory that has lifted the burdens of many

His shoulders have borne the burdens of many responsibilities
His back has remained strong and erect; that others may stand tall
He has put his hands to the plow
He has guided us all through the mine fields of unseen danger

His countenance is the look of experience
His eyes reflecting years of perceptive intuition
His mouth speaking wisdom, bringing understanding

His knowledge is ever increasing
Because his wisdom and understanding is ever growing
He is the pinnacle of the enlisted force
The embodiment of Air Force wisdom

WHEN HATRED ABOUNDS

When hatred abounds... none shall prevail
When hatred abounds...life becomes a living hell
When hatred abounds...a nation is bound
Bound by intense desire, peace never found

When hatred abounds...blood now boils
Heart now tainted, and spirits now soiled
When hatred abounds...souls now fail
Destruction, agony, and fears assail

When hatred abounds...Countenance glows red
Unholy redemption leaves us all dead
When hatred abounds...anger and rage
Eyes become blind, a beast is now caged

When hatred abounds...fury's unleashed
Unrestrained wrath, the beast is released
When hatred abounds...where is control?
The gird of restriction loses its hold

Reign in hatred that love may abound
Victory and peace will surely be found
Love is the key to hatred demise
Transforming its energies to love pure desire

THE CHIEF
(Mighty, Massive, Majestic, and Noble)

He is Mighty, being great or supreme in power
Turning the wheels of a well oiled machine

He is Massive, being imposing: In quantity, scope, intensity, degree
and scale
Full of wisdom, understand and knowledge
Spanning the spectrum of a diverse and ever increasing mission

He is Majestic, being sovereign in greatness and authority
Regal...dignity...splendor and grandeur
He is the all encompassing glory of the enlisted force

He is Noble, being of high hereditary rank
Showing greatness and magnanimity of character
Illustrious... grand... stately and magnificent
He is...THE CHIEF

BLOOD ON THE BATTLEFIELD
(How It Cries Aloud)

Blood on the battlefield saturate the soil
An Earth already corrupted; now given greater toil
Cries of the wounded piercing through the night
The all sickening sounds of war's anguished fright

The voices of men and women screaming in pain
All bleeding and dying, broken; pierced and lamed
Splattered and spilled, oozing and dropped
Fall to the ground, a fountain unstopped

The voice of the blood in a torturous silent scream
Cry from the earth, for one to redeem
Some poured out in violence, fury and rage
Screaming out in anger, a wild beast un caged

Others cry for vengeance, but not for itself
Only against injustice and the ravishes it has left
The cry is heard loudest in those who death draws near
Seeing no life thereafter; summons many fears

The Earth will ever mourn as she drinks in life's blood
What once flowed warm, now a cold and lifeless flood
Blood on the battlefield, how it cries aloud
Poured out like rain from a dark and stormy cloud

MOLTEN RAIN

The skies are clear on a starless night
Nothing shines but the moon so bright
The silhouettes of thunderous birds appear in the dark
Through the nigh skies can be seen vibrant sparks

Unsuspecting people mingle below
Now peering into the darkness, but little do they know
Fire from the darkness piercing the night
Streaking through the air, for the moment, a beautiful sight

People marvel, *what could this be?*
The Northern Lights over a desert sea
Now turn excitement into blood curdling screams
How molten rain is now what it seems

Peace and tranquility now turn to war
Vengeance or vindication, which can be sure
Molten rain from heaven does pour
Flesh now in anguish, and hearts bitter sore

Molten rain created by man; streaming down upon desert sand
When the storm is over will any yet stand?
Molten rain turns sand to glass
Stained red by the blood of the mass

FAR AWAY, TIME SPENT ALONE

Far away, time spent alone
Another day in forever, singing Lang Syne song
Isolated from the people I love most
In a land that is foreign, a guest, not a host

A pilgrim, a stranger in a land not my own
Toiling and laboring, trying to keep strong
My heart can't but wander over the year that has passed
Trying to draw strength, for inspiration I now gasp

A room that is silent, my thoughts are all I hear
Echoing of my loneliness ringing in my ears
No communications, the phones today are dead
An unfortunate occurrence, now nothing can be said

Reflecting on my loved ones, and what they mean to me
Wanting to be with them, but this is my reality
This day will pass, and the feelings dark and low
There will be a brighter a day to set my heart aglow

Praying for the dawning, a new day to begin
This dark and silent night shall soon come to an end
Wit it will come the laughter of all that is new
My heart will now rejoice over the darkness I've come through

COUNT THE COST

Count the cost of traveling in the way
Pain and pleasure are meted day by day
Open your wallet and empty your purse
This natural sacrifice gives believers eternal worth

Late night vigils and early morning prayers
Pouring out one's soul, laying the heart bare
Eyes still sleepy and body so weak
Words cannot be uttered, but the Spirit doth speak

The steady voice of thou shalt and shalt not
Will the crucifixion ever be stopped?
Wanting your way, yet having it not
The flesh is torment seething and hot

You've grown to maturity in the Stature of God's Son
Surely now the victory I've won
Now God's servant comes to inform you again
This, dear mature one, is not the end

Now you must know the mysteries of the Father
Through the midnight darkness the Way seems much harder
I thought I had been to God's Throne of Grace
Now, I am told...there is more to this Place

The Son is Day...and the Father is Night?
In His darkness I'm told not to fight?
Violence and fear in me do rage
You asked me to rest while trapped in this cage?

Empty me of all that I am
My flesh keeps asking; *how'd I get in this jam?*
The way to victory is in my defeat?
In a bottomless pit buried beneath?

Looking back behind me on all that was done
Turning back now nothing to be won
I resolve within me to again count the cost
Without daylight and darkness all would be lost

My brother...my sister...do remember this
Delight in the Father and the Prize you'll not miss

70

O WHEELS
(How They Roll)

O wheels, how they roll
Like thunder in the heaven, quaking the soul
None can stop you, for your power is within
A life of infinity, you'll roll without end

O powers of the wheels come carry me
Swept in your centripetal force, moving free
Spinning, swirling, ever moving on
The power of the Spirit to whom you belong

O wheels filled with fire
Carrying the Almighty with vehement desire
Come swing low whirlwind of fire
To me, man of dust, and lift me higher

Celestial substance in my terrestrial soul
Immortal dust has now made me whole
Coming from afar and transcending time
Seeking and searching, the lost you did find

WHEN FOR WHATEVER REASON

When for whatever reason...life takes a change
When for whatever reason...events turn strange
When for whatever reason...we don't understand
These are the times to grip our Savior's hand

When for whatever reason...tears fall from our eyes
When for whatever reason...we can't understand why
When for whatever reason...our light becomes dim
These are the times to just trust in Him

When for whatever reason...love seems to fail
When for whatever reason...peace seems like hell
When for whatever reason...we have shattered dreams
These are the times to drink from Christ's living streams

ANOTHER TIME TO SHARE
(Moments and Words Together)

Another time to share moments and words together
What a miracle, act of Almighty God
Able to put a voice into a written word
What a delight to have the joyful
Resonated sound of God's Word ringing,
Singing in our Souls!

Vivid images of truth,
Love...romance...passion...and compassion
Stood up erect in our minds and hearts
The brush of the artist
The needle of the weaver
The chisel of the sculptor move in our soul

The brush strokes are gentle yet determined
They caress the heart
The needle is piercing as it infuses us
Infusing us with soft linen righteousness

The chisel is mighty as it strikes
An indelible mark of beauty upon our will
An edifice of love is now created

BILLIE'S BOOK

OF POETIC

MEMORIES

(*Both Now & Then*)

by

Billie Beck

ABOUT THE ARTIST

Life has been good to me and I feel richly blessed through experience. I have been a proud wife, mother to seven talented children, Grandmother to an equally talented twenty-three, and Great-grandmother to another 17 wonderful people. One may well imagine that holiday gatherings in my Missouri home, congers many familiar visions of *The Walton Family*, filled with heart-warming stories such as seen on *Little House on the Prairie*. At seventy-six years young, poetry is just one of my many interests. My inspiration comes from God, Family, friends, and nature. As a retired registered nurse, I also enjoy reading, gardening, and modest success with gourmet cooking. Every day in my life finds a humble appreciation of such things.

Poetry comes in many forms, and my homespun reflections focus on family values, poetic expressions, and Japanese haiku. For me, writing poetry is much like turning off the technological world, sitting on the front porch, and enjoying the truly valuable things in life – shared experiences, among family and friends amid a beautiful sunset – and sharing too, the collective history that makes up the strong character of those living in America today.

Much of my development both artistically, and as a person, comes from growing up during the Great Depression. Times were difficult (except for the extremely wealthy) at that time. There were very few jobs available. Imagine not being able to afford so much as ice cubes for a favorite refreshment, or relentless worry over how to feed and clothe your children, and keep a roof over their heads while the unemployment rates peaked to 25%. That is how things were for the majority of people back then. Those who survived such trying times can attest – anything is possible with belief, hard work, love, and dedication. Such is the American spirit that continues to influence our country today. I love my family and believe in God - I couldn't have come this far without either of them. God, family and close friends inspire me. My favorite quote? Psalms 23: *The Lord is my Shepard ... He restoreth my soul.*

While I have been writing poetry as a means of artistically recording moments in my life (that are both great and small) for many years – this is my first book, and I wish to sincerely thank Dr. Harris "Cole" Vernick for my first merit-based scholarship publishing. May readers both enjoy, and find inspiration for their own unique books of poetic memories.

The Lord Is My Shepard ~

He Restoreth My Soul (Psalms 23)
Billie Beck

TABLE OF CONTENTS

CHAPTER ONE – FAMILY VALUES

MY HUSBAND – THE AVIATOR

With each wing shift, a silver spark
Streaks overhead like a dart
That pierces the foam of tumbled clouds
And scatters the mist apart

I see its white smoke churning
And fancy its spray in my face
Like touch of rain moistened gossamer
Or bits of dew drenched lace

I strain to follow in distant haze
The scintillating course of your flight
But only thunder in muted waves
Rambles down from the heavenly height

My feet are cowards and must always feel
Beneath them the earth's hard ground
But my spirit is bold and at your side
Rides with you - adventures abound

Author Comments: We were in the United States Air Force for 25 years. My husband was a B24 pilot and flew 35 missions over Germany. The last plane that he flew was the B52. I used to watch him take off and wonder. I stand in awe of those big steel birds. My spirit flies with him every day.

Musical Dreams

Lying in bed wrapped in your arms
watching shadows dance across my window
on a soft sensual breeze of spring
listening to the music of Mozart & Bach

Intoxicated, we listened to Eine Kleine Nachtmuisk
delicate touches serenaded my yearning body
kisses as sweet as the fragrance of Magnolia
on a warm spring breeze, danced upon my lips

Where was the music of the masters coming from
as it waltzed in and out of our souls and kindled desires
docile fingers ~ untying the ribbons of my silky robe
passion igniting as The Marriage of Figaro played on

Mozart took a bow and offered the stage to Bach
drowning in a liquid pool of passion, not missing a beat
Symphony No.40 in G Minor waltzed in and out of our souls
on a sensuous spring breeze and in a musical dream

Author Comments: Special thanks to my editor for helping me make this poem flow
with a rhythm and smoothness such as found upon a silent creek with nary a ripple on
a hot Missouri day.

DEPARTURE

While I was gone, they said
Seeing him being laid away
Under the flower-strewn earth

Let us store with reverent care
All the things he used to wear

Here, his coat upon the wall
Full of lively contours still
Beneath, his scuffed shoes
And from the shelf above
Odorous and satin smooth
The pipe he loved

They were so kind
I could not let them know
How futile all their toil
When I returned I saw
All was as before
You smiled as usual
From your favorite chair
And raised a hand in greeting

Author's Comments: Your spirit remains - gone but not forgotten.

PARENTHOOD
For Christina & Henry

Is this - he asks – *fulfillment?*
Years of earthbound days ahead
Now that first ecstasy has fled?
With proud humility he sees
His child upon its mother's knees
Sees her lift a tiny hand
Still wavering and weak
To feel its warmth and smoothness
Like velvet next to her cheek
Then to her lips and press
With many a soft caress
Tenderness wells up in him
The pattern falls into place
He looks above the child
In snowy lawn and lace
To read the answer there
Upon his dear one's face

KATIE'S GOODBYE KISS
For My Granddaughter, Amanda Katherine

Katie said goodbye and kissed me
Took my roughened hand in hers
Pressed her warm young lips
Against my wrinkled cheek
Something in this childish gesture
Love, spontaneous and kind
Brimmed my eyes with sudden tears
Someone once said that feelings sharp
In youth grow dim with age
And unused tear ducts dry
Then explain a rush of tears
When Katie said - goodbye
And kissed me

Author' Comments: As we age - we aren't as youthful and full of energy as once was. But, don't assume because of that we have lost the ability to Love, Mourn, and Cherish our memories. All are still working well. I didn't just have tears when Katie left to fulfill her dreams – I boo-hoo'd for days!

TEACHER & STUDENT
(For my daughter Liz – a Special Ed Teacher)

With bashful mien he stood beside her knee
And opened up his hand so she could see
A strange and shapeless thing made from the clay
That she had given him to mold that day

It was so crudely formed no one could tell
What childish concept he had meant to spell
She thought to find grave fault but saw him raise
His wistful eyes and changed the blame to praise

Assured he cupped the clay and turned to go
His shoulders stiff with pride, his face aglow
She never knew a spark was fanned to flame
That was to flare in time and bring a sculptor's fame

Author Comments: All children need praise and encouragement as they are clay in our hands – we are their teachers.

BIRD WISDOM
(For Aunt B)

In the lamp's pale light
That cut the darkened night
I saw him as he clung
Close to the sheltering wall
Oblivious to winds
That swirled and beat
To sting him with their barbs
Of cruel and pointed sleet
For in his breast he kept
Memories of storms that swept
Across his small bird life
And so he learned to know
That all storms pass in time
The churning turmoil ends
And with the sun once more
Will come day's welcome peace

Author Comments: My favorite Aunt B used to tell me, when all was not well – be patient, as all storms pass. Wise lady this aunt of mine!

DILLY MAN DILLY

Why such a clatter along the street
Screen doors slamming and running feet
Nappers tumbling from rumpled beds
Shaking dreams out of tousled heads?
They heard the Dilly man's bell and woke
Eager for popsicles, bars and coke;
Dashing outside waited in line
With Spot at the end, his eyes ashine;
Each day when the children went out to play
His Dilly man friend would say - okay
Then he would do his roll over trick
And get a leftover bar to lick.

Author Comments: Written in remembrance of when my kids were small. They lived for the sound of the ice-cream man's bell and would wake from a sound sleep to run and greet him. Yes, we had a dog (Spot) that went with them and also got a treat.

COMPASSION

Whenever there's a holiday
And I have time to play,
I often skate across the street
And on the other side I meet

An old man with a cane ~

He drags his feet along the walk
And never stops to have a talk
But always looks down at the ground
And makes a curious rustling sound

With every breath he takes ~

It must be hard when old and slow
To see how fast a child can go

So, passing by, I creep along
As though I'm not so very strong
And wait to skate with all my might
When round the corner out of sight

THE 13TH COMMANDMENT
Thou Shall Not Commit Abuse

(To All Who Have Suffered)

Screams
through-out the night

Weeping
as silent as still water

Spirits
shattered and torn

Sinking
further into a
black hole of despair

Scars
and pain will always be there.

FORGIVENESS?

Author's Comments: There are all kinds of abuse in this world-be it physical or verbal.
The end result is the same - DEMORALIZED

FAMILY TREE

Family tree
Sprouts from a
Miracle seed and

B
L
O
S
S
O
M
S

CALL FOR CHRISTMAS

Come Star; send down your clearest light
To guide man's footsteps in the night
His eyes adhere so close to earth
He cannot see beyond its girth

Come Seraphim, sing loud, and clear
Man's ears are dulled; he cannot hear
Your song of peace above the din
Of earthy sounds He glories in

Come Christmas Spirit, circle wide
The need is great this Christmas tide
For greed and lust rule man's hand
And hate grows rampant in the land

THE SILVER COBWEBS

One Christmas Eve, long ago
A dormered house with shades drawn low
Stood waiting in the dark and quiet
For the Christ Child's coming in the night
When lights were out He came to see
If homes were ready and to bless each tree
Since dawn the maid had scurried about
In search of spiders to put to rout
She swished her broom and made them go
Into the blustery wind and snow

When the Christ Child came, outside the door
The spiders huddled on the floor
They gazed at Him, their soft eyes brimmed
With longing to see how the tree was trimmed
He felt so sorry to see them sad
And let them in; what fun they had
Inspecting the trinkets on the trees
Until not one was left to see
Then, creeping down, outside they went
 Into the storm again, content

But the Christ Child viewed the tree aghast
For wherever their tiny feet had passed
Not a single string was bright and gay
But webbed instead with dusty gray
He mused, a bit, then with His hand
Changed every web to a shining strand
Since then we twine through Christmas green
Long threads that glow with silver sheen

100 YEAR BIRTHDAY GREETING ~ MOTHER

On your special day of 03-17-05
We gather to celebrate your life
Celebrating as we have in the past
By sharing our experiences of growing up
With you as our mother

We wanted to tell you this
As children there was so much we couldn't understand
The depression of the thirties was difficult for many
And our family was no exception

You worked late into the night as a seamstress
Using your treadle sewing machine and your skills
You turned out tailor made clothes and expensive gowns
For the wealthy

We realize now how much you sacrificed for us
Your dreams were put on hold and never came true
As you encouraged us to pursue ours
And you never complained

Being a seamstress couldn't be considered an exciting career
You didn't own expensive clothes
You didn't even own a diamond ring nor drive a fancy car
And you never got to travel

Every day regardless of how you felt you looked after us
Worried about us, fed us and loved us
Never expecting any thing in return
You taught us about unconditional love

You see mom, we know now and understand
That you actually gave each of us two lives - our own and yours
From the bottom of our hearts we thank you
We love and miss you so

Happy One Hundredth Birthday until we meet again
Your grateful and devoted children
Mary and Jack who have joined you in heaven …

~ Newell, Billie and Charles

MEMORIES OF THE GREAT DEPRESSION

(Circa 1929 – 1941)

It seems so easy to take so much for granted - there was a time in not so distant history, when such luxury simply, did not exist. Those who lived through such times, and survived, understand the value of – appreciation.

I remember the great depression
My Dad lost his job as a Barber
Things fell apart at our house
This seems to be what I first recall

Two men came to our house one early morning
Taking our new refrigerator with them
It had been repossessed

Now had to use our old one
It used blocks of ice
Couldn't use this ice for tea or water
Didn't have money - for that kind of luxury

My Dad looked for jobs but they were scarce
Most folks had their hair cut at home
Only the rich could afford a barber

WPA was created to help provide economic relief
My Dad didn't like the work – he took up drinking
There was little left of his check - after his "nights out"
He left … and Mom divorced him

Mother raised five children by herself
She was a seamstress and a very good one
She supported all of us on her income
From sewing, and selling home-made pecan pies

Sometimes she would be up at all hours
Finishing a garment for one of her clients
She worked so hard
Food was scarce - and we didn't have to be to told
To eat what was put on our plates

We all had chores so Mother had time to sew
My sister and I were responsible for the laundry
No there wasn't a dryer - just the air and the wind
The younger boys helped by cleaning house
Older brother found a job after school to help out

During Christmas holidays
Mom's family always had a large gathering
We each got one gift and a bag of fruit
I do believe we were happier with just one toy
Than kids are today - with so many

My brothers followed the wheat harvest
Up north as far as Nebraska
The pay was good but the work exhausting
War II was declared and things changed
All over the world

My Mother remarried and finally
Had some one who would appreciate & love her
We had a player piano with all the old rolls
We had one called *Don't Fence Me In*
That piano entertained us for hours

In the Fall, our large family gathered
At the park for supper
We had chili (which Mother made)
Others brought desserts and tea and coffee

These times were devastating for so many
Families were separated and marriages ruined
Unable to cope with the stress during that time
My siblings and I learned to take care of each other
My one and only sister, Mary, was like a Mother

We learned to appreciate and respect every thing we had
From food to clothes and the few toys that we received
Aunts, uncles, cousins, & friends - all shared what they had
With their less fortunate kin

Author Comments: Living through this depression during my childhood and early years
- enduring all the hardships that were shared by all, shaped me into the strong person
that I have become. I like to think this generation of survivors has helped to contribute
to and influence, the strength of character that we see in America today.

CHAPTER TWO – POETIC EXPRESSIONS

THE POET SINGS HIS SONG

The poet sings his song - he has no choice
Inherent in his soul, the melody
Beats like a pulse until he gives it voice
Unnumbered times he sends out winged words
To ring with cadences a crested peak
Only to have them ricochet and fall
Bereft of harmony, wingless and weak
At each rebuff the pulse wells up anew
Until he sings again - he has no choice

Author Comments: This is how I felt after working on a poem - forever trying to make it come together - and still not satisfied … Frustration!

THE POET'S DREAM
To All Poets

Inspired by a dream, the poet's thought
Flared high, and flowed in words of light
Each vibrant verse well fraught
With truths designed to help the world unite
And live in peace

Years it lay unread
The yellowed page furred thick with grime
Until a fumbling youth paused on his way
In search of some Utopia sublime
And found untouched within the ancient book
The poet's matchless ode

He filled his cup with all the singing words
And from them took the sustenance he craved
And drank it up

Awareness brought the Poet's soul release
He knew at last, Eternity's deep peace

DECEPTION

Our eyes
Reveal
The way
We feel
Toward those
We meet
And if deceit
Lies deep within
Take care
Lest friends
See through
Disguise
And all
Love dies

Author Comments: Written after reading a story about a romance during the civil war-
when much romance was carried on through eye contact.

CHRISTMAS EVE IN IRAQ

In Iraq, men will not see
The Star of the Nativity
On Christmas Eve; no candles shine
For them through windows wreathed in pine
All silvered bright in filigree

Instead, only a potpourri
Of bloody sickening debris
Car bombs exploding
Parts flying through the air

Let not one word we say malign
The task they do and undermine
Their faith in true democracy
They risk their lives to keep us free
From foes with sinister design in Iraq

VETERAN'S DAY
To All The Soldiers Of The Past, Present, and the Future

The rhythm of marching feet
A parade, and high on it's standard
The Flag
Of the USA
Trailing its starry folds

Stand tall, son, when it passes
Throw away that cigarette, and salute it
The symbol of your country
Holding a precious heritage
Your birthright

Think what that means
Freedom to live and grow unhampered
Freedom of speech
Freedom to learn
Freedom to love

It's yours to enjoy
Be grateful and proud
Stand tall and salute
When she passes

Author's Comments:

With sincere thanks to all that have fought and the ones still fighting to protect our freedom. It's a sad day in my life when I read of Flag burning in this country. I think of all the lives lost to keep her flying.

THE LIL' GIRL ON THE DOOR

Little one I see you there
With Golden flocks of flowing hair
Wings of silk reassuring smile
Come closer sit with me for a while
You look like someone I know
My memory fades me some although
You come to me each passing day
Make me feel content someway

Little girl upon my door
Come speak to me - Oh tell me more
I know you have something to say
Is it my time to fly away?
I know I've had my time on earth
Lived and love its all been worth
Every moment that I've had
I remember now I felt so sad

Little sis I loved you so
The angels came and took you though
It's nice to see you here once more
There upon my closet door
Sweet little sis I'll take your hand
You've come for me and this is grand
Within my heart I'd always pray
I knew you would return one day

Author Comments: While taking care of my friend Erika who was dying of lung Cancer, she would ask me numerous times during the day if I knew that Lil' girl on her closet door. I discussed this with Erika's husband and daughter. They informed me that she had been asking this same question for several weeks. He told me that Erika had survived World War II in Austria but her little sister who was 5-6 years of age had died from untreated pneumonia. They assumed that the Lil' girl was Erica's sister.

Of course we never saw the Lil' girl and Erika passed away the next week. How can one not believe in Angels?

NIGHT & DAY

The hooded night comes in on slippered feet
To snuff the blazing sun's bright candle out
And in its place above the shadowed street
Sets gentle stars that put the dark to rout
And soon, the world, by day so rough and bold
Is soothed to rest, and like a monk devout
Withdraws to ray, mysterious and old

Author Comments: Inspired by watching the bright sun sinking and dark shadows dancing throughout the sky.

NIGHT'S CUP
(Cinquain – Dedicated to M)

Night's cup
Is brimmed with stars
And glistening on top
A limpid yellow slice
Of moon

SKY
(Cinquain)

Sky
Grey clouds
Of trailing mist
Are veils that brush the hair
And leave wet stars entangled here
And there

ICED WORLD

All night the cold rain fell
Now glittering in the sun, the glazed earth
Gleams like an enchanted ballroom
Each tree is fringed with crystal pendants,
Sparkling with iridescence - A giant chandelier
Entranced I reach to grasp
The whole ephemeral loveliness
But a jealous wind stands guard
Fearful least I gaze too long
He sends the tinkling prisms crashing
And plies them underneath the trees
In splintered glassy heaps.

Author Comments: This was written after 2 beautiful ice storms here in Missouri - I can always find beauty in Mother Nature, in spite of being without power over four days!

A LETTER TO SPRING

This year, Spring when you arrive
Bursting with exuberance
Do not be in a hurry to leaf the trees
And spread the earth with bloom
We like to anticipate
Purple crocuses in the snow
Or gay jonquils
Green mist over the willows
White lace in the plum trees
Linger a while
Let us hold and savor
Winter was so tiresome and long

Author Comments: The long winter, with two long-lasting ice storms, inspired me to write.

NAKED AMARYLLIS LADY
Maryllis Belladonna
A flowered species native to South Africa

In nudity of coolest green
So every slender curve is seen
Between the tidy garden rows
A shameless naked lady grows
She flings her petalled tresses high
And flirts with me as I go by
Then whispers to herself and winks
Behind my back, the naughty minx
Although I think it's a disgrace
To flaunt her nudeness in my face
When showers blur my windowpane
I shiver with her in the rain

THE WEAVER

Spring drifted through the garden yesterday
And left the tree foam-white against the sky
Like maidens dressed in virginal array
Who tremble lest their lovers pass them by
I thought Spring's tapestry complete, but I
Forgot the April magic of her loom
This morning purple lilacs spill their bloom

Author Comments: Inspired by one of the late spring snow showers that we get in Missouri. Just beautiful to see the lilacs against the pristine white snow.

RENDEZVOUS

Oh, I must roam the woods today
No matter what the weather
Lest autumn beauty reach its peak
Before we get together

I would not miss the glowing gold
That overflows each hollow
Or scuffling through the crackling leaves
With ne'er a path to follow

My eager eyes will gather in
The loveliness around me
To hoard against the certain day
When winter winds have found me

So, I must roam the woods today
No matter what the weather
Tomorrow I may be too late
And miss it altogether

Author Comments:

If you haven't taken that walk or drive -hurry or you will miss all the beauty of autumn!

MIRROR, MIRROR ON THE WALL

When starting on a shopping tour
I fancy I have great allure
But my feelings of elation
Quickly changes to deflation
When I see a sober face
Staring from a mirrored space
And find its mine, grown
Commonplace

Author Comments: Written in remembrance of my sister and best friend, Mary - who used to accuse me of being vain. When we were out I would stop at every mirror to "primp." Now, I avoid every mirror when I shop!

TEA ETIQUETTE
(Limerick)

When a caller admits he has thirst
If in good manner's you're versed
With an offer of tea
Everyone will agree
The tea bag should be given to him first

A YOUNG MAIDEN
(Limerick)

There was a young maiden from Sutter
Who took a long ride in a cutter
She carried some cream
That her frisky team churned up into rich
Yellow butter

Author Comments: During the hot summers (no air conditioning-just fans and Mother Nature to help cool us), my brothers and sister (and me) would sit in the shade and make up rhymes and limericks - some unprintable!

TO GOD

Life held to my reluctant lips

I had tasted the bitter cup of sorrow

I turned aside and begged for help

Until some vague tomorrow

In vain I plea

For I know who holds tomorrow

Through it all

I learned

Humility

Author's Comments: God guided me through a most difficult time of my life-He was with me all the way and walked beside me until I could again stand alone - He has never left my side.

THOUGHTS FOR THE DAY

To All Poets ~ Great & Small

Peace on earth begins within
How you live
How you share
How you give your self
Makes all the difference in the world

Author's Comments: We don't have to wait until Christmas to give - Follow your passion and get involved with causes that touch your heart and benefit others. Blessings to all!

CHAPTER THREE - HAIKU

Haiku may be defined as a short Japanese poem (in the neighborhood of 17 syllables spanning one to three lines) that may embrace humankind, which is part of, rather than separate from, nature. Written outside of Japan, haiku may also utilize the language tools in which it is written. The term haiku is both singular and plural.

Maxene Alexander – Executive Editor

CHERRY BLOSSOMS
For my daughter Pamela

soft as dew drops
petals of pink rain
shower down on me

Inspired by a gift of Japanese Cherry Blossom that included lotions, bath gels, and powders with a heavenly fragrance that left the skin silky smooth - I guess poets are inspired to write about any thing!

⚬⚬⚬

SEASON TO SEASON

autumn leaves
bind the pages of summer
frost tightens the clasp

⚬⚬⚬

PENNIES FROM HEAVEN

golden leaves falling
pennies from heaven
from the oak tree

Inspired by a lovely sight that awaited me one morning ~hundreds of leaves falling like pennies from the 100 year old oak tree (beauty prevails - over the work!)

⚬⚬⚬

GREEN FROGS

greenish frogs
leaping in water
mating time

MY ALARM CLOCK

playing hide and seek
across my tiled red roof
playful squirrels wake me

❧

VOLCANO

hot steaming lava
pouring down the mountain side
volcanus erupts

❧

HEADING SOUTH

pristine white egrets
silhouettes against blue sky
southern migration

❧

FLIRTING FIREFLIES

winking yellow lights
Illuminating dark nights
Frolinking fireflies

❧

THE GREATEST SHOW ON EARTH

arrows of fire zigzag
across dark skies
thunderous applause follows

❧

THE WORLD
To My Great-Grandchildren

baby blue skies above
velvet green fields below
world on a merry-go-round

OF

GRACE

AND

GRATITUDE

By

Allen Gail Brady

ALL LOVE...

FLOWS FROM GOD
Allen Gail Brady

POET'S PROFILE

Pinball, anyone?

Pinball machines were my business for many years, playing, repairing, servicing and enjoying all aspects of the 'coin op' industry! Why then was I so surprised when the game of life took me for a bouncy ride? You think I would have seen it coming!

Randomly, I developed cancer; hit the bottom when I was told it was inoperable, bounced right back up when my surgeon managed to save my life by a miracle operation, then went right back down with seven months of aggressive chemotherapy.

Back on the upward ride, although too sick to continue my business, and hitting the wall a couple of times with bankruptcy and painful neuropathy, I discovered a God given talent for expressing myself in poetry. I hit the high marks when I joined a poetry website, and discovered a whole community of poets, diverse, friendly and welcoming, each with the same love of words which I had discovered in myself. I found healing and pleasure in writing and sharing my creative expressions.

The Giant pinball machine of my life rang high scoring bells when I met and fell in love with another poet. She and I became close, sharing our poetry and friendship online at first. I soon became involved and in love with her large family too. Then, in another spectacular downward dive, my cancer came back, this time in my lungs and bones. Devastated, I stared into the long downward spiral towards death. I was given four months to live without more Chemotherapy, which I refused.

Mary invited me to get very real, by coming all the way out to Florida to meet me! Before she had even arrived, I had taken her at her word, and sampled the delights of parasailing! Hard to look death in the face, whilst whooping with joy at several hundred feet above the sea! Mary's visit was a wonderland of reality mixed with the sublime. We lazed on beaches, shared sunsets and smoothies, and were children for a glorious day at Disney. "Paris next" she smiled, and Paris it was! Up the Eiffel Tower, down in the bowels of the metro system, over the Seine, Through Notre Dame, and scaling the heights of Montmartre. Life became a joyous bounce as we took in London, Brighton, beautiful North Devon and some time spent with my new English family.

In February, Mary came back to Florida, this time armed with four big empty suitcases and her large son Tom. We spent ten wonderful days together and at the end of their visit, they packed all my worldly goods into the cases, and simply brought me home with them! Here I am, surrounded by loving family, all my needs and wants provided, still going strong, nine months later.

Whatever the flips and the bounces, whether I hit the top score or the bottom, I have never been alone in this life. I know I have loved and been loved, and have truly lived.

...Reality? It's all just a game of pinball!

TABLE OF CONTENTS

Atop A Rhinoceros

In Africa; quite drunk I was,
atop a rhinoceros.
I grabbed for its horn
as it started to buck...
no horn, HIPPOPOTAMUS!

AUTHOR COMMENTS:
This poem was created from a challenge which I was given "rhinoceros" as a word to be rhymed in the poem—I used it as the title as well. It is my first "formal" poem.

The Abandoned Farm

A dust-clad, rusting tractor stands alone,
among the straw and spider webs that hang
from wooden rafters rotting in the sun,
illuminated in the shadows of midday.
Between the cracks in walls and ceiling high,
slivers of light slip deep into the dark inside.

A land once pure and proud, this empty world
is left with weeding paths and unkempt fence;
where living green grew tall and turned to gold,
harvested in dreams of someone's happiness,
forgotten now by those who came this way;
remembered long ago by those who could not stay.

A house without its curtains; without charm,
sits weathered on a hill by the abandoned farm.

AUTHOR COMMENTS:
This was one of my first poems written. I used the sonnet form as a base and adjusted the line length for effect. It was one of many poems I wrote raising the concerns for our farmers.

Counting Bricks In A Wall

In idle hours my thoughts drift back
to cooler days of fall,
no frosty winds or shoveling snows,
just counting bricks in a wall.

Some forty-foot high in shades of gray
with yellow, orange and blue
built near the middle of years gone by,
for people with nothing to do.

The bricks and stone, quite cool to touch,
where numbered men left stain,
frustrated tears and hard played sweat
grow darker with the rain.

While many a day I'd lie in green grass,
the wind-blowing high through trees
and swirling leaves, running so fast,
pretending like me, to be free.

When down from blue sky its white caught my eye,
an ever-so-hard-hit ball,
distracting attention from this, my ambition,
of counting bricks in a wall.

AUTHOR COMMENTS:
In America, baseball has been a traditionally loved sport and pastime for boys and men alike…there is a sense of freedom and artistry associated with the game; the ball flying high through the air…boys testing their physical skills and abilities while learning to play and work as a team…many lessons learned which carried over into life. Chicago's Wrigley Field is a great place where bleacher bums worship that freedom, youth and camaraderie. Only forty miles east on the lake Michigan shoreline stands another wall, forty-feet high, Indiana State Prison, serving as the backfield of their baseball diamond…both places were fields of honor where numbered men left stains upon those walls…under the same blue skies and wind-blown clouds…with the sound of gulls close by…I've seen both these walls…men longing to return to childhood, searching to be free once again.

All That Is Left

The papers served today
by the county sheriff,
say that I must leave this
land my family owned
for more than a hundred years.

On this porch, the chair
that my grandfather built,
its legs worn short with time,
sits like a monument
to the American farm.

Out by the road, a stone
lies left unturned,
where once a tractor broke
and fell upon my dad,
pinning his life to the earth.

This night, my last, I take
those memories with me
that gave my life its worth,
made this land my home,
and all that is left, I leave.

AUTHOR COMMENTS:

This was one of the first poems that I wrote, one of several inspired by taking a trip back to where I grew up as a boy. It was farm country in Indiana. Most of the homes and farms were still around, with a look of having never been touched. Many of the farms were out of business or sold out for developments…the little farming left was big business. I knew several families who had to sell out and file bankruptcy or barely broke even. I was behind the times in doing this, but I only just realized what it must have been like thirty years ago.

When Winter Turns

When winter turns and weeps its frozen tears,
this farm will close its gate and clear its field.
Within my loneliness, death finally nears.
The hour is close to join my fallen peers,
in loss by power that the bank will wield,
when winter turns and weeps its frozen tears.
That living song a farmer feels and hears
is stripped from me just like an apple peeled.
Within my loneliness, death finally nears.
A bitterness, white-hot within me sears,
my heart, so wounded as this fate is sealed,
when winter turns and weeps its frozen tears.
Before the mirror I must face my fears,
drop to the floor where I will pray there kneeled.
Within my loneliness, death finally nears.
At last, my dreams can rest, after long years
of struggling with crops for greater yield,
when winter turns and weeps its frozen tears.
Within my loneliness, death finally nears.

AUTHOR COMMENTS:
This is a villanelle, a beautiful poetic form. It is especially useful for dramatic effect with its strong repetition. It is true mirrored passion! The poem is one of the series I did on the plight of American farmers...this was a time in the 70's and 80's when many people were speaking out. The situation was one of progress. The expense to produce food for the table was increasing while the ability to raise the price of the product was not. Foreign supply was becoming easier, large corporate farming was sweeping the country...the small farmer was a thing of the past...had America allowed it to happen naturally, then all might have been well...we could have helped individuals restart their lives...but artificial economics were put in place that only made it worse...same outcome.

The Ghost of Wildcat Rocks

A childhood long ago when I was small
did leave my life with many memories,
of West Virginia's mountains standing tall,
and shadows dancing 'round the dogwood trees.

Out on my grandpa's porch in fading light,
we'd sit while Uncle Orn would tell his tales,
that kept us up and listening half the night,
about the dangers working on the rails.

His friend and he had ridden their handcar,
a stormy night too loud to hear the train
that crashed head-on and knocked him just as far,
as his friend's head went rolling in the rain.

Asleep, I dreamed with sounds of ticking clocks,
those footsteps from the Ghost of Wildcat Rocks.

AUTHOR COMMENTS:
This is a sonnet consisting of fourteen lines of iambic pentameter. I chose line breaks. Many modern sonnets do this, whereas, traditional Shakespearean sonnets are made of three quatrains and a rhyming couplet without line breaks. I enjoy the spacing to allow us to take a breath and feel less overwhelmed by such long verse. I also enjoy the separation between the parts. Sonnets tend to present a story or problem in the first couple parts of the poem, and then the last quatrain brings a resolution or further addressing of what has gone on...the last two lines then close the poem. In this case, I told a true story of my childhood. My Uncle Orn was a story teller...more likely, a teller of tall stories! But they were fun and entertaining. I added the ghost part to take advantage of the setting and how such fun could be. I dedicate this to Bean and Pip.

Upon The Christmas Tree

There's something very special about this time of year,
the frosty nip that bites the nose as winter draws so near.
Gaily decorations hang for everyone to see.
And lights are shining brightly, upon the Christmas tree.

A wreath of pine and ribbon adorns the hallway door.
Children lick Mom's candy spoon wishing there was more.
Cookies with large chocolate chips, fruitcake red and green,
but best of all the lights are bright, upon the Christmas tree.

Dad tickles Mom with Santa beard laughing, "Ho! Ho! Ho!"
And artfully maneuvers her near the mistletoe.
While tiny hands feel packages to see what they might be,
beneath the lights that shine so bright, upon the Christmas tree.

The room is warm and cozy with kids sprawled on the floor,
counting tags all marked for them wishing there were more.
Mom says that it is bedtime, on appeal Dad does agree,
and lights once bright grow dimmer, upon the Christmas tree.

A hug and kiss says thank you, then grownups fall to sleep.
But sleigh bells often interfere with children counting sheep.
At last, young eyes begin to close with dreams of what will be,
while lights are gently fading, upon the Christmas tree.

All is finally quiet, the house is very still.
Snowflakes do a magic dance across the windowsill,
while tinsel spark like fireflies, floating as if free,
giving life to shadows, upon the Christmas tree.

AUTHOR COMMENT:
This poem I wrote many years ago when I first starting writing. I wanted to put on paper what Christmas was like to me...and the Christmas tree was the best way to do it. This is a portrait of my childhood.

An Ode to Meatballs

(I'm not crazy about odes)

O, to have a song to sing
While throated by a nightingale,
a soaring on an opus wing,
this ship, about to sail.
For beauty's eye is love's sweetheart,
with touch of velvet fingers near.
My smile drawn tight is but the start
to closure of all lonely fear.
Beseech ye children of the flower.
Let open petals' glory glow,
while spilling nectar from their tower,
here, deep within the row.
So, echo not forever song;
be still in quiet time.
My throat is toadish and so wrong
to sing the glories' rhyme.
But fragrant, grease-smoke tingling,
brings gift inside my nose,
erasing tears of eyes that sting
while taste for meatballs grows!
For love me with your body's touch,
then cook my final dish.
And fill me with your love, so much,
that you're my dying wish.

AUTHOR COMMENTS:

Mary and I work as great inspirations for each other. We even give challenges to each others to write poems with a word in it and maybe no letter (e)...often the challenges are silly and meant to force the other to work within tight limitations... One such challenge is to pick a style and a title and for both writers to write a poem using this. While discussing what form to use during one of these times, I made the comment, "I'm not crazy about odes". This statement became a popular saying around the whole community. So I was challenged to write this poem about Mary's meat balls, and to name it, "I'm not crazy about odes".

Whispers Of A Rainbow

Heaven's breath fell silently this day,
as raindrops cried their morning dew,
wetting flowers and blankets of autumn leaves,
turned yellow by the rising sun.

Caressing breeze touches gently
with such tender hands as angel wings,
tugging at the collars, pulling them upwards,
pressing faces away from that touch.

Crunching leaves and twigs give way to steps.
Shoes pick up cut, wet and clinging grass,
leaves too, but fall aside with moving feet,
left again to dry and blow away.

A bugle cries and tears the morning air,
echoing against reverberating rifle fire,
first one, then two, then three.
But still the bugler sings his plea, taps for me.

Symbols wave and flap, softly tossed about,
but few have shown to salute or honor,
other than those fallen, called
so long ago, brought home at last.

Emerald eyes stare vacantly,
lost among those wooden chairs.
Wonder looks; take in her shoeless feet,
dirty toes wet with mud, peasant blouse.

Powder-born smoke dissipates with clouds,
taking away somber tones, as brightness
displays a haunting sound across the field,
from far horizon, whispers of a rainbow.

Poet Tears

Tonight, I feel tears flowing,
those that will not stop,
nor wet the cheeks nor stain
the clothes...but fill the hollowness
Inside.
Tears that cry behind the eyes,
where no one sees,
that never dry.

AUTHOR COMMENTS:
This is a descriptive write in which I studied the feelings of sadness and tried to describe it...I found that passion, and created this beautiful little poem.

Dying of the Rose

Browned, but on an edge or two,
the rose begins to spread its wings
towards the sun,
drying its freshness but the more,
unknowing that its life is near an end...
fragrant and so sweet.
Breathe in more life, and fill your stem
 with freshest, dew-drenched water,
 pulled from deep within the crusted earth.
Tilt your beauty skyward,
as though anew.
Open more, as leaf and petal fall.
Try, as nature asks you,
to be beautiful,
yet feel the lonely whisper of the wind.
Is it cold within your withered, dying heart?

The Pond

Sunlight reflects upon ripples in the pond,
like flags waving gently in a breeze.
Turtles float aimlessly
in quiet currents.

Live oak blossoms seed the water,
like powder sugar on a pie,
while a gray, white throated duck
splashes himself in cooler shade.

Wooden posts rise from the surface,
wetted green with algae and moss,
crisscrossed support braces looking
like a railroad sign.

Walkways built with warping timber,
graying in the sun and wind,
carrying the memories of
those who crossed.

Beyond the shoreline, rising to the road,
a drain pipe weeps earths tears
through washed branches
and pond debris.

Pine needles carpet a shaded room.
Birds dig with yellow beaks.
Branches sway, and on one tip,
a butterfly.

AUTHOR COMMENTS:

This is another form of free verse. I use no set line length, meter or rhyme. I do have quatrains with line breaks, so it could be given other labels. But I prefer classifying it free verse. In this case, I wrote this poem as an exercise in observation and description. I wrote this at a local restaurant. The restaurant, "The Road House", this road house going to and from boardwalks sits atop a pond. It is a picturesque place with great food. One day I asked my waitress for a pen. I then wrote this poem while sitting there observing the pond. I simply wrote about what I was actually seeing. I made a challenge out of this with a group of my poet friends and many of them did similar poems. They all told me that it was a fun challenge and learning experience for them. Mary joined me there once.

Waiting

Beneath the oak tree waiting
A small piece of carpet lies unrolled

Upon the ground; distant sounds
Of waves crashing against ancient rock.

Gulls cry in search of food; picnic smells.
The wicker basket is filled with wine and cheese,

Crackers, grapes and chocolate nuts
Nestling one cold piece of chicken wrapped;

Waiting too, beneath that tree planted
Some years ago in place of cut flowers.

Blue sky fills the breeze with warmth from
An autumn sun, shaded by the growing oak;

Pulling at the napkins, rolling an empty cup
Stilled for a moment by another sound…

Rustling leaves and the crunching steps
of one, or perhaps, another.

AUTHOR COMMENTS:

Mary and I were waiting to find out the results of tests being done for cancer. Neither of us knew if she had cancer or if mine had returned. We planted an oak tree and decided that we would return to have a picnic when it had grown into a shade tree. She didn't know if my cancer would allow me that opportunity, and now there was the chance that she, too, might have cancer. We simply agreed to meet…I wrote this poem as the outcome of that waiting…years went by, the tree was shading a lovely picnic spot…and someone was there.

Tomorrow, When I Waken

Now listen to the dreams as they unfold,
forever fall in place, as one might say.
Where once the breeze's touch grew stark and cold,
just look around and sense this warmth today.
Alive, I feel, enjoying one more play,
and to the water I am once more drawn,
to see the emerald green of warm gulf bay.
Tomorrow, when I waken, I'll be gone.

But never mind the frightened, feeling old.
For from this celebration I'll not stray,
with such surrounds of beauty makes me bold,
and grizzled fur is all that's looking grey.
Upon the sands, my troubles, I will lay,
pull tight this sweater waiting for the dawn.
I whisper to my love that I will stay.
Tomorrow, when I waken, I'll be gone.

Reach out to me and pull me close to hold.
Please share with me the happiness I weigh,
upon those scales of wishes that were sold,
to reimburse encumbrance I must pay.
So turn and share your laughter, I do pray.
And bless me with the pleasure of your yawn,
then giggle till I'm laughing and am gay.
Tomorrow, when I waken, I'll be gone.

Malady, know that I will never stray.
Just smile on me and king this knightly pawn,
and toast with me a glass from mica tray.
Tomorrow, when I waken, I'll be gone.

AUTHOR COMMENTS:
This is a ballade form of poem. I wrote this the day that I had tests taken to determine if the finding on my latest tests were cancer…or the return of my cancer. If it was back, it would be Stage IV, final stage…the prognosis would be that I was dying. So tomorrow I would be a different person. But today, while happy and free of such worry, I chose to go to the beach and enjoy a sunset, go to a nice restaurant and have a great meal, write this poem.

Chloe's Sonnet

How could there be a child more beautiful,

a flower rosy as your cheeks' bouquet?

Could softness be as soft as new lamb's wool.

or laughter like an angel's voice to pray?

Should rainbows dry their eyes and turn to smile,

while thunder curls a lip in voice to sing,

each time, in storm, you stop to pass the while,

with song of peace, releasing tears to wing?

For bubalilly's grow to wonder's height,

afresh of thought in ageless parallel,

to cast a softened hue on all that's right,

no thought to fear the all that such might quell.

While watching you grow up we've been allowed,

in blessings of what's you, to be so proud.

Adrift

Adrift
in
the silence
of
the tide,
motion filled
yet unmoved by
currents
or waves,
that
forever sweep
distant
shores,
pulled by the moon,
waiting
for
that one special night
when she
brings
me
home.

AUTHOR COMMENTS:
This is an example of free verse poetic form; there is no set rhythm or rhyme scheme to follow. Line length, syllabic count, and rhyme is completely non-essential to the poem...the key is the freedom to use the words, phrases and punctuation to control the movement and sound of the work. In this one I was floating out in the warm Gulf of Mexico to find this inspiration and to get much of the poetic language for it.

Beside The Fire

Embers glow and sparkle red,
deep into the shadows of night,
while dying flames dance their life.
Illuminated spires of smoke
give backdrop to bursting sprays
 shooting outwards, upwards,
racing with the heated draft.
Both warmth and hour
burden my eyes with sleep,
though drawn to stay and watch
this hearth beside the fire.

Hermosa Morning

Drooping eyelids of morning clouds
hide the hazy dawn.
Distant fire of orange and crimson
backdrop the horizon of pine-topped mountains.

Birds announce the awakening,
chilled slightly in the cool morning air,
shivering with the pine needles,
stirred by a gentle northern breeze.

Black Hills caressing this quiet time
like a child holding a cocoon in the hand's palm,
eyes held in awe by its opening,
revealing the spreading wings of a butterfly.

The Dakota Trail

East of the Black Hills lies a region to see
where trails find their end and friends sometimes meet.
A land stretching outward barren and worn,
worse than a desert where hearts are still torn.

Land is eroded from too many droughts.
Chokecherry thickets, pasque flower sprouts,
dried out farm with a dried out man,
not much else left in the Dakota badlands.

Sun scorching earth at one-twenty degrees.
Winter brings down a harsh sub-arctic freeze.
Beauty is scarce with miles in between;
the star-filled sky is like out of a dream.

One day while I traveled those trails headed west,
Stopped at a saloon for some much needed rest.
A smile and a drink from the owner was thrown.
And I got my first glimpse of that red desert rose.

Legend now has it when you're ridin' the trail,
you'll come across friends that never will fail.
And if you ever must lose them you might call it fate,
for on that long trail another one waits.

AUTHOR COMMENTS:
This is a quatrain. I wrote this poem about my trip to South Dakota. A friend is a rancher and owns a bar called the "Trails West Saloon". So this poem was in honor of her, and the nature of such oasis to the western ranchers and travelers to have a place to stop and cool off…a place to have a little recreation and companionship. She once told me that even if we lose a friend or someone we love, that there will be another one waiting on the trail for us. So I included that lovely sentiment in my write. And I found that the land is exactly how I described it. But it is beautiful and the sky is like a sea of stars.

Diamond Fly

Brilliant, white diamond, drifting

at the meeting of the blue,

emerald green sea pulling,

pulling me to you.

Lost among its swells,

too far from shallow shore,

could there be a turning back

more distant than no more?

While life's lightening thunder sounds

grow fainter, quiet,

peacefully,

reminding of another time,

a time not meant to be,

when I was not the one I am,

nor you the one for me,

when you were in a prison

and I was standing free.

So float away horizon,

fill the billowed sail,

know that I will follow

eternity's travail.

Summer

Coming home for the summer,

to be with family again,

taking walks and riding horses.

These are from what poems are written.

Fabric sewn in colors of June

and mountains' winds

tossing buckskin tassels about,

with horse tails brown and paint.

Leaving behind tomorrow,

making our own yesterdays.

Walking hand-in-hand right now.

New colts...new friends

giving hope...breeding new blood

into the tired hearts of those that meet

in these lands of spirits,

of ice and fire...

of summer.

AUTHOR COMMENTS:
This is another free verse. The poetic form allows the writer the license to use any line length and any rhythm. Each line is independent of the other lines. If rhyme is used in such a poem it is called free style rather than free verse. The poem is written more like prose, but uses language that is more beautiful or colorful than what is commonly spoken. In this poem, I am going home to a ranch in South Dakota for a summer vacation. A bunch of friends and family are meeting. I wrote this in their honor, to remind them, and myself, of the importance of this time...of the relationships...of the land.

Tandem Hearts

From its case first opened
comes familiar smell.
Wood's oil aroma drifting,
rise within her well.

Deep tones echo in her
sound whole, hollow beating,
harmonic tones pulsed in hand,
melodic interlude fleeting.

Touched, for only a moment
by velvet's soft embrace,
her blue, royal beauty
mirrored/ in his face.

Adjusting, gently, each string
of that heart inside,
tuning the rhythm of two beats.
Tears drop from two eyes,

falling on one string that touch,
echoing of two,
overtones in sadness,
twelve-bars played in blues.

Amplifier squealing,
distortion feedbacks' reign,
crying in rejection from
two hearts born in pain.

When finally lights go softly down,
and there upon the stage,
he stands alone with love in hands,
naked, unafraid.

Singing, soft vibrato strings,
touched with silver darts.
Pulsed harmonic melody,
beating tandem hearts.

EDITORIAL COMMENTS (Yvonne Marie Crain)
Tandem Hearts, authored by Allen Gail Brady was first published in the UK, within the book entitled
Tandem Hearts, ISBN-13: 978-0955537431, June 2007.

The Pilot

Stout against the wind he stands.

Cold is the arctic reach that penetrates

his woolen coat, the layers of cotton shirt and vest.

With hands in pockets, he braces his body and mind

against the harshness of the night.

He'll board the ship, bound for berthing,

and take it home with a skill and bravery

honed to sharpness by his life.

But, for now, he stares upon the waves.

Their bitterness warns him, with an icy spray,

that there is no forgiveness

on the North Sea.

AUTHOR COMMENTS:
This is an example of free verse. Such style serves well poems of descriptive nature and those of great storytelling. Here, I wrote a poem in honor of my friend, Ian Travis, Master Pilot in Sheerness, England. Proven seamen, these captains earn a job of bringing ships in and out of harbor, and to do it safely with the lives and property in his hands worth more than can possibly be imagined. Parking ships from fifty meters to three hundred and fifty meters require a delicate touch and concentration of a surgeon. The depth and tides, such amounts of water and their movement is crucial…how long will it take to stop such monsters of the sea, how much power will it take…for off by just a fraction can be disaster. Thank you, Ian, for showing me the poetic nature of tugs and chewing gum.

End of Summer

Thoughts, chilled along with
cooling waters of the gulf,
drifting laterally like sea grass,
uprooted by the waves.

Images of summer dance
amongst honeycomb reflections
of sunlight beneath the water,
illuminating white sands.

An angel fish touches me,
then two, then twenty-two.
Surrounded by a school,
inviting me to follow the swim.

White gulls float gracefully,
unusually quiet in their goodbye,
respectful of the freedom
shared this season.

Friendships, here amongst the wild,
reminiscent of those found
along the vacation trail,
bonds to be never broken by time.

Looking down at empty arms,
pulsed by the sea's caress and touch,
that heart once held now free,
released into the safety of the womb.

Back to the shore, I step from the water.
Weighted again by life's reality.
Distant thunder calls to me, "Come back."
Salted tears sting my eyes as I walk away.

AUTHOR COMMENTS:
Summer was nearing its end…I was either going back to work or my cancer had returned. It was soon to be decided by the tests taken in September of 2006. The amazing year was at its end…or so I thought…it had really just begun.

For Those That Stop

There is a rose,
a single rose that sits
upon a wall of thorn,
a rose of black's deepest hue,
trapping all the light,
reflecting none
but that which
a single tear sends
in sparkling reach
to those that pass
and dare to touch
her living softness,
not seen but felt,
in ways unimagined,
opening a world
of glorious,
sensual pleasure,
fragrant fingers
teasing laughter
from within,
awakening new life
and awareness
for those that stop.

AUTHOR COMMENTS:
This wonderful example of a flower serves as a metaphor for those times when someone or something is so hidden or unattractive that we simply pass by with them unnoticed or us not wanting to stop to look. But what of those who do stop? What do they find? Perhaps nothing…perhaps a wasted effort, but what if we do find something? Is there an opportunity to meet someone special or something of value? As an artist, I notice things that others might not see…I see the details. As a musician, I hear the sound and rhythms around me. As a poet I tell their story in an artistic and beautiful way.

My Words No Longer COME

Words come easily to me.
Was always able to express
the way I feel here in my mind,
in this world I've ruled so long.

But my world has made a change.
My quiet thoughts are restless now.
There are ripples on that stream,
flowing gently by.

The words can't fill the void
that is left each time you leave,
no matter how hard I try,
however long I cry.

Do you remember the time when I
could hold your heart within my hands,
tell you softly how it beats,
make you know I understand?

Well now I've let you come inside,
where all my thoughts would come my way,
where I'd find the words to say
how much you really mean to me.

I feel empty without you near.
Yesterday was never here.
So today could be the one...
but my words no longer come.

Narcissus

Legend tells of a reflection that stole
a man's heart for the beauty
he saw.
And in sadness, he died
for such beauty.
None can be restored by the cultivar,
straight and tall,
who tends her garden,
in shades of tan and cream,
cultivating his soul
with her perianth touch,
nourishing him from her corona,
while the stone nymph, Echo, cries.
But feet of clay
and eyes of green
try
to bring him back again.
But it was not his beauty, lost
in sorrow,
but the reflection of her,
in his eyes,
upon the water.

AUTHOR COMMENTS:

This is a free verse poem written to give a romantic look at the old myth. I wished to tell the story of a man in love with a woman, a woman whose beauty simply stole his heart each time he saw her. But circumstances prevented the two of them to be together, yet he still ached and pined at her beauty and at the thought of being together. In the myth, Echo loves this man. But the other woman did not...so the myth says that he starved to death because he so loved his own reflection in the water that he couldn't eat. In my story, it is her reflection in his eyes that he sees in the water that is what caused him to sit in a hopeless state, unable to eat, no desire to live. So after his death the other woman became a gardener who tended daffodils, those flowers representing him. It was her passion to bring him back to life through those flowers, her curse. This is just my imagination at work...I could see myself in the myth, and how hopeless love can be...for I could also see myself dying with a broken heart. I thought this story needed a romantic ending.

Exhale of the Night

Quite glorious, this sunset we behold.

Within its falling shadow, colors hang,

as evening turns the warmth of light to cold,

and stars replace the crystal notes once sang.

What ending could be better for this day?

Just watch the dawn pass slowly to the west,

arising in the east so far away,

allowing dark to bring much needed rest.

But in the dying embers of such fire,

a sky still glows where ashes only lie.

Should every sense of time, thus far, expire,

then feel the tandem breath that passes by?

For though the blazing inhale is quite strong,

The exhale of the night lasts just as long.

AUTHOR COMMENTS:
This sonnet was written as a challenge to use the last word of each line in the poem by Shakespeare, Sonnet #73. I first started writing a poem about some poor boy being lynched by his girlfriend's father for refusing to go away. I told Mary that it was hard to take the challenge seriously with such a poem and restrictions to use another poet's last words only. She suggested that there wasn't a reason I couldn't write a serious and meaningful poem...one to rival the original. At that time I changed my attitude and threw away what I had been working on. I then decided that I could write a sonnet, and that fourteen words had already been written...I then wrote this poem...for the sunrise can be such a glorious beginning to a day, a day filled with excitement and challenge...only to be toasted by the most beautiful of sunsets...what greatness exists in a day...but then the rest...but more than that...the night!

Clock

Upon the wooden mantel set,

atop a rough-hewn, gel-stained oak,

good time be kept for all that care,

this gathered party of good folk.

For whisper silent is the show

upon the wooden mantel set.

While palms are scratched to sweating brows,

each eye is fixed like all the rest.

An old man clears his drying throat,

while one clears lying conscience found,

upon the wooden mantel set,

with pointing hands and little sound.

Should fate or justice find their way

into this room where good folk met,

to stare upon the passing there,

upon the wooden mantel set.

AUTHOR COMMENTS:
This poem is a quatern in poetic form. I wrote this from a challenge in which we agreed to write one using the title "clock". In mine, I thought about a room with an old mantle clock, perhaps in a courthouse or place of similar somberness…a jury room…a waiting room…where men and lives were judged, perhaps…while waiting for that time to pass…waiting for the judgment to be made… for whatever reason one finds himself there.

The Bushman and the Boy

Down under, a place or a heart to be filled
with the fierceness and greatness of awe,
where the cry of a wind or the whisper of echoes
will reach to your eyes at the dawn.
For the legend of men are instilled in the children,
growing them hearty and tall,
longing to see to both ends of the rainbow,
awaiting, first sound of the call.
Be it in the pursuit of a sporting day's race,
or climbing a mountain so high,
could one find it embraced in the arms of a woman,
listening, intent, to her sigh.
Perhaps at a school with some lasting degree,
astute, in a library's realm,
carrying a friend, both he and his rifle,
or fighting a storm at the helm.
For the legend of poets and warriors down under,
a bushman, hard riding, in joy,
begins with the dreams first read in night's shadows,
detailed in the mind of the boy.

AUTHOR COMMENTS:

I wrote this poem in honor of a friend of mine, Mike Walsh, who is a writer and engineer from Australia. He and others have a roughness to their writing that I jokingly call bushdog style. They often write with varied length lines, giving a stop and go rhythm, less metered feeling. I like this with poetic license to be able to use the words, phrases, and punctuation to control the flow of the write, rather than a strict meter. In line eleven, "could one find it embraced in the arms of a woman," I have intentionally added a couple of syllables to the line length here to change the pace, to force it. I use things like this for emphasis, or to change the feel if the mood is to change, or if direction is changing...such tools we have are fun to work with...take a look at this line in particular to see what happens here...you might stumble on the first reading, but see what I have done, if you can. Read it a couple of times and see if you can understand my intentions. It speaks of boys becoming men... this line brings romance into the mix for the first time...I wanted to slow the read there for effect... but only an emphasis...and then the poem got on. I hope you do enjoy.

POETRY RAQS!

By

Amanda Dawn Vanessa Cianci

Music Seeps Into Writing

Just as Worlds Emerge from Dance

Amanda Dawn Vanessa Cianci

ABOUT THE ARTIST

I was born and raised on the Canadian Prairies. My Mother, Deirdre, introduced me to poetry at a very young age. She often wrote song lyrics and poems and shared them with me. Her demonstrations of written art were my first step into creative writing.

I displayed an easy understanding of poetry, and a flare for art in general, while in elementary school, as well as a musical inclination. My true fire for poetry, however, did not ignite 'til my adolescence when I discovered a book in the school library entitled *Flint and Feather: The Complete Poems of E. Pauline Johnson*. This remarkable Canadian poet inspired me to further develop my skill. I read her complete works multiple times in an effort to absorb as much from her inspiring words as possible.

The third stepping stone in my poetic exploration was in meeting another poet—Christopher William Cianci—who became my mentor in poetry as well as my closest friend and companion. Without his help my poetry might not have made the leap that it has into a richer, clearer expression of my creative mind. Since our marriage, in 2006,, Christopher and I still continue to encourage one another's artistic endeavors.

Despite an ease with the written word, my first artistic passion is dance, particularly American Cabaret Style of Oriental dance—Raqs Sharqi (*Raqs* meaning 'dance' and *Sharqi* translating as 'Eastern' or 'of the East'. It is pronounced *rawks shar-kee*.) or, in other words, Bellydance. For me, these two art forms, dance and poetry, perpetually inspire one another; music seeps into writing just as worlds emerge from dance.

In addition to these artistries, my interests also extend into the areas of health & fitness; pen art; Latin, African & Polynesian dance; and mysticism. I'm ambitious to pursue both dance and literature to greater heights and am preparing the manuscript for my second poetic publication, as well as a co-authored poetry book with my husband.

I derive inspiration not only from my own life's experiences but also from the lives of those around me. Nature, love, philosophy, mythology, spirituality, and fantasy, all fuel my quill, as do the challenges of form poetry. As such, my poetry shouldn't ever be viewed entirely as a 'diary' of my personal life. I write mostly for the pleasure and meditation of doing so.

I've assembled a collection of favored poems for this publication, to share my creative personality with the reader. I hope that the varying themes will provide something of interest for all who take the time to explore my poetry.

Special thanks to my Mother, Deirdre L. Tolson, and my husband, Christopher W. Cianci, for their love, help and encouragement.

TABLE OF CONTENTS

Sublime

Do my adoring poems, penned for you,
paint a portrait's glimpse into my soul?
Whilst sweet songs grace lips of zeal—
do you hear? I'm sound, soft, and whole.

What awaits us in tender silence
should we dissolve all need for words?
What wisdoms might you impart to me?
How fierce should our wildest fires burn?

Were my verses arrayed as flesh to you,
would the warmth therein be touchable?
If you could not search, deep, my jade eyes,
Sweetheart, could I still be as lovable?

Can I dance for you with total heart,
show you vividly a spirit sublime?
What portal's gates would part for your entry
to this lush fruitful haven of mine?

Where in your heart will you take me to
amongst unexplored landscapes within?
What adventures will you whisk me off on?
How deep into ocean's depths might I swim?

How far dare we delve into such pleasures?
What beauty with words can we write
when whispers, caresses—such pleasures—
are sensations hidden far in the night?

What bares lovemaking if we touch just
raw passions and expressions inside?
Where find we desire and where the spark,
when in imagery's hive such honeys reside?

If the only fertile grounds upon which
our intimate ambitions may play
are the sweetest words and fine poetry,
Lover, could you still take my breath away?

Ghost Ball

Slumped o'er wine or fluent on the floor
with dance steps which mimic a skill long before...
Transparent gowns—glimpse no figure beneath.
The music's collapsed, brought time to its knees.
Memories, all, that won't soon decay—
the waltz of longing that won't ebb away.
Decor of this hall, long faded, revived
by hands of the living—by the dead was denied.

Each night modern day slinks out and hides.
Drab walls bloom flowers which have long since died.
Gents 'round tables jest with passionate 'life';
Their laughter falls soundless—how bladeless a knife.
Night mistresses glide, their toes never land.
Pretty like dolls, those young Tragedy-Anne's.
Mists of old passions hang stale in the air,
like once-sweet perfumes, of their sweetness now bare.

Such an ending befell them—a crime never solved.
What desires still lure them, so unresolved?
Ghosts of this hall whisper secrets unheard.
This party's demise, perhaps, best never learned...

Crème

Taste love's milk of my lips' lyrical praise.
Whilst pressing deep, resistance shies away.
Our promise sought in such seductive ways—
taste love's milk of my lips' lyrical praise.
Alchemic influence of your touch so stays—
pure ivory breast of mine shant betray.
Taste love's milk of my lips' lyrical praise.
Whilst pressing deep, resistance shies away.

Sunset

Fading heart sinks beneath the sea—
troubling memory follows.
A last light on the horizon—
fated path accepted, it drowns.

Troubling memory follows
as stormy day raises the waves.
Last light bleeds crimson into night—
too devout a love not to rise.

A last light on the horizon,
wisdom of the predestined dawn.
Asleep, shall dream of joyous lands—
wake strong to climb aloft the clouds.

Fated path accepted, it drowns,
renewed with each self-bound cycle.
Emoting light shed in nurture
of soul's landscape, tending faithful.

The Bellydancer

Immersed, she's drenched in melodic rhythms.
Cascading tresses spill to a toned waist.
Song's foreign fingers stroke undulations,
painting focus on her soft-featured face.
Her spine, a regal serpent now waking,
slithers smoothly across drum's charming beat.
Hands proudly grace each meaningful Mudra
while hips rock their steady percussive heat.

Marble floors—cool and creamy hues seep forth,
like liquid richly paving dancer's path.
As though on sleek ice glide those practiced feet,
traversing space, appears effortless.
Stone pillars ascend, lifting her prayer—
dance encircled within sanctuary.
Thick velvet falls from domed ceiling, aloft—
granite etched with visions of royalty.

Satiny gales of finely stitched fabric—
a rising spell of silken mists and lace.
She adorns a cloud of most vibrant shades.
A ruby bindi—gem kisses her face.
Bejeweled chain shifts on muscled belly.
Engraved bells, in concert, hug rounded hips.
Halter richly fringed with glass beadery—
strands fired from the desert dunes of Egypt.

Wafted sheer veil frames her hypnotic form,
painting fluent language of skilled physique.
One curved motion melts into another—
lithesome limbs in waves of elegant ease.
Her abdomen flutters, accenting trills.
Winged arms lift strong, release slow in descent.
Controlled hips 'tick-tock' into four point locks.
Deep into this lush inner realm she's sent.

Middle East torch lit a fuse in the West
and by this guiding light, she celebrates,
illuminates all feminine delight—
a radiant rose poised in relevé.

The Bellydancer (Continued)

Body encouraged by drummer's quick hands,
her vivid poetry deftly hastens.
Earthly symbol, a woman's rolling hips
praise creation with quaking expression!

Veil released, billows, a cloud overhead
raining gently to pool, spent, on the floor.
Drawn into tempest—dancer's wild cyclone—
her mind quiets in the eye of the storm.
Magnificent beauty—heightening winds
of shining hair, skirts, skill, pride and passion.
Music's grip, at last, yields abrupt release—
she poses, appears void of exhaustion.

Catches her breath while thoughts reawaken,
as though emerging from deep lucid dreams.
Pillars dip back into swift dissolving
marble stage, seeking lands from whence they came.
The long draping carmine of plush curtains
once again dons a pastel floral print.
Pillowed furnishings of her living room
find their way back from vision's banishment.

Her glittering, fine, elaborate garb
now a cotton bra, loose-fitting plaid pants.
Sweetest dazzling smile upon her lips
remains charismatic—luxury clad.
A flask of oasis, precious in hand
as she hears her three-month-old baby wake,
The Mother, born to cuddle and nurture,
with spirit renewed for another day.

Twilight Vision

Soft painted auras melt
against a silver sky.
Soulful owl echoes his chant.
Loon plays her woodwind sigh.

Cricket's orchestra wakes
each newborn star of eve.
Mists moisten lush flora
whilst on sweet breezes, weave.

The trusted touch of dusk
strokes the slow treetop sway.
Deep shadows permeate
released in the fading day.

Hushed lunar reflections
dance on musing lagoon—
their dreams illuminate
in rippled crescent moon.

Veils thin, that divide worlds,
as realms of spirit reach—
touch, through this backwards hour,
those Shamans whom they teach.

Time's inhaling deeply,
shall exhale the night's rise,
don its charms to beguile
whilst daylight closes eyes.

The Hawk

When the wind blows hard
and the hawk's wings spread,
her focus is sharp,
she's sky bound in red.

The lift takes her high—
her course strong and stead.
With her wildest cry
she takes strength to head.

Vicious is beauty
when it causes dread.
Silence shall hurry
to fear's place instead.

The wind's wisdom wakes
while stroking her head.
Her great speed enflames
to strike her prey dead.

No question of will,
it's her realm to tread.
The wind will blow shrill
beneath feathers red.

Author's Note – *This poem was written for, and is dedicated to, my step-sister, Jessica Tolson. Jessi, I hope this totem carries true meaning for you and encourages the strength I know you harbor.*

Mistress Pleads ...

Judgment swayed,
an honest heart dismayed—
drowned victim to her own loving want.

Ring's symbolism broken, continues to haunt—
her memories of his touch which bitterly taunt.

Love's passions exceed loyalty's needs.
Her heart wails while it bleeds.
Mistress pleads...

Another Shattered Prism

(Acrostic)

A
note
of longing
trickles down
her pale parchment;
everything scrawled upon
red flushed cheeks and in silent
sorrowful eyes. Behind phantoms of
history are beautiful timeless memories.
A whisper's end, a shuddered sigh, releases
teardrops, imprisonment of blinking starlight.
Their sad beauty bathes in evening's ambiance.
Each night, she locks her gaze with the moon's—
recalls how it once hung over them so proudly,
emitting soft luminous light on their true love.
Dwelling in this cosmic company, she again
promises him her undying devotion, and
remembrances. She will cherish their
infinite union, that of love and
spirit, which shall live ever
more in her heart.

Poetic Galatea

Quill quenches desires
craving fingers seek.
Dip into fire,
inkwells ember deep.
Draw heart upon parchment—
prayers beg into being.
Words set atop alter—
wishes tempt to create.

Echoes my soul,
"Undress love, release!
Let me tremble before you
in love and of need.
Feed me, preserve me,
take all that pains.
Renew—revive!
Bound to you—bidden free!"

Wonderment breathes, awed,
animates dreams.
Arms wrap my waist, weaken my knees.
Heart wakes—mind falls to sleep.
Body aches whilst spirit weeps.
Gods speak of joy, how we please—
divinity seeps wherein we keep.

Adrenalin's penned into poetry,
lifting flesh and blood from raw fantasy.
"Hold me, unfold me,
wipe tears from my eyes!
I, your Galatea—
art loved into life!"

Sculpted of verse,
stroked warm and embraced.
Gratitude's drank, igniting praise.
Stepping from page, to nude reality,
held fast, tightly—
Devotion's decreed!

Her Ancient Dedication

Dancing—primal heartbeat flows—
past wild aurochs on the wall.
Their bodies sway, pulse and leap—
grace stroked to life by firelight.
Melting amidst lively troupe
of ripe ochre reds and gold,
shadows dash in from outside
escaping glacier-cooled night.

Excited, abandon mounts
melding with drummer's rhythm.
Sacred deities, beckoned
to partake in gathering.
Eerie hollow bird-bone flute
wails in spirit voice to bring
honored ones, coaxed lovingly,
to their caves festivities.

Dancer's full hips meet each beat
and melt into percussions.
Bone and ivory carved beads
rattle, tied loose 'round her wrists.
Collecting eyes, her bare feet
fall assured on trampled soil.
Her dedication displays
joy of Mother Earth's fine gifts.

Chanted song, magic and laughter,
thick as wood smoke lacing the air.
Impassioned so, the dancer,
her own celebration brims.
All the night fermented brew
passes 'round from hand to hand.
Bountiful, ripe harvest shared—
fruitful summer's last light dims.

Predawn shall find hearth fires banked
'neath vaulted limestone ceiling.
Dancer curled in lover's arms,
their riches wrapped in buckskins.

Before I Wake ...

Clasping my hand
you pull me forward
from sleeping form
drawing me toward
your astral realm
and floating gardens—
lunar spectrums
showering fragments
of light, like tears,
upon our faces.
Gather me near.
Love interlaces.

Dusk deepened with
immortal romance
enwraps my heart
in ethereal dance.
Your eyes, My Love,
their laughing spring green
streaked with violet
and pure golden sheen,
view my rainbow
and darkest shadows.
You kiss my light
and soothe my sorrows.

Devotion treads
upon cosmic soil.
Canopy crowns
above us, royal.
Emanating
with warm ecstasy,
we breathe in hues
of intimacy.
No deeper touch
may possess my soul.
Intricate love
so seduces whole.

Before I Wake (Continued)

Bathed in rivers
of cascading sparks,
in starlit glade
our union embarks.
'Midst lucid dreams
transcends time and space.
We're interlocked
in tightest embrace.
Lovemaking weaves
vivid tapestries.
Our bodies paint
with love's artistries.

You smooth my hair
with luminous hands—
unbridled gifts
of our fruitful lands.
Coursing tender
electricity,
I'll not deny
this absorbency.
Yes, dawn comes swift
with our burst of song—
before I wake
know we won't part long.

Winter Romance

Moonlight glitters on fresh fallen snow,
drifted upon icy windowsill,
whilst lovers bask in warm afterglow.

December snowflakes glide—whirl in show,
beckon cold drama's beauteous thrill.
Moonlight glitters on fresh fallen snow.

Golden flames lick in the fireplace, low.
Watch the world transform, tranquil and still,
whilst lovers bask in warm afterglow.

Trees lulled to sleep by winter's song, slow.
Wind chimes whisper their soothing night trill.
Moonlight glitters on fresh fallen snow.

The season's magic two hearts bestow,
dance in contentment of soul's fulfill
whilst lovers bask in warm afterglow.

Cuddled and wrapped there in quilted throw,
as nature dons white blanketed chill,
moonlight glitters on fresh fallen snow
whilst lovers bask in warm afterglow.

Vantage Point

Pushing past spruce and hazelnut bushes,
avoiding loose gravel on steeper slope,
she climbs the path to her place of refuge—
quiet mountain ledge where she flees to cope.

Settles onto folded woven blanket,
pulls her wool wrap tight, warding off the breeze,
closes her eyes, allows shoulders to drop,
then looks out to those far sparkling seas.

She breathes in pine scent and fresh morning dew,
vision nourished by panoramic spread.
Her village below, where many still sleep,
not yet risen to the conflicts ahead.

She bows her head to humbly acknowledge
those grand spirits who richly gift the land.
Thanks them for lessons which bore her patience,
though she oft' still struggles to understand.

The last faded star blinks out in the sky
yielding to the flawless blue summer day.
Nature's unopposed cycles united
yet, in her village, such wisdom's astray.

She basks in silence melded with birdsong,
wishes that the home-bound duals would cease,
to which she'll return, singing all the while,
grateful, at least, for her own inner peace.

Not to Forget

Sol - amber jewel adorns wintry morn,
perched aloft yond stand, tall pine and spruce,
whilst softly sings Zephyr, whirring on past,
who's journeys cross hushed Canada.

Maple and birch, in slumber's wake,
rest nude 'neath blanket of white.
Rivers, slow to don frozen night cap,
commit jackfish to secrecy.

So crisp the breath a child breathes,
that of beloved rich northern home.
Warm dens fashioned of wood and brick
shield dozing folk in quilted cocoons.

Frosted forests guard our cozy keeps,
where red fox curls in burrow's nest.
Padding bobcat prints snowy drifts
by marathon of brown bear's dream.

O, peaceful dawn, wild geese have flown
as beauty reigns, coats leaf and limb.
Those crystal spires drape prairie's crown—
shall ever thaw heart's memory.

Tempestuous Choreography

Black silk tornado—
dancer whirls, enraged.
Expelling fury,
wild, defying cage.
Steps etch granite floor.
Curves slither fiercely.
Craving shattered chains.
Escape sought blindly.

Frustrated tears bleed
from nigh-hateful face.
Struggling spirit
fights tightened restraints.
All windows locked, but
shall bust should I reach.
Amidst dungeon walls
desperate to breathe.

Song's thunderous growl-
anger bid welcome,
seeps into veins whilst
sanity's ravaged.
Moments of retreat
found in art's shadow—
dance keeps heartbeat strong,
hope in tomorrow...

Lovers' Lullaby

Lay me in lavender gardens to heal,
relaxed beneath an attentive caress.
Lull me into dreams that your eyes reveal.

Crescent moon's misted veil, bids thin conceal—
silver midst mauve of twilight's evanesce.
Lay me in lavender gardens to heal.

Cradled in your arms, this eve so surreal,
rhythm of two hearts fondly coalesce.
Lull me into dreams that your eyes reveal.

Touch ivory flesh with loving appeal.
Pale stars look on while two lovers undress.
Lay me in lavender gardens to heal.

Soothe me with a kiss; your devotion's seal.
Your hands gently smooth each fine brunette tress.
Lull me into dreams that your eyes reveal.

Fragrance wafts of lilac and chamomile
upon sighing breeze, where flees all distress.
Lay me in lavender gardens to heal.
Lull me into dreams that your eyes reveal.

Lady Golem

Secluded self-outcast
pines for her addiction.
Deforms in dank caverns—
internal confliction.
Piteous creature wails,
clefts hold tortured echo.
Fights in vain—her lover
will no longer follow.

Features split, distorting
in unending dual.
One bleeds crimson vengeance,
its twin pleads, a poor fool.
Cursed vicious, a nightmare,
condemned from deep within,
decays slow for one vile
irretrievable sin.

Suffers in bleak ruins—
shrine built of obsession.
Steep-burrowed void swallows
merciful redemption.
Hope pit-trapped, peace hunted.
Child weeps, warped inside.
Neglects light nigh smothered,
fades wherein she resides.

Claws fierce at rotted walls,
screams in shrill wretched shame.
May reap none other's greed
to host self-gotten blame.
Wrapped in thin ragged lies,
perpetual digress,
she hungers for one ring
that she'll never possess.

Barren Shore

Cold and gray
as the beach
those skies
reflect, desolate,
on my eyes.
Course grit sand
with raspy touch
on weary feet,
weakened as such.
O, salty waves
weep with fury!
Express my heart
for I'm unable!
Life sustains
by breath's acquiesce
of aching breast—
my tightened chest.
To stand hit
by bitter gale—
behaves as though
a hurricane—
not to quell,
nor grant heart pity,
thus, in failing paradise
I remain…

That Old Black Rum ...

Drinking in her pain,
shoots back that poison,
won't reflect upon
her bitter reason.

Release delivers
a rush, then she's numb.
Heartache's toxic brew
blends well with straight rum.

Deep midnight thickens
within dying heart,
whispers unheard words
from which mind won't part.

His tender touch fled,
her desire remained.
Foul clouds well and churn.
Clarity refrains.

With that final drop
her soul seems as ice.
Won't melt until morn—
her demons entice.

Howls fierce denial,
her shrill anguished cries.
Smashing glass to floor,
she closes her eyes…

Searching Closed Eyes

Shadows linger once sunset cast—
stains on stone, frozen silhouettes.
In silence, lime's parchment erodes,
clouding sight of lost ancestry.

Still, dates bespeak untimely truths,
whence mother rests o'er three new babes.
Riddles scrawled amidst fading clues,
whilst wind emotes low requiem.

Husband waits cold 'side empty plot.
One century gone, wife ne'er joined.
Four siblings lay—three daughters first,
just brother survived passed twenty.

Born 1850, nine years lived,
her grave etched by acidic rains,
effecting form—shoulders and head—
as though unquenched, shadow's restrained.

Stepping soft by worn epitaphs,
sad finales and queried ache,
young woman, fluent in grief's tongue,
interprets tales with sober ease.

While walking verdant memories,
her path unsure with no home claimed.
Mourns her daughter, since stolen ill—
her heart reads clear, those dwindled graves.

Simply a Rose

It's simply a rose,
a gift he offered to me
freely as his heart.

Sharp unhidden thorns,
just as true beauty and love,
unashamed of flaws.

Warm colored petals
soft as the finest velvet,
tender as his touch.

Full and blushing bloom
atop proud elegant stem,
yet surrendering.

Open as his heart,
his affections offered whole
as he welcomes mine.

Petal's arrangement
as though by an artist's hand,
presents natural.

Something beautiful,
feelings incomparable
when it draws my eye.

A token of love,
it's simply a rose, and yet
something so wondrous.

From Under the Muck

Long after skulking off, your smog still lingers thick.
That foul and putrid stench—Invading residue
wafts from stoop up stairwell, seeping 'neath bolted door.

Casting unnatural, acidic cloud cover
you smother my domain—light snuffed and fresh air chased.
Tainted showers entrap, drenching my atmosphere.

Had once thought you swampy, unpleasant, but of no threat.
Now, nightmarish tendrils swirl mad—your noxious raid—
black tentacles probing any means of entry.

Return to stagnant pools of your wicked wasteland!
Dwell shameful and deformed amidst disgusting slime!
Be gone, rot-swaddled beast! Move on, and let me be!

Legacy

Whilst setting sun 'pon sinking ship
sprays antiqued gold of western dream,
regretless breath, sweet on my lips,
praises rare bliss my heart has seen.

Briny winds message foreign coasts.
My song crowns even Neptune's roar.
Soul's gilded waves embrace my toast—
Cheers, fine sea! Passion to yond shores!

ROOTS

A
N
D

WINGS

by

Joy Ann C. Lara
(JJG Cabanos)

DEDICATED THOUGHTS

To my family and friends who encourage my creativity, my deepest gratitude. A special dedication to *my mother, Ced:* Throughout my childhood she ensured that I had the best teachers. She was the moving force behind my first solo painting exhibit held at *City Gallery in Manila, the Philippines*. It was a unique celebration of my 18th birthday, and a life-shaping success that pointed me toward artistic horizons.

Since then, I have had various exhibits in the Philippines and internationally. In the UK, my 3rd solo exhibit entitled *New Eyes* featured my poetry alongside my paintings. In the USA, I recently exhibited with the Westfield Art Association Drawing Group in Westfield, and the Visual Arts Center of New Jersey in Summit, New Jersey.

At this time I extend my gratitude for the scholarship grant I received from Dr. *Harris "Cole" Vernick, Founder of the Cole Foundation for the Arts*. I am honored and deeply grateful for the opportunity to share my love of poetry through *The Baker's Dozen, Volume III*. Also, I thank *Yvonne Marie Crain, Senior Editor* for her sincere interest and gentle guidance as editor.

The Roots of my life run deep providing a strong foundation which holds me as I stretch and test my Wings in art as in life.

This collection of poetry takes the reader through a journey of artistic growth. *ROOTS* features poems I wrote while in late elementary and in high school. *WINGS* is a gathering of poems written in recent years.

I sincerely hope these poems share the *groundedness* of being well-loved, and the *exhilaration* of flight as expressed and experienced in poetry.

Joy Ann C. Lara
~ JJG Cabanos ~

Strength in Vision:
Focused ~ Firm ~ Forward-Moving

Step by Step ~ Ferociously

Joy Ann C. Lara

AUTHOR'S PROFILE

By:
Yvonne Marie Crain
Senior Editor

Joy Ann Jalnaiz Guerrero Cabanos, or JJG Cabanos for short, was born, raised and educated in the Philippines.

She came to the States in 1989, worked for a publishing firm in New York City before settling in Pittsburgh, PA with her family. Husband Ed and sons Jaime and Javier are all strongly creative individuals, whose interests in art and literature mirror her own, and range beyond to include photography, theatre, film and sculpture.

In 2004 the family moved to the UK for three wonderful years. Having since returned to the USA, home is now in Westfield, New Jersey; yet Joy feels at home in various countries including the Philippines, the UK, France and Greece. Joy finds much of her inspiration comes from her family and her travels in different countries.

Joy was blessed to grow up in an extended family atmosphere that valued and encouraged creativity and expressiveness. Home is where her lifelong love of reading, writing and artistic talent blossomed. Although Joy thanks everyone in her family, she especially thanks her mother, *Ced,* for encouraging and supporting her education academically and in the various fine arts.

Through elementary and high school, Joy had classes in piano, art, and ballet. She continued her education and received a degree in Business Economics from the University of the Philippines.

In the visual arts, she was taught by renowned Filipino painter *Fernando B. Sena* and in ballet, *Leonor Orosa-Goquinco,* Philippine National Artist for Dance. These mentors nurtured and honed her natural gift of expression. Joy discovered that her painting and poetry complimented each other; as you find Joy's art, you may find her poetry as well. Words and images are many times married on a single canvas and expression.

Although Joy has a very sensitive side to her personality, she also has quite a wonderful sense of humor and her heart is filled with love for her family and mentors. These qualities are necessary to enable an artist to provide visuals for the readers.

Joy has expressed that she is *lucky number thirteen,* chosen in this wonderful trilogy. Although she may not be placed as the last poet of this wonderful piece of poetic works, it was not luck that brought her artistic poetry here, but definitely was her wonderful God given world of beauty and creativity. It is my pleasure at this time to present JJG Cabanos to our ancient and accepted craft of poetic literature.

TABLE OF CONTENTS

PART ONE: ROOTS

A well rooted system of growth will be found beneath a solid, encouraging and loving foundation. It comes and remains healthy through continued nurturing and well formed direction. Self-assurance sends the roots deep for strength. Self-reliance encourages the expansion of feeders. Both equally important to enable a lifetime held steadfast. How fortunate are the ones who understand and give this important deliverance. How grateful are the ones who openly receive it.

Perspective

There once was a student of Maryknoll

Who abnormally grew very tall

With head in the clouds

She looked down on crowds,

And wondered why things were so small

Author Comments: I studied at Maryknoll, a private Catholic school for girls attended by many students from well-to-do families. Maryknoll can be found in numerous countries around the globe, i.e., the Philippines, China, and the U.S.A., and more. It provided education from elementary through university level.

Editor Comments: Limericks are usually considered humorous, nonsense or off-color. *Perspective* is a subject about young people living a sheltered lifestyle, perhaps untouched; therefore oblivious to the reality of poverty around them. *Perspective* begins in the direct and usual pattern of most limericks; however, it ends with an unusual twist that will bring a smile to your face (Yvonne Marie Crain ~ Senior Editor).

Prayer in a Storm

I feel so much like rain today
in a desert parched by sun.
Inside I'm cold and wondering
if my feeling heart is done.

Day-by-day my life goes by
like raindrops cast away.
My tears continue on
as rain I cannot stay

and dwell on mem'ries of things held dear,
they echo sounds of pain.
I want to run far from them,
I live in rushing rain.

Now where am I to go?
What am I destined to do?
God ~ I yearn so much to learn
to safely come home to you.

Rain ~ if you only show me how
from clouds you find the sea
I'd brave the ebb and flow of life
then surface to find me.

If only you'd dispel the fog
sun's warmth I may behold.
Because I need a chance to feel
youth before I grow old.

But rain endures ~ life's streets shine wet
and onward I must plod.
I fear ~ lest lightning strikes my dam,
release a mounting flood

of bitterness with sad regret
my rain has washed on down.
God~ I do feel the strong currents,
please don't let me drown!

A Living Voice Inside
(A Poem for Mom)

Mommy dearest ~ Mommy sweet,
Mommy good and mild…
These were words I wrote to you
when I was but a child.

Time has changed me; change has made
a diff'rent melody…
Have I sung it to you Mom?
At times I sound off-key.

But still the words ring in my soul
the feelings swell and flow…
They are what I can't hold back
I just want you to know.
That now you're more than dearest Mom,
more than a friend and guide
you've grown to be a part of me
a living voice inside.

I'd like to let you know, dear Mom
it's rarely that I do…
I value all you've done for me,
and Mom ~ *I do love you.*

A love like mine for you is strong
because it stems from yours…
Thank you Mom ~ this love you've grown
is *magic* we'll call ours.
For like you say, *time is too short*
and *every moment counts…*
Now I leave behind the past,
my childhood, sights and sounds.

You will always be with me
throughout life's changing weather.

Come what may, I shall remain,
to you ~ your loving daughter

Author Comments: This is a thank you poem I wrote for my Mom upon my high school graduation.

For You ~ For Us ~ Forever
(A poem for Dad)

To the greatest Dad a girl could have
my watchful lord protector.
Ever faithful ~ always caring,
none better could I wish for.

To my fav'rite clown who always
cheers me up with laughter.
Never failing Savior… when
my troubles runneth over.

Dearest Dad, how could I be
here or now…without you?
Yet, such times come rare and few
when I say, *Thanks; I love you.*

So here is a chance for me
to say what fills my heart,
thank you Dad for everything;
I've loved you from the start.

I love you here…I love you now
tomorrow you will see
how all your love and sacrifice
has made a better me.

Some day you'll be proud to show
the world your "little" daughter.
I in turn shall not forget
the debt I owe you, Father.

For time flies fast, you will change;
I shall grow old too.
The only thing that will remain
is what love like yours can do.

My special thanks as I leave
this small world for another.
I'm not afraid; I'll make it through…

For You ~ For Us ~ Forever

Author Comments: A thank you poem to my Dad upon my high school graduation.

156

Reverie in the Rock Garden

shade and shadow

in my woodsy hollow

cascades of green

showers of yellow

disquiet or peace

in worn paths to follow

the brilliance of color

conceals secret sorrow

Author Comments: This piece I wrote as a high school freshman. It appears that I was highly aware of color and all its nuances even then.

Editor Comments: A special hideaway place found, perchance to knock on the doors of secrets; finding the normal simplistic ebb and flow of all lives, both joy and sadness (Yvonne Marie Crain, Senior Editor).

Comets

My dreams are comets in the sky,
Streaks of brilliance passing by
Lighting up the darkest night
Then quickly vanish from my sight.

Dreams have wings so swift you see,
They fly too far and fast for me
To reach ~ to clutch ~ to hold at last
  Before they fade into my past.

That's why my friend I look to you,
For help before they bid adieu
It's time to catch this falling star
Before it falls away too far.

Before its light has swiftly flown
And dares to leave me all alone,
Let's catch that *Comet;* make it stay
Help make my dreams come true today.

WANTED: A Place

I need a quiet place for me

where there is friendly privacy.

Peace and quiet; without loud noise,

a spot where I can hear my voice.

And talk with Him who makes all life

a haven from the reach of strife.

A place where I can feel I'm one

with nature…*GOD*… the stars and sun.

A Shangri-la where I am free

to live and let myself be me.

Found Peace

Beauty lies in everything;

just there and waiting to be found.

Wonders are here; right before us,

if only we'd stop to look around.

If only we'd stop warring

and take time out to think and breathe.

We'd find love and beauty everywhere,

above us ~ among us ~ beside ~ beneath.

PART TWO: WINGS

With Roots lovingly nourished and lessons well learned; time is now to stretch and test one's Wings. Adulthood ushers in an exciting passage of life.

Everyday experiences create highs and lows; life swirls gentle as a breeze or whirls wild as a tornado. One learns the importance of drinking deep from wellsprings of creativity. This provides sustenance and resilience for the journey, which when taken with courage and faith, opens up a world wider and more wondrous than the imagination can intuit.

What Do You Want To Be
Now That You're All Grown Up?

I want to be
like the tree in winter:

> Unadorned
> Unafraid
> Survivor of snows
> Believer in spring

Claiming my place in the cycle of seasons

> Rooted
> Steadfast
> Ever-reaching
> .....ever-reaching

Ode to Wildflowers

I admire the wildflower

because it spends itself

in unabashed bloom,

undeterred and self-affirmed

even if…

it is a mere pinprick of color

in a nettle-choked corner where nobody goes,

even if…

it is unwelcome

in the well-tended beds of blooms deemed worthier of our gaze.

Tiny Seeds

This is the thought

That keeps me alive through winter:

      Tiny seeds patient in the darkness

Tiny seeds prepared to blaze forth in their time

Their time always comes,

With the ceaseless cycle of seasons.

Swift Sunrise

It's gone, where is it?

Quickbright shard of flashfire

that razed this scaffolding of branches

holding up my morning's leaden sky.

(Oops, lost the rest of this poem. I'll have to find it...)

Editor to Author: Joy, did you find the completed version of *Swift Sunrise?* "(Oops, lost the rest of this poem. I'll have to find it...)" this is very funny. I believe most people can relate to misplacement of paperwork or other articles, and sometimes a frantic search to find them (Yvonne Marie Crain, Senior Editor).

In the Louvre without a Camera

One day, I was
in the Louvre without a camera;
the most stupid mistake a tourist could make.

But then Spirit did not intend
that I walk those halls a spectator
snapping *I-was-there* souvenirs.

That day I was swept up
by ghosts of artists past.
Spoken to, shaken and screamed at
by brethren who have trodden that road
I dare dream of taking
…yet fear taking.

Fateful day! I am
dizzied ~ engulfed
in the almost-physical embrace of
those who came before me.

*"Come drink, come be,
WHY DO YOU NOT?"*

And my naysayer falls in a crumpled heap;
turned to dust that scatters in the footsteps of the crowds.

New day, I was
Reborn
In the Louvre without a camera*!*

Twins …Firenze

I returned to my room past sundown;

the heat of Florentine dusk on my cheeks.

I am weary…

but filled.

Names gush with my breath in rivers of awe and reverence:

Michelagnolo ~Brunelleschi ~Giotto ~Botticelli ~Rafaello…

She returned to her room past sundown;

the heat of Florentine dusk on her cheeks.

She is weary…

but laden.

Names gush with her breath in rivers of awe and reverence:

Fendi ~ Armani ~ Versace ~ Coveri ~ Ferragamo…

Children Learning to Walk

Come little brother,
I'm learning to walk
and how to rise when I stumble.
Here's a handhold
across this vast divide of ocean,
I am here… I must walk this road.
You are there…you must walk yours.

Please…take my hand and hold it;
step one-foot-in-front-of-the-other along with me
Onto each our own separate journeys

    Hold on… but feel the earth solid beneath you.
    Hold on… but feel your strength gather.
    Hold on… but feel your horizon pull.

Know we are stepping into surefootedness,
find strength ~ even if sometimes afraid.
We all fear passing shadows or stones that might trip us.

Come then, brother, take my hand.
We can grow steady together
and when we let go…
I will pause ~ watching you with love and pride
as you walk, run, then fly into the promise of your dawn.
I will smile ~ hit my stride and blaze into mine.

Author Comments: For JJ and Jan; for brothers and sisters everywhere who are learning to love each other.

Lasagna a la Lola Auntch*

Although she cannot be with you, 'Vier, **
her Love remains sustained.

Manifested
in al dente layers of comfort:

> *Béchamel ~ Marinara*
>
> *Meat and Spices*
>
> *Melt-in-your-mouth Cheese*

All baked into this fragrant feast:

> *Self-Sacrifice ~ Strength*
>
> *Gentle Smiles*
>
> *Caresses ~ and Care*

Her Love journeys over our separating sea.
In celebration and assurance
always to remain:

> *Nourishing*
>
> *and*
>
> *Constant*

Lasagna a la Lola Auntch,
whenever… wherever…we may roam.

* *Lola Auntch* is a nickname meaning *grandma-aunt.*
** Short for *Javier,* my youngest son's name.

Author Comments: This poem came from a bedtime ritual I have with my youngest son. As he drifts off to sleep, I whisper a litany of how my parents, my brothers, my aunt (his grand-aunt whom we fondly named *Lola Auntch*), love him even though we are half the world away from them. One of Javier's favorite comfort foods is lasagna, which happens to be a specialty of *Lola Auntch.* My childhood memories of New Year's Eve were made more special by her uniquely creamy lasagna. Today, I continue to follow her recipe; *Lasagna a la Lola Auntch.* This will always remain the incarnation of her love wherever we are and however far apart we may be.

Praying in the Garden

Flowers are prayers
and prayers start healing;
we entrust in the Lord,
this grief we are feeling:
helplessness, anger,
vengeance and fear,
despair and questioning,
Where is GOD here?

Let flowers remind us,
yes ~ hope stays in reach,
in simple ~ in small things;
in the kindness we teach
by our good examples,
and prayers we pray;
by actions of loving
to all ~ everyday.

So, though we can't be there
to battle the fires,
to save shattered lives
as we surely desire,
our challenge is Here ~ Now
our call is to show
that Good springs eternal
just as flowers grow.

So look to the flowers;
let them help us pray,
may our prayers for Peace come alive
in all we think, say and do today.

Author Comments: In Memory of all who died in yesterday's attacks and for all victims of terrorism around the world, especially those who have gone unheard and unmourned.

In Companionship and Sympathy to all people whose lives are shattered by violence in any shape, form and scale.

In Gratitude to the courageous people involved in all aspects of rescue, investigation and rebuilding in this tragedy and all like it the world over.

In Hope and Encouragement as we each move forth in ways large and small, learning to keep hope strong. May we bravely seek Peace, unceasingly, and in our own way.

Today

(For the mornings when I'm at war with the world)

...and so, Today

Do I add?	Take away?
Destroy?	Create?
Spread love?	Spread Hate?

Build up this smoldering pile of injustice,
or bolster the pillars of small honest joys?

I have	Mind
I have	Heart
I have	Will
I have	Freedom

it is

it is

a choice—my choice

Today

Editor Comments: Many thoughts and feelings were derived from the terror experienced worldwide on September 11, 2001. Alas, to live in chaos or peace, to love or hate is a choice we all must daily make. Which is it that you choose?

Introduction: Broken Crayons

It was but a few days past September 11, 2001. *Celebrating Diversity,* a Pittsburgh-based community organization I was a part of, responded to the tragedy by hosting a gathering for support and sharing. I was assigned to organize the children's craft activity.

As crayons were needed for this, I requested friends and neighbors to donate crayons they no longer needed. As the time approached to setup the activity tables, I began to wonder if the children would be interested in used odds and ends of craft material. After all, they are accustomed to new supplies.

A thought then crossed my mind; *these castoff crayons, when put to paper, continue to color as pure and true as when new.* These broken crayons, a metaphor of the human condition, conjured an image that captured the polarities of wrenching fear and timid hope I felt at that time. This poem came forth as an encouraging salve for all broken hearts, including mine.

Broken Crayons

We are all broken crayons,
but we can still paint a picture of peace.
Though shattered
though crushed
WE ARE
STILL,
       the purity
       the vibrancy
       the life-force
of colors
that can hold the vision of a world
beautiful and peaceful
as it was meant to be.

Author Comments: I read this poem later during the *Celebrating Diversity* gathering to begin the healing share. I hope it will continue to remind us that whatever shape or form we are in, shiny new or old and broken, we still remain *the vibrant colors that can hold a vision of this world… beautiful and peaceful, as it is meant to be.*

Broken Crayons was also read during "Colors of Peace", an ecumenical Service held for the first yearly remembrance of 9/11, by the *South Hills Interfaith Ministry* in Pittsburgh, PA.

Non-Traditional Prayer

won't find me

praying in grandmother's manner:

Veiled, bowed

walking on knees and feeding on pain,

rosary beads ~ rosary beads ~ rosary beads.

I'll pray

with breath

of winter branches forcing bud.

The anguish of tonight's internet headline

my lament and griefcry:

Kyrie!

Eleison!

Kyrie!

Requiem

The cherry blossoms were blooming
when you left.
I was not by your side,
but I can picture

how labored breath and ebbing will
found release
from the measured drip of medicines
and tearful prayers.

I'd like to think
you gained the freedom
of this burgeoning springtime
on this far side of the world.

Was it pink, Uncle?
Through pain,
and fear of the unwanted parting
was it lush and many-petalled?

Blue-skied and green-budded,
this new;
this everlasting life
that has reclaimed you?

Sunflower Said

Even those who bloom,

glow

and shine their light into the darkness

will tire

and fade;

living out their season

their unrealized dream-seeds calling in the wind.

Who will answer?

Who will answer... will you?

Nilaga ni Venancia

Soup…
simmers memory.

Hearty sustenance
ladled by *Lola* *
to warm and calm
on thunderous typhoon evenings
long…long…too long ago.

Now served of me,
heady with flavor and remembrance
to warm and calm
on blustery frozen nights.

Filling, soul-bracing proof
that love spans generations:
 …Thick
   …Nourishing
     … Undiminished.

* **Lola**: Tagalog word meaning *Grandmother. Tagalog is spoken in the Philippines.*

Author Comments: Nilaga is a soup made with beef shank, cabbage, potatoes, carrots and plantains. As I was growing up, this was my *ultimate comfort food* during the rainy season. My Grandmother*Venancia* serving this soup is an indelible image of love.

Rondo Alla Turca

My warmed-up fingers dance the keys;

reliving a youth decades gone.

Years melt,

and there he is ...*Juan*...

shriveled into the mutt-yellow couch

to my left.

His gap-toothed grin fills the room,

gnarled hands applaud

granddaughter in concert.

Lolo* gloried in my gifts.

Why did it take me

forever

to do likewise?

*Lolo: Tagalog word meaning Grandfather. Tagalog is spoken in the Philippines

Author Comments: *Mozart's Rondo Alla Turca* is something I love to play on the piano. One day, after a particularly "on" practice, I looked up to see my wisp of a grandfather seated nearby, applauding even as his hands no longer had the strength to clap audibly. What struck me most at that moment was how unclouded and bright his eyes seemed, and the pride I saw there is a source of strength I can count on when I feel doubt.

Swift Sun

It's gone –

where is it?

Quickbright shard of flashfire

that razed this scaffolding of branches

holding up my morning's leaden sky.

Gone –

Pierced right through me-

exploded

into sparkled flecks of firefly glow,

settling unbidden

on lonely unlit corners

of remembrance.

Author Comments: I found the remaining verses to *Swift Sunrise!*

Editor Comments: A day moves through life much too fast… sunrise to sunset, I noticed the title of this completed piece was changed from *Swift Sunrise* to *Swift Sun*. This poem may have disappeared for a while; however, as the sun always does… it returned and was found (Yvonne Marie Crain, Senior Editor).

IN CONCLUSION

It was a pleasure to work on a collection of poems for *The Baker's Dozen, Volume III*. Once again, many thanks to *Dr. Harris "Cole" Vernick*, who offered me this chance to share my work, and to *Yvonne Marie Crain, Senior Editor* whose gentle and wise guidance resulted in the completion of "ROOTS AND WINGS".

I have been writing poetry since childhood, and see myself doing so for the rest of my life. Being published is a special gift as it gives a poet a voice in the world. It gives readers a chance to experience another's voice and perhaps converse in an informative and creative debate.

I certainly look forward to writing and sharing more poetry with you in the future. I wish the best of luck to everyone involved in the creation of prior, present, and future *Baker's Dozen* anthologies.

JJG Cabanos

Throughout *ROOTS AND WINGS* you will find *Joy's* gifted expressions of love, encouragement, hope and faith, and at other times, lamenting sadness. Sparks of humor and playfulness are displayed in *Perspective*, a limerick, and within the conversation between author and editor in *Swift Sunrise* and *Swift Sun*.

Working with *JJG Cabanos (Joy)* is a delightful experience. For your enjoyment, she delivers and leaves a piece of her heart and soul within each poem. As a reader, you will understand and enjoy her poetry, using all five natural senses, if read several times quietly and then read aloud.

Thank you for stopping by, we hope you enjoy each piece of polished write by *JJG Cabanos,* a gifted artist and poet with a bright future.

Yvonne Marie Crain
Senior Editor

WALKING

WITH

WORDS

By

Mary Merryweather Travis

A POEM IS ~

A DANCE...WITH WORDS

Mary Merryweather Travis

ABOUT THE ARTIST

As a child, I would look for the patterns in words; savour the sound of phrases, looking for rhymes, rhythms; searching for the music in the words.

The more I learned of language, the more I realized that there was to learn. Creating feelings in words became second nature to me and, although not yet branching into poetry, I wrote many short stories, and creative essays.

But life has a way of getting in the way, and writing took a back seat, making way for a career and then children, who came thick and fast until there were five of them. Sam, Chloe, Tom, Bean (Anneliese) and Pip (Joseph), ranging in age between 23 and 8 years old.

How fulfilling it is to be the mother of so many wonderful people, I find it impossible to describe. Maybe one day, in a poem, I will be able to convey the depth of my love for them.

With the passing of time, I find that I now have time to pick up a pen and to continue my interrupted walk with words. These poems are just a few of the joyful steps which I have taken, on the road to becoming a poet. I invite you to linger for a moment, to share my God given love of words and to accompany me on my walk.

My future endeavours as a poet are to continue writing books and to share my words with the world. In November 2007 I had a book published entitled, 'Live 'til I die'. Also, soon to be published are two books entitled, 'Warm up the Winter' and 'Long way from home'.

With gratitude, I dedicate my works to Dr. Harris (Cole) Vernick, the founder of The Cole Foundation for the Arts. I extend my humble thanks to every member of The Baker's Dozen Family, especially, Maxene Alexander, Executive Editor ~ Yvonne Marie Crain, Senior Editor ~ and Vivienne Harding, Art Director and Editor Assistant. Your hard work made this publication possible.

TABLE OF CONTENTS

COMING HOME (Quatrain)

for Hartland Point

Triton thunders outraged roar
and dashes fury at the shore!
The cowering rocks, the trembling sand,
buy dear their freedom from his hand.

White lighthouse screams, with beacon's breath
stark warning of impending death
at mawkish seabirds thermal flight,
from rugged rocks on cliff top height.

These fortress cliffs, this gallantry bower
which claims crossed lover's final hour,
hold back by force of rocky strength
King triton's war, along their length.

Wind whipped sky of mangled cloud
resounds aggressive thunder, loud
while lashes rain like cutting knives
and jagged edge of lightning thrives.

Take hard my hand, and join my cry
of sheer defiance at this sky!
Come fight with me through every storm
upon this place where I was born.

STORMCHILD (sonnet)

For Kaya Clara Thindwa, my God-daughter

Born just as lightning rips its jagged way,
with blinding purple fury, through the sky.
Steel rolling mountains blacken light of day
and drown, with thunder, infant's piercing cry.
Amidst the bloodied pains she takes to bear,
with fierce primeval cries of life newborn,
defiant tiny fingers clutch the air
as though to draw the power of the storm.
Such savage storm wind whistled, wild and hurled
the rain's relentless lashing in its rage
as ancient soul, reborn to older world,
reopens eyes upon a newer age.
She gazes with a look of wisdom old,
as joyous mother offers comfort's hold.

I WANT (sonnet)

I want a storm wind worthy of a fight,
majestic cliffs to awe me with their height.
I want white horses, riding crystal waves
and tears enough for all neglected graves.
I want to ride the sunset's fiery glow
and gift a lifetime to a dying child.
I want to know what makes you love me so,
and where the book of right and wrong is filed.
I want to feel your strong arm at my back,
To know you're there to catch me, should I fall.
I want to have the patience which I lack
when life decrees I cannot 'have it all'.
I want, as evening falls, to touch your face,
To promise you we'll have our time, and place.

FOREVER REIGN (sonnet)

For Ed, the president of the club

The great hall rang with merriment and song,
with jesters' bells, and hale and hearty cheers,
as silverware competed with the throng
of several hundred royal cavaliers.
The Queen, in lilac satin, graced the feast,
and laughed with glee at jester's foolish wiles
whilst every cavalier, from great to least,
dreamed, longing to receive such radiant smiles.
A hush preceded trumpets, heralding
with fitting splendour, pomp and circumstance,
the entry of His Majesty, the King
to lead his smiling consort in a dance.
As royal hand took dainty lilac glove,
she whispered, "I see only you my love."

OPIATE (sonnet)

If I awake, betimes, to find you gone,
and just the distant pounding of my heart
to bring to mind that body courses on,
then must I seek, clearheaded, other art;
distraction from the absence of your touch?
Avoiding by pretence, that which I long
to hold, to taste, to breathe, and tight to clutch.
Can such obsessions to sane mind belong?
I read, but words can point me only back
to where my empty arms feel sore the need
of warmth, of physicality they lack.
And so, my Love, with poppy's milky bleed,
I soothe the troubled psyche of a mind,
which would, within this crystal, solace find.

UNLIT (sonnet)

Dim, the shaded grasp of your affection,
conceals the needed sunrise of my dawn.
Darkly now I see but in reflection,
that suffocating night will follow morn.
For in your airless shadow, I must weep.
To live, to breathe, I must embrace the light.
Imprisoned, in captivity I sleep
beneath the shifting trickery of night.
Take this kiss I offer you, in leaving.
I travel now to seek a brighter place.
Soon the dying day shall sing her grieving.
Insidious, the evening shrouds her face.
Inside my soul a voice speaks, soft but clear,
"You shall no more find light, should you rest here."

CONFOUNDED (sonnet)

Confound me not, as I confound not thee.
Kind distance keep from all that I would be.
Seek not my thoughts, my eyes, my heart, my mind.
Keep not my words, nor follow them behind.
I feel your eyes burn hard from every place
I would, in peace fly free from choking grasp
and sing my songs without such jealous clasp.
In all attentions spare me of your grace
lest I divine, somehow, your sad intent
to live, through one who owes no debt or word,
a life which should in worthy cause be spent.
Take nothing more from me that I demurred
to give or lend, to one whom I preferred
approach me not, with any soft relent.

NIGHTGLADE (sonnet)

for my wonderful Pip, my own joyous sprite

Bright teasing, darting shafts of lilac light
dance freely from between the windblown limbs
of moon washed silver dryads of the night,
and sprinkle haunting spells of lunar whims.
From slender argent fingers, starlight filled,
hang gem encrusted ropes of diamond lights
so intricately structured by the skilled,
who weave their treasured strands upon the night.
Full sung, the whirling rushes from the east
bring dancing dervish bounty of dry gold
which gathers, gossip laden, in the least
of shadow rooted, mossy, dew filled fold.
Perceive the joyous being of the sprite
who, in the very moonbeams, wings his flight.

STOPPED (sonnet)

for Mossy, always in my heart

She chimed her last, with one great weary sigh;
a dozen dulcet bells to end a time
when life held more than mockery or mime
of moments danced across an endless sky.
Her tireless cogs by age and effort stilled.
Those golden hands now covered sleeping face,
no longer keeping time, but keeping place,
where once they held each passing hour we filled.
Uncaring in our shameless waste of years,
we scarce remembered once to count that bell.
Her timely wisdom rang to heedless ears
and made no loud lamenting where it fell.
How could we know what only Time could tell?
That only he who truly listens, hears.

SEA SONNET (Italian sonnet)
for Ian, the pilot of this vessel

How silent sleeps the sea, beneath the night.
Her subtle swell a symphony of dance,
where white maned horses ride the peaks and prance,
unshadowed, in the sapphire shades of light.
Enticing siren song sends soft invite,
to sway, with haunting sweetness and romance,
those lonely souls forlornly seeking chance
of happiness with some capricious sprite.

A sleepless seagull's sad and speechless cry
plays mournful echoes over moonlit lands
and rises to the distant starlit sky.
Unceasing in their tireless ebb and flow,
the soothing waves caress the timeless sands,
permitted but one kiss, before they die.

THE ANCIENT (sonnet)
for Spooky

Unseen within the shadows' deep conceal,
a blending of the dark, and darker still.
Such presence but a mere discerning feel
of rising hairs from dank unpleasant chill.
Awaiting, with the absence of the light,
extended fingers clawed with grim intent,
more ancient still than those which haunt the night
and have, at least, the day for their relent,
the Old one blows his foul and fetid breath
upon the joy and innocence of youth.
A song devoid of all but whispered death
to chill them with mortality's harsh truth.
Whilst knowing his embrace a fatal clasp,
each soul staves off this fearful, final grasp.

FIRST CHRISTMAS (sonnet)

In early dark of frosted winter night,
as windows show their decorated face
my eyes are drawn to tiny coloured lights
which cheerfully adorn each willing space.
I sit and gaze with wonder at the sky,
as if it were the first time ever seen,
and watch as tiny snowflakes twirl and fly
to mantel over autumn's gold and green.
The stars seem brighter now than times before.
Anticipation's magic fills the air
as in this waiting heart, an open door
swings wide to welcome joy, now you are there.
Within the softened glow of candles' light
I sing with you our song of silent night

Author Comments: This poem and the next are dedicated to my dearest Allen, who showed me the magic and then taught me the words, with my love and thanks for the gift of Christmas joy.

SOFTEST SILENT NIGHT (sonnet)

With quiet joy this Christmas Eve unfolds
in dancing glow of warming candle light
whilst tinsel gleams with shining greens and golds,
each adding to the beauty of this night.
A tree stands proudly dressed festive cheer,
bright candy canes reach high to star of joy.
Sweet voices herald ending of a year
and tell the story of a baby boy.
A chair beside the crackling fire stands bare.
Before it, on the rug, a figure kneels
and gently bows a grateful head in prayer
of thanks for overwhelming love she feels.
With all the words of softest silent night,
a voice, which once was silent, rings out bright.

CONTENTMENT (sonnet)
for Ian

In walled secluded garden, hidden deep
beneath the leafy branches, dappled green
from gentle sunlit shafts which softly seep,
a cool, idyllic fountain plays, unseen.
Each perfect diamond drop, a single note,
harmonious in continuity,
which ripples where the waxen petals float
who dared escape their formal symmetry
to kiss the living water with their dance.
Star spangled jasmine perfumes fading light,
whilst butterflies come late, to take their chance
to feast before the soft advance of night.
Serene, in setting splendour, sinks the sun
before the evening star. The day is done.

REMEMBER (sonnet)

Can we outrun the shades of falling night?
Or think to guard, to us, one scrap of day?
Oh no, my Love, such dreams are but a flight
of fancy, for all times must pass away.
But would that I could slow the hand of Time
to snatch one golden minute from his palm.
I'd hold it 'gainst a later, harsher clime,
to comfort me with sweet nostalgic balm.
For in this shining moment's stolen glee
I would but hold your hand, and breathe your name.
Perhaps with thirsting kiss you'd answer me,
reminding me of passion's warming flame.
My love, when I have served my time, alone,
I beg you, light a lamp, and guide me home.

EVER YOUNG (sonnet)

for Annie May Bartlett-Jones and Thomas George Jones
Beloved grandparents, together at last

In looking back from lavender and lace
when innocence and youth, like roses, bloomed,
this glass reflected once a younger face,
where joyful smiles, amongst the dimples, roomed.
How come these hands, once fair and smooth, now claw?
What can this mirror mean? Does it yet tease
with spots of age that fragile beauty flaw?
Whence come these lines? What silver threads are these?
Smooth you this cap, old hands, and tremble not!
And look, old faded eyes, full in this face,
lest dignity and pride should be forgot,
not sweetly wrinkled 'neath this cap of lace.
For know, within this frail and twisted frame,
still blaze the fires of passion's scorching flame.

TALL SHIP (Quantrain)

Give me but a tall ship, built of clouds,
a cold and ghastly sea of moonlit sky.
Then I shall set a course, by heartless stars,
and sail the opal moon path 'til I die.

And should the day dare show its sunlit face,
or dawn on me a welcomless tomorrow,
I'll travel silent to a darker place
and drown each sunlit ray with tears of sorrow.

So follow not this darkened course I'm bound,
lest all the light you see, you should imperil.
Guard well your tender ears against the sound
of icy tears, from shattered stars of beryl.

MOONDANCE (silver switch)

For my forever Toad, may I have this dance?

In silken silvered sapphire shades of night; pale moonlit dancer raises graceful hand.
With barefoot patterns softly sketched on sand,
she lightly swirls a slip of breeze blown white.

As dancing shadow weaves in wraithlike guise,
to music of soft water over shore,
creating an impression of much more,
a simple trick of moonlight in your eyes.

Pale moonlit dancer raises graceful hand,
a simple trick of moonlight in your eyes
as dancing shadow weaves in wraithlike guise
with barefoot patterns softly sketched on sand.

To music of soft water over shore,
she lightly swirls a slip of breeze blown white,
in silken silvered sapphire shades of night,
creating an impression of much more.

Author Comments: (Silver switch a new style created by the author, 16 lines [four stanzas] in iambic pentameter Rhyme scheme abba cddc bccb daad line repeat pattern 1234, 5678, 2853, 6417)

AND NO MORE SEE (triolet)

How sad, to close one's eyes and no more see
the beauty of a morning, filled with light.
Nor take delight in Nature's company.
How sad to close one's eyes and no more see.
To miss the dew drenched rose, kissed by the bee.
Nor follow, hushed with awe, the osprey's flight.
How sad, to close one's eyes and no more see
the beauty of a morning, filled with light.

WINTER SUNRISE (Free style)

for Tom, my wonderful Chig, who was there

Close pressed, my face, on icy pane
as rose the sun in fiery blaze
and lighted every crystal chain
with diamond points in frosted maze.

A thousand tiny rainbows shine
and for one moment, each is mine.

TOUCH (Nonet)

Pale pink blossom weeps from graceful tree
upon the fresh dug grave, beneath.
Nature offers her beauty
to soften last farewell.
Gentle petals drift
over bowed heads.
Sorrow lifts
at their
touch.

HE WROTE

He wrote to leave his honest thoughts, to give
some insight to their mad and frenzied plight.
He offered them a creed by which to live
and ways to hold the standard in the fight.
He left inspiring lines to lead them on
and offered up his soul in phrase and rhyme
with courage, to inspire them when he'd gone,
in syntax which would stand the test of time.
Within his mortal limitations jailed,
yet still his mind flew free above the pain
and even when his strength had failed,
he rallied to the battle once again.
Iambic strains and paper as his sword,
he wrote, with tears for ink, his final word.

OUT OF TIME
for Auntie Gracie and Uncle Nicky

Upon her finger shines a ruby ring,
put there so long ago by one who knew
the bitter sweet of borrowed time to sing
his song of tandem hearts and lovers true.
She twisted it to catch the better light
and gazed within the ruby's crystal blush,
reliving in nostalgia's rosy sight,
that moment when the gentle loving brush
of tender lips took hers with whispered kiss
and question of forever's lasting vow.
She smiled, in tender memory of bliss
they stole from out of time and lived, somehow.
Despite the Reaper's merciless advance,
a short but perfect step in tandem dance.

WINGS OF THE WIND (rhyming couplets)
For Tom, my amazing Chig

I feel warm winds of distant lands blow soft across my face.
They bring me tales of worn brown hands, of guardians of this place,

who toil, to live, in deserts dry and wide, far sloping hills
Whilst tiny round faced babies cry, love wrapped and carried still

On backs of loving mothers keep who pick, to earn a wage
and lullaby their babes to sleep with calm of sainted sage.

From far away I hear the song of creatures, old as time.
Their wild crescendo calls their young with love, as I do mine.

Hot winds bring colours, bright and true, red saris, bangles, gold
against a sky that's painted blue with artist's palette bold.

I shiver, as the breeze grows chill from frozen glacial tower,
where all is white and cold and still, devoid of tree or flower.

My arms flung wide, what can I do? I have no wings to fly
"Wind, take me there! I beg of you!" She carries but my cry.

SUNSET

for Sam, artist, musician and poet

With azure blue serenity
across the bay, as evening fell,
a hazy calmness soothed the sea
with whispers of a softer swell.

By unseen brushes, painting free
that sunset scene we loved so well.
More colours than the eye could see,
so bright the daylight's closing knell.

We watched in awe with artists' glee
such flames as could the sun repel,
and made to sink beneath the sea,
as though the sky were fiery Hell.

As though the sky were fiery Hell
and made to sink beneath the sea,
such flames as could the sun repel.
We watched in awe, with artists' glee.

So bright the daylight's closing knell,
more colours than the eye could see.
That sunset scene we loved so well
by unseen brushes, painting free.

With whispers of a softer swell,
a hazy calmness soothed the sea
across the bay, as evening fell
with azure blue serenity.

191

SERENITY (cameo)

Also for Sam, who leaves the gift of happiness wherever he goes.

Happy,
he dances slowly,
a joyful dance upon the sand.
The sea smiles
as placid waves lap the shore.
The boy with the serene face
smiles back.

THIEF (Brady's touch)

Trace then your gnarled and dying finger
gently down the soft curve of my cheek
Look full into my loving eyes
and brush away these diamond tears
of grief.

We found the kind of love that lingers;
poems of which, loving hearts could speak.
Our time to sing this song of love,
alas, with your advancing years,
was brief.

Could I, with woman's simple power,
halt the reading of life's fragile rhyme?
Reclaim one single precious day,
by merit of this tender role
I bear?

Oh no, my Darling, nor one hour,
so relentless marches Father Time,
although into my soul he saw
and knew exactly what he stole
from there.

Author Comments: Brady's touch; a new style created by the author in memory of **Allen Brady.**
A two stanza poem with a syllable count of 9,9,8,8,2,9,9,8,8,2 and a rhyme scheme of a b c d e
aw b f d e. The rhyming need not be identical in both stanzas. This poem had first print under
my personal copyright within the book entitled 'Live 'til I die'...printed November 2007.

ANOTHER TEAR (free style)

To my beautiful Chloe

A mother cries another tear
and dusts the empty shelves,
where once stood coloured books which told
of fairy folk and elves,
then changed their coloured spines to show
a scholarly array.
But even those now obsolete;
no reason left to stay.

A mother cries another tear
as pictures tell a tale
of tiny princess dressed in pink
and ballet at a rail.
Wild haired rider on a horse
gives way to party girl,
then joyous student standing proud,
diploma all unfurled!

A mother cries another tear
and clears another drawer.
The crumpled gown of bridal white,
the veil still on the floor,
are signs of happy exit made
by fledgling, now a swan.
A mother dries another tear
and smiling, carries on.

DARKWOOD (quatrain)

for darling Bean, the brightest and most magical of Faeries

Oh darkened glade wherein bright faeries play
admitting only dappled hints of day.
Amidst thy green and secret arbours hide
deep places where elusive elves abide.

Upon the moonbeams' filtered shafts of light,
dance forest sprites in joyous tiptoed flight.
Wild, timid creatures, tranquil in such place
lie hid away from danger's hostile face.

The graceful elm, in spirit form, entwines
her comely limbs with ivy's luscious vines.
Sweet dryads weave such dances as would blind
the eye of mortals to all earthly mind.

The eerie song of silver moonshade fox
calls softly from amongst white granite rocks
and soothes with nature's unadorned console,
such pain as ever troubled mortal soul.

Should, in your heart, harsh clouds of darkness fall
or pain and sorrow take you in their thrall,
I'll sing to you of Darkwood's healing air
and with bright hope dispel such foul despair.

VEILED (Rondeau)

Soft swirling silks in muted shades
of lavender and silvered jade,
enticing with exotic glance
beneath concealing veils' enhance
her supple weaving form arrayed.

With lightest graceful movements made
to subtle sitar music played
whilst sunset sang its soft advance
in muted shades.

The veiled enchantress dipped and swayed
with ancient movements well obeyed.
Whilst those who waited on the dance,
firm held in fascination's trance
by mystic ritual portrayed,
in muted shades.

OUR FATHER (sonnet)
for Kirsty

The tiny child closed soft her sleep filled eyes
upon the faces watching by her bed,
and with the closing, bade her soul to rise
as gentle grieving hands stroked golden head.
She heard no wrenching sobs or helpless tears
of mother holding lifeless little hand.
But free at last from pain and earthly fears
she turned her face towards a brighter land.
She stood before the golden stairs alone,
her infant legs too small to climb their height,
then stretched her baby arms towards that throne
where sat the King of Kings, in all his might.
Descending to her side with tender care
He took her in His arms and stroked her hair.

NEITHER PHRASE NOR RHYME (sonnet)

On tranquil water's calm reflective mood,
low hung by willows' weeping green refrain,
where ancient oaks in darkened spinneys brood
with stately beeches drenched by summer rain.
Beneath the water's soft and sunlit screed,
where fathom's acres sift in murky mud
and gentle currents dance with feathered weed,
swim soundless, silvered fins in season's flood.
With pen in hand, I laze in cushioned boat
in hopes to capture, by some word or line,
the essence of this scene from midstream float
where overhanging branch and sky combine.
But neither phrase nor rhyme could hold the sight
of pure white swans in silent outstretched flight.

TANDEM WORDS (sonnet)

Each word joins hands with that which went before
thus forming line to influence the 'all',
that where your pencil marked with blackened score,
you gifted us your heart in tandem call.
In every softened syllable, or sound
of poets tears, of counting bricks of rhyme,
each carried tales of inspiration found
in offered thoughts you dreamed from borrowed time.
Not once did scrivener, upon this stage
begrudge one single phrase, one given word
but spread those tender thoughts upon each page
in hopes that such nobility be heard.
And so, my friend, I give you what you gave,
a voice which triumphs over any grave.

LEAD ME (Kyrielle sonnet)
(For Sam, Chloe, Tom, Bean and Pip)

Dry with faith these tears of sorrow.
Shine Your light towards tomorrow.
Restore me. Let Your spirit blaze.
Thus lead me through life's twisted maze.

Such wickedness this world holds dear.
Lord, cleanse my soul and keep me near.
I pray You take these hands I raise.
Thus lead me through life's twisted maze.

I leave temptation at Your cross
and suffer, by such act, no loss.
Wait with me through my darkest days.
Thus lead me through life's twisted maze

Let me with honour sing Your praise.
Thus lead me through life's twisted maze.

Fresh Lands

by

Christopher James Rhodes

In Stillness Speaks Hope

Christopher James Rhodes

Author Biography

Professor Chris Rhodes (www.fresh-lands.com) is a writer and researcher who became involved with environmental issues while working in Russia during the aftermath of the Chernobyl nuclear disaster. He studied chemistry at Sussex University, earning both a B.Sc and a Doctoral degree (D.Phil.); rising to become the youngest professor of physical chemistry in the U.K. at the age of 34.

A prolific author, Chris has published more than 400 research and popular science articles (some appearing in international newspapers: The Independent, The Daily Telegraph and The Wall Street Journal). Non-fiction book publications include: Toxicology of the Human Environment (Taylor and Francis, 2000), Radicals on Surfaces (Kluwer, 1995), Jagged Environment (JEpublications, 2001), and the novel University Shambles (Melrose Books, 2009).

Chris additionally maintains a weblog which discusses contemporary energy and environmental issues (http://ergobalance.blogspot.com), which has garnered a strong and growing international readership, and on the strength of this he gave a recent invited lecture tour of the United States. He also writes a regular monthly column for the internet-based magazine Scitizen.com, on the theme of world future energy provision.

In addition to his many scientific pursuits, Chris is also a prolific poet and Chairman of a Peer Review Panel for an on-line poetry workshop; he received a merit-based scholarship grant from the prestigious, Cole Foundation for the Arts, to produce a collection of 45 poems which are now in press for publication in The Baker's Dozen: The Cole Foundation Collection, Vol. III (AuthorHouse, 2009).

As a registered Media Expert, Chris has given a variety of radio and televised interviews concerning environmental issues, both in Europe and in the United States -- most recently on BBC Radio 4's Material World. Latest invitations include a series of international Cafe' Scientifique lectures regarding the impending depletion of world oil.

Chris has formally left academic life in order to pursue his own consulting firm (Fresh Lands), which works toward improving environmental conditions both in Europe and in countries of the former USSR (www.fresh-lands.com).

Honours and Awards: President of the Royal Society of Chemistry (ESR Group), and the award of a Higher Doctorate (D.Sc) by the University of Sussex (2003), which is the highest mark of esteem and recognition any researcher can attain. Fellow, of the Royal Society of Chemistry and Vice-President of the St. Paul's Trust Centre (a Liverpool based, Christian charity), and member of the Royal Society of Literature.

TABLE OF CONTENTS

Quantum Reality

Within the speckled lantern of the Earth
burn such primordial forces of the void.
Surface scourged by Sun, storms
and dust,
it cracks and blisters,
but endures.
Perceiving it motionless, we do
not spin giddy in the round.
Time does not overwhelm.

Instant by instant the
quantum world corresponds
into everyday mechanics,
seeming so utterly
commonplace, whatever
philosophy may underlie it all.
Reductionism becomes futility,
leading into dark disconnected
Minutiae...

There is no truth at the end
Of each single narrow track;
And the absurdly large or infinitesimally
Tiny, converge upon a single
Reality...
A unity, where strings become
Zen,
And that which illusion has made solid
Boils into light.

The Miners

In that intention a cloud was forged,
emerging from thickest bracken,
like lovers sharing a shy glance
of mingled nudges.

Rising high on the tall hills,
which knew our adolescence,
and where we lay
among filtered sunbeams,
on a terrace of ochred promises,
casting back strewn dreams
and lullabies for children
never born.

Clamorous, amid grey slates
of rain,
the crow coughs its
guilty secrets of ascending glory;
wings flashing spangled black,
like the dust on miners'
faces,
as they rise from the seam.

The wheel spins no more,
set solid in the past
tense of Wales,
but the cable will not break
from the muted winding-engine;
turning its face in a
shame of redundant expectation,
and its coal lies still,
under the foot of Monmouth,
waiting for the oil to run-out,
and still the world.

Author Comments: I grew-up in South Wales, where almost one million miners were employed - now there are practically none. Yet, as the supplies of oil and gas are threatened to run short over the coming decades, some of the mines are to be reopened, but these communities as I once knew them, are lost forever.

Existence

Days that burn and shout as one,
Underlie my being.
In the ancienty of ancestral moves,
Or pivotal resolutions,

As to how future cards may fall;
cast down upon each
face of love or hate,
among the dark and light,
tendrils by which we are all
bound.

Eternity is but a croaked whisper.
The shadow of a cough.
That which remains unbound,
and falls on either face -
the two sides of illumination.
Too luminous to
glow.

The Living

The living have no darkness,
bound in this Earth of splintered light.
No fathom shall still them in the
deep,
nor break them into shrapnel.

No hills may hold them
back - shall they not look,
forgiven and forgiving,
to find each one?

Amid the seething chaos that we see,
unvanquished in the sense of source,
of who we are, or were, or
may become;
but are not extinguished
like the waxy fingers,
smouldering in bewildered pain,
in smoky palls,
that burn as in a moment's loss.

We are cast through prisms that dissect
each corpuscle of the murmured
part.
Creation cannot forgive the individual
elements it is bound from.

Above the limits of one state,
we glimpse with a lent eye,
from him who reads the text
in word or Braille;
feeling the underlying force,
to be ... at all.

Divorce Proceedings

"His lovemaking was not of the
tenderest kind, M'lud."
He nodded at the euphemism of her
brief,

while the court sniggered,
imagining. She looked ashamed,
dirty underwear alluded to
if not downright laundered in public.

"Objection," patted back the defensive
manoeuvre,
but the ground remained
unswallowingly firm.

Invaded and abused, beaten and blindfolded -
even he was ashamed
in the cold light,
and could not bear the reflection
her eyes uncovered of him,

so, tying her into position
he first bandaged all evidence
of soul,
into anonymity,

rendering her as meat,
flinchingly compliant
to do his deeds.

It was only later,
seeing a hurt beyond physical measure,
untethering her pain,
that he signed the divorce papers,

sighing out the words:
"I did love her, you know?"
And inasmuch as he could love
anybody, it was the truth.

Ein Langer Kuss

(A kiss that lingers)

Ein langer kuss - long enough -
wishing that time could stand still,
for long enough to really feel the now.

Amid the darkness of these nights of snow,
weaves illumination in the
reflection of those eyes.
Now I am sure, that eyes
have never looked at me before.

Fluency - the fluid quality of flow -
is marked by such rare instances;
Rare eyes, rare kisses on my breast;

Open so, the uncluttered hand
of trust, negotiates the surfaces
and the depths we are;
the kiss of blind fingers reading Braille.

Shadows

Shadows lengthen in
this bizarre conflagration
of coral seasons.
Cards fall open that were
sealed shut for so many
entombing years,
whose messages may only
now be read.

Sounding-in the winding whirs
of penitent denial,
which waited in the
wings of a sub-plot -
or so it seemed -
but really was everything,
and should have been
allowed a bow on centre-stage,
for its rich-deserved applause,
before the crowds shuffled-out,
amid the encores.

Dark in the Asylum

Dark in the asylum (as it has become)
the demon objects to a quiet demise.
In her final hour,
it is all that remains
of those marshalled personas;
ever unresolved.

Fear remonstrates with peace,
and rising accordingly,
she lashes-out her frail violence
at other
such poor disconsolate souls,
who will not remember
where the bruises came from.

Now locked-within (all privileges
tucked-onto by-roads
arterially from harm's main drag)
a hefty dose of librium
and behind the glass
where the orderlies can see her,
she stares...
unseeing but unrepentant.

Thunderstorm

Thunder vibrated the black sky
as though the electric atmosphere
was poised in space for you
and me to make our moves.

Will she or won't she come back?
I pondered over that odd conundrum,
and if "yes"; is it such a good idea?

Perhaps better to leave yesterday's
performance as an act on a single stage,
and smile awkwardly in polite denial...
then I knew it was you, before I used my eyes.

Some sense of you - a fragrance
perhaps? - hesitated in the doorway;
then closed it behind and put its invisible hands
unwisely over mine, almost innocently.

Walking back, through the moist grass of expectation,
uncareful and enriched in the warm rain.
From green unmown waves rose the fresh scent
of earth; in ascending visceral knowledge -
ours the only pulsings of iron-Heme.

Mammals stepping around the inexorable
green, sun-driven circle of light.

Birth, life and re-birth without end,
calls for some sporadic self-reaffirmation.
Within a primordial fluency,
older than subjective mores,
ignited in the skyward flash of instinctive will.

Towers

I saw it change its course
and then the rubble
and the noise rolled down

into the concertina
cloud of dust and ashes.

In the flick of a blade
the world became mutable.
I didn't know how finely
it was poised,

there on that giddy edge
of familiar trust,
crumbled into a sequence
of slow stills,

trembling past each window,
frame by frame,
tumbling on down.

Individual lives ended
where a levelled age began.

Sundials

The dawn opened on a decadent world.
I opened slightly hazy eyes to see:
sling-backs tossed
separately into corners;
a couple of empty bottles
of champagne - one standing,
the other on its side.

I looked at you - still asleep and quiet -
and watched the Sun reach in,
to touch your hair;
igniting it into a copper flare,
then pass its shadow on,
over the cast-off party dress;
the scattered underwear.

Passing segments of a sundial,
marking time upon its face.

Balance of the World

Death does not discolour
the shades of face or form.
Light absorbs the entirety
of all you are, or were...

Death does not discolour
all shades of billowing darkness,
nor the influence of calmer
facts...

 Straining against the rain of
force and there, in the dark
interlude of aspects cruel
or accidental, for that matter.

Perfect in each symmetry,
as when that energy condenses
into the simple dews
on flowers.

Schrödinger's Cat

Impossible? Doubtful.
Desirable? Who Knows?
Floating conceptual states -
both at once, in pervasion -
like Schrödinger's Cat -
the poor dead beast!

Poison in the box, it would
have died - believe me;
ultimately all nine of its versions
would be culled simultaneously;
boxed-up or not, and the
smell would have given
the game away, before the
Herr Professor opened-up
the new reality.

We know the direction of all things -
some excuse them by entropy -
that is a real cop-out!
But what about you and me?

Directed and directfull -
desirable or not...
who knows, again?

If one of us could accelerate
at near light velocity and then
look back upon the other,
and realise, in his absence,
what he had left behind,
to grow-old, while he pursued
such astral fractals of some
philosophy he didn't understand,
but pretended to anyway;
he would, in all conscience,
wish to die,
having proved himself
so utterly right.

Words

Storms and waves and winds
are the conflict of clouds.
Definitions falter upon the
wings of words that fail.

Such a crash of fragments
splinters into glassy directors
of entropy - of convolution;
catching the inscrutable
pieces:

small and broken to
an atomic limit of dimension:
and within rest, when they do,
those embers of love pervade.

Finding Freedom

Bending my back like a willow
I will not break but bear,
and give and forgive in a
gesture of benign acceptance.

I weather intrusions of status,
of storms and moments that
cast me amid future memories, and
memorials of benign acceptance.

I flow, falling, caressed by all
sweeping airs, breaking
unbound through this thin
atmosphere of benign acceptance.

In malleable form where only the
spirit keeps no solid record, among
the persistence of time, I hear such
echoes of benign acceptance.

Serenity Prayer

Calm has replaced anger and hence love
has emerged from the guise of fear.
A state of grace enduring, but mainly
hidden behind walls of hate
and well-fed malcontent.

 This is serenity, perhaps the kind
that underpins 12 step programmes,
ACIM and other connections to
a Higher Power; to improve
my conscious contact with God
as I am to understand the word "God."

It is also acceptance and wisdom -
and moral courage to change
the old bad habits of assailing
oneself with attack thoughts;
to cast-off the loathing of fellows.

Even if they did hurt you (without shadow),
admitting the possibility that the pan
of their own pain just boiled-over
and scalded an innocent onlooker.
So, today I choose peace, and forget
them all; letting-go of fear.

Love has no counterpart in fear.
Fear is not the opposite of love.
It is small ephemeral pieces of darkness,
that together conspire
to obfuscate the truth of light.

Miracles

Miracles happen, in the shifting
moods of winds and seasons.
In the rise and fall of rain,
blown among mountaintops,
our sins and other false premises
are drenched into a fresher baptism,
and by such ceremony restored to light.

Amid the geological upwelling of granite
the spirit reflexes in renewal;
the phoenix-cycle of metamorphosis -
fire and ash, wings having done their job;
once soared then set-down
bent beneath the collective massivity
of five hundred years (or so legend has it) -
casting the solid form amorphously
in an anonymous shell of death.

Flying from dark spaces,
connecting to the Source
of all power, where eternal life
might be prodded or intruded-upon,
if not immediately evident.

Tom Cat in the Sun

He blinks his eyes, amid
all consternations of which
only humans are aware.
He rotates, apparently
a ginger phantom of
mysterious forces
that transcend, at least
this dimension that eludes us.

His fur warm - to a hand as
a casual thermometer that
rolls on its back, purring
and being - mostly being, as
cats are so truly Zen - and
oh yes, you can scratch
my chin...

Peak Oil? What's that?
Who cares?

"Peak Oil" is the maximum in world oil production beyond which its supply will decline inevitably. We are at that point now, and so civilization will most likely relocalise into small communities if no substitute fuel can be found. However, cats don't care about things like this do they - Zen creatures that they are?!

Chicago Winds

Winds turned over the spirals
you had wound within my mind
four years before this odd interlude,
and four thousand miles distant.

Though a mere bystander, Michigan's breath
called back memories but calmly,
cooling my borrowed embers of passion
in the propitious vastness of its waters.

As I wandered among new friends
and unfamiliar sidewalks -
high on Big John, ascending
a thousand feet, battling vertigo -

our energies seemed
once again connected,
and I could feel you with me, there...
I swear.

 Haunted, I flew four thousand miles
and one day back, leaving your essence to wander,
and someone asked me, unbidden:
"Did you know she was in Chicago?"

...and only then, could l let you go,
knowing the truth.

Perhaps when we love we remain connected.

The Blind Ego Sees!

In shone a finely resurrected light
which woke me from a deep, deluding haze,
and brought me here, among the heavens bright,
in unity profound for timeless days.
Though valiant, my blows had been in vain;
detached, yet bound in dread by fear and storm:
the purest spirit poured on me as rain,
now I perceive the power of its form.
I did not know the nature of true love -
the state of stillness that we find within -
it is not gifted to us from above,
nor shallow, as a game we play to win.
The falling ego keys the realm of peace,
and from our broken cares we find release.

Big Bang

Weaving among the tireless boundless spaces,
stretch all tendrils of light and dark matter.
Switching between the alternate echoes of
sound and silence, are the vibrations -

the single clicks of all creation,
crammed into a unity of sweeping hands
and counterparting stillness;

of mirrored freneticness and calm;
turmoil and peace, stretching into infinity;
coexisting to balance the universe -
yin and yang - You and me.

Fossil Era

In a mad excess we lit the torch,
and without much thought ignited
the Earth's bestowal from
five million years of effort.

And in the pyre that stretched
up to the Moon,
throwing atom-bombs;
killing horses and millions on its way,
enlightenment still eluded us;
blinded by the glare of technology.

At once, it is nearly over,
that flash-in-the-pan -
the momentary illusion
of man's omnipotence.

We almost believed that Nature had begun to look up to us
and God was in a retirement home somewhere,
out of sight and out of mind -
now an ironic future yields in the retracing of steps;
in making peace with the older ways.

Prague

Twisting through the lanes of the old town,
spirited the choked segregation
that drove Kafka's paranoia.

Shuffling through Wenceslas square,
sweeping past the Astronomical
hands of the dividing clock, ornately
covert from an instrument of measure.

The Vltava churns its waters
in a smooth sweep of the eternal,
dividing Vysehrad from Hradcany.

The flat dogged plain lies down subserviently,
providing unquestioned compromise;
the gilded heights and towers of the castle,
walling history within its clutches.

Reflections

When you left, I felt bereft and lonely;
cored-out again, like an apple.
We were a bare pair,
borrowed from other canvasses;
bound to return and paste-over
the patches evident in those
incomplete landscapes.

Sometimes it is as though
dimensions warp and connect,
through worm-holes of
our wishes; linked points
of infinite gravity -
the residues of formerly
great stars gone-out -

binding their illuminations in maximal inertia;
appearing dark to a casually unbraided
glance, as though they were never really there.

Yet, there tails an inescapable fragrance of
persistently insisting memory,
at the very least... that much still shimmers,
if I shade my eyes.

Alzheimer's

"Is anybody there at all?"
The lights have fused and flickered-out;
so far, it seems, on down the hall

"Have you gone?" I want to call,
but who would hear my meagre shout?
"Is anybody there at all?"

Your face takes on a sudden pall,
no sentience that I can rout;
so far, it seems, on down the hall.

In your prime you gestured tall -
your lips framed a disarming pout:
"Is anybody there at all?"

I wrap you in a woollen shawl,
routines that I will never flout:
so far, it seems, on down the hall.

Once, manically, you'd scream and bawl,
raving, throwing things about...
"Is anybody there at all?"
so far, it seems, on down the hall.

Deathbed Scene

She lies still, and greyly silent;
almost in pale rehearsal
of what must come.

A mirror would be barely fogged
by these rattled leavings of her
breath, reluctant to skim-out,
pretending (hoping) it to be
all finally over, but that time
is not quite at hand.

There are no happy memories,
but plenty of the other kind -
though it is in poor taste
to dwell upon them now.

At such moments we
are bidden to summon love -
to recall it from another time
and graft it onto here;
actors learning lines -
aping scenes maybe,
wishing they were fact.

So, I take your frail paw
with all its power gone,
and your eyes open -
we exchange a look
that is reminiscent of
affection, and feels like it too.

How could it be otherwise;
I have a heart, you know?
You do, of course, having
delighted in breaking
it moon in, season out.

My later lovers patched
it up with plasticine;
and that's how it remains.
You silly, sad old woman -
we should have been friends.

Cold War

We imagined it over:
solid concrete walls
and political screens of iron.
Partitioned nations and peoples
crushed by a polished, heavy stomp.
In Budapest they kept
the mighty bronze icons,
cast molten into the surly
face of Hungary,
unmanning even murmured
postures of insurrection.

The Berlin Wall was built
to keep them out not us in,
so shone the brilliance
of a regime that crumbled.
The Czechs were broken from
all sides, first sewn-in
with Slovakia (lands later amputated);
murdered by Heydrich's memory -
though they did get rid of him,
in a bitter snatch of triumph,
fleeting as a fly.

The boot trundled back to kick
them into touch in '68,
breaking poor mild Dubcek's heart.
One boy set himself on fire:
a torch that yet beckons
to the mindset of Prague;
among those vestiges of history
that are unforgettable,
but at least not yet forgotten.

From the rubble of Der Berliner Mauer
we saw the cold-war end.
Each of us holds a piece of
its stone, within us somewhere,
like relic wood from the cross;
making a million tonnes or so,
if its provenance should be believed.

Wavelengths

I stepped-out into a newly apparent world
in its dawn; half relieved, yet half afraid.
The past only too well known but over;
with what next, a matter to be guessed.

Time is odd - we generally miss the present
moment, feeling it to be a fulcrum -
a node between wavelengths of fear.

One, casting back, remaining afraid
though logic demands it is forever gone;
the other, extending into an invisible
ultra-violet, or burst of gamma-rays;
dreading great forces we cannot yet feel,
if indeed we ever will.

And yet "now" is the only place we ever truly are,
and the one setting in which to find peace.
Time is an illusion, as is fear;
a state of disconnection from
the Source of all power.

Blessings

He came, blessing a union thought barren;
slipping into this world like a shimmering star.

An angel's wing brushed its sparkling dust upon
that wondering pair, infusing them with light.

His hand cold - they found the infant blood turned to ice
in tiny fingers of unheld joy - seemingly a gift rescinded.

"Does God have no heart?", is an obvious question to ask,
but its sense deludes us.

God bless you, little boy, for igniting love
where it was not before.

Author Comments: To Elijah, a friend's child who died last year, aged 3 month

When the Rain ...

When the rain licks windows,
rolling its rounds in droplets,
pouring against the scaffolding
of an oddly configured sky,
I notice its sheen, like the
yellow edge of silver;
densely-packed, lead-bound,
as the Atlantic weather
carouses our bay.

When the rain drenches,
toward that close of day,
shot through a sepia still
of non-metallic means,
I feel the separateness
of such weighty cast-offs,
beyond the gravitas
of internal light.

When the rain unfolds,
pouring darkness on the external
sense of eternal shadow,
it confides in the space
of the dark demons that are gone -
fled from the essence of light;
but magically mere shadows
even of them are lost,
consigned where they at last belong.

Oh, when the rain cascades,
life becomes...

One Remembered

In the pitted flicker of your eye
pauses the shadow of a white room,
enclosing a bed - made and unmade;
with clothes strewn and unstrewn.
Whispered promises adopted but not believed.
Protestations made to sanctify the will;
due distance to disempower the ones at home.
Casual faiths, like cats and urgent lights,
put out at night.

The Leader's Lament?

I have let the side down.
So the flickering messages whisper to me
in the truth telling darkness,
where disappointment becomes dismay,
and then appal.
Sifting through grainy fingers in body bags,
those residues of consequence passed into
another's hand,
through a cold impersonal chain of command.
Side to side we stand, flicking bombs -
murders and suicides in equal measure.

In equal justification - now too
desensitised for shock value -
WMD[11] or a dictatorial barbarian?
The excuses are confused now
amid the unstultifying ooze
of blood and oil.

Lightning

Lightning strikes an essence of pain
far more than any illumination
that could finally fall our way.
Odd, we are here - in this room
of dark glory, strangely frugal -
a mattress, strewn clothes
and casual tissues I had remembered
to buy from the all-night store.

It is strange - as I stand alone at
this window; staring over the
anonymous brilliance of a city,
blinking silently above sirens
such as you - I see a bubbled
face, glimmering as a ghost
of who I thought I was.
Present dreams and definitions
turned to consensually
impersonal anonymity.

---

1   Weapons of Mass Destruction

Perfect Day

Moving and clinging comes the intention
we have known all along would arrive,
in lips and thoughts and subtle
accepted arrangements of words
and looks and sounds of provocations.

Pheromones could probably be
blamed - a far distant extreme
from love - let us not
delude ourselves on that particular
score and just accept this matter
in all its aspects, manifesting:
masquing in a familiar disguise...
just so you know it.

Doors close onto colluded
streets of dark cold;
a pair of shadows huddled
amid all the rest, are we -
an arm placed appreciatedly
back, around a leather coat:
"Kiss me", you say, as if
surprised by the first one.

"I never thought..." words are
really a delaying irrelevance;
feeling spot-on and distracted
from who we are and where we
should or might be,
now, or in five years.

A door opens into inevitable
light, clothes strewn in a
familiar irregular pattern.
I am always amazed by perfection -
and in this moment all is
utterly perfect and oddly still;
awaiting furore - soft, familiar,
that gentle, awkward, round
edge of human appetite.

There is no Death

There is no death,
merely sleight of hand.
Scattered rains, at once
strangely focussed,
soaking into the dry sod,
bring forth the living
Earth from ashes -
the organic realm
flourishes,
according to the cycle
of the Sun.

Recast, atom by atom,
each molecule of me
becomes the great ocean,
boiling into the atmosphere
(making lions or hippos)
or filling-in the empty
spaces that Nature
apparently abhors;
but bound on this
eternal wheel,
there is no death.

Brighton Beach (1982)

Rolling in waves, our undulations
crash against pebbles,
as the afternoon dissolves into
these distillations of the Sun.

Breath condensing into the sea:
fragments of the atmosphere
snapped into droplets,

snatched from the rising vapour
of one moment, into the solid matrix
of this point of reflection.

A beach-ball beckons from the horizon -
red and molten - its golden tendrils
incontestably flamboyant, sweeping their figurines,
hastily prepared, into the deep ocean.

Swiss Love Song

Viewed against the immenseness of mountains,
all other scales pale and stand still.

A window frames the vista: wall cables
(presumably electrified) on which roses grow -
to prevent the thorny issue of undue ascent
and protection of the Jungfrau (presumed a virgin).

A ginger cat keeps guard asleep below:
one eye open, while an ear flicks at a raindrop.
He rotates without raising a paw.

Boats paddle past, their wheels threshing water;
whistling-by, peak-capped and polished,
buttoned-up in shiny uniforms
until the guard shifts at four.

A teacup storm chatters on the lake,
without spilling a single drop,

while the village worthies flint-up
the amber warning lights just in case,
spinning in the merest splash of rain.

As the wind ruffles fur, sheltered among the toy houses,
and shakes the single wooden bridge away,
model citizens run along on shiny clockwork trains.

Author's Comments:
It could be any small community; but I am fond of Switzerland.

Chink in the Curtain

Against the morning,
the whispering shadows call,
as light glimpses the mechanism of day,
and night and memory are separated
in departed anonymity.

You call revision and false guilt,
while I revel in the lingering sensation
of consensual wonder;
mapped upon the pulsing framework
of eternal shade and time.

Black and White: 1913

After ninety-two years,
you still turn me on.

I'm quite amazed.
Unlike flesh, your image has
barely lost a tone.

Hair black and thickened
into fingers, scented by desire.
Eyes bright; breasts unbowed;
buttocks tight; thighs strong;

eyebrows full on olive cheeks,
their bones Slavonically high.
Dark beauty; proud Balkan belle;
where did your flesh retire?

And did you leave a grand-daughter...
somewhere, in this fourth dimension?

Gathering Storm

The wind whoops and groans for yet another nail
to keep the fence from blowing down.
I listen, earnestly and irked
for the slapping of wood,

the creaking of posts,
the reverberations of corrugated
iron sheets,
rattling on the shed roof,
but holding firm.

I never think of the slates;
they have proved robust, covering
our home these thirty years,
deflecting harsher storms than this;
funnelling rain into the gutters,

baking dry when summer
brazed the oak of the door so hot
it burnt my touch.
Withdrawing my fingers into
the cool deeps of *status solidi*,

the frame of our marriage unyielding,
yet softly tolerant beneath its surface,
moulding to the fingers of change,
but holding secure
against the strongest gusts
of foreign invaders.

The Oil of Progress

Barreling-on, fomenting the black rivers
that metered-in an age of gold,
the planet spins against a thousand suns,
drawn upon a fragile canopy of time and space.

Horses chew-on calmly in the pasture,
made redundant generations back.
These unemployed, reluctantly drawn out
for a wedding or village affair on the green.

We struck it rich! Upwellings in unheralded Texan fields
murmured in a European war... the first to come.
The new century rolled its eyes aloud
at Quantum Physics and tanks,
which generally broke down,
or sank in soiled mud around feet forever bound.

Depression came, blowing grains to swirl
dry and unsown in the dust bowls of wrath;
the razor-shards of oil plundered the land,
ploughing into the furrows of a second, greater war.

Reparations and expansion; populations grew.
Thirteen billion hands (working in pairs you understand)
of oil-fed fingers now abstract their attentions,
in blind faith, this cornucopia could never end,
each squeezing the Earth like a hollow stone.

Loosing the old ways and stuffy values...
now oil-fed bombs fall on the swollen lands
of its source; doodling about the jigsaw-map
and shading-in the missing pieces, state by state;
tweaking the beard of an older faith.

Buckling-up the belt of quirky geology around the Earth,
to secure the ring of fire into more democratic hands;
lacing Nature's midriff tighter and tighter,
until the final phantom sputters
a farewell flame and is blown-out,
like the last smoking candle on a birthday cake.

Give them a lump of sugar from your hand,
and a hearty slap on the flank - entice them, with whispers.
Call the horses back again, sooner, not later.
The oil-party clock struck twelve, while our backs were turned.

Author's Comments:
The world is running out of the cheap oil that has fuelled the modern age.

Echoes of Love

A real and realistic love sweats from the soul;
it holds its breath in dread of the egg-shell sound -
the cracking, creaking of the heart.

The love, no longer new, prays -
for at least the continuum of words,
of hollow sounds that are undisturbed...

and undisturbing; even false reassurances
that no dreaded cards will turn a silent sudden hand,
are enough to quell its nerves.

A sigh ruffles pages on the table:
watching one go out and not look back;
the "accepting love" that is true love

hedges only a wistful nod at "in love",
becoming the love that bears only numb witness
to ears and lips... now it is no longer of love.

Swan

Turning the white swan-plume
like an exoskeleton
of bleached coral,
your neck pauses in an unbidden
nodal calm of still grace.

A serene wing rises -
all renditions of fair beauty -
yet each belies the true
inner spirit that is you.

When the swan settles,
covering its eyes in rest
from an ever-subsuming view,
it releases the unmoulded
inner space of you.

COME

WALK

WITH

ME

AWHILE

By

Sarah True

I am taking this opportunity to thank *Dr. Harris "Cole" Vernick*, founder of *The Cole Foundation for the Arts.* The Merit-Based Scholarship Grant you so graciously gave is a once in a lifetime opportunity to come my way. I don't think I can completely describe how grateful I am that you found me worthy of publishing my sometimes rambling poetic thoughts.

Also, I want to thank Yvonne Marie Crain, Senior Editor; Maxene Alexander, Executive Editor; finally, a thank you to Vivienne Harding, Art Director and Assistant Editor. You have all been so helpful with your input; willing to answer my million questions.

You are heroes, one and all

LIFE... A COLLECTION OF MEMORIES

LOVE ~ LISTEN ~ LEARN

Sarah True

ABOUT THE AUTHOR

My name is Sarah True. Honestly, it really is my name and not some nom de plume. I was born and raised in Texas back when it was still the largest state in the U.S.A. No, I will not divulge my age. I am old enough to remember days before the computer but young enough not to remember the Woolly Mammoth.

I attended high school at a boarding school located in the state of Virginia. This is where I met the love of my life who was attending a university in a nearby town and he has remained the love of my life for over forty years.

We, somehow, managed to beat the odds. We married the day he graduated with a degree in Electrical Engineering. I guess you could say that I was his graduation present! We went on to have four children ~ three sons and one daughter. Was she spoiled rotten? I shall leave that up to you to figure out.

When all our children were finally in school, I went back to school myself; becoming a somewhat aged nurse. My main purpose, aside from humanitarianism, was to help pay for the education for all these little hellions running around my house. It was actually in nursing school when I fell in love with writing. That was spurred by my English instructor, when she told me that I was entering the wrong profession: That I should be writing instead of nursing.

So, began the writing. I did, however, work as a nurse and did manage to educate all of these rascally offspring at long, long last. After the final graduation, and sigh of relief, my husband took an early retirement.

Was he going to sit home while I continued to work? Not on your life. Now we are the proud owners of an inn located in northern Pennsylvania, and are finally content and happy being our own boss. Of course, that leaves us with no one to blame but ourselves should things not go well.

When our daughter was a teen, memory I would like to keep buried, I placed upon her *The Mother's Curse.* I went one step farther by saying that I hoped she would have two just like herself. She did! Now we have two beautiful granddaughters who are much nicer than their mother was, because I can send them home.

My favorite form of writing is to tell stories. I enjoy writing historical prose, quatrains and rhyming couplets with the odd limerick thrown in for fun. I often like to walk the dark road, to be honest; I *very* often like to walk the dark road. If I make you laugh, cry or scare you to death, I will happily have done my job. I have been published in poetry magazines and several anthologies and have a series of children's books with a literary agent at this time. She will own ten percent of me, but only when and if the books are sold, so she does have incentive. I write because I have a need to write, and I do not try to frighten the little ones.

TABLE OF CONTENTS

CLOCK
(Free Verse)

He was ready to go.
Just days before he had told me so.
He said that the days were simply
For winding the clocks.

Once so big in my eyes;
Now... shriveled on white sheets
With tubes and bleeping machines
That counted his life on greenish screens.
The nurse said I should talk to him,
"You never know," she said.
"Perhaps you'll reach inside his dreams."
When she left, I leaned across
And kissed his sunken cheek.

I love you daddy, I whispered.
I was startled when he whispered back,
"I love you, too."

He only spoke one final time.
With a murmured; breathless sound
I can't be sure, but I think he said,

The Clocks... Have All... Wound Down.

Authors Comments: This is a true story

PEACE AT LAST
(Rhyming Quatrain… of possibility)

From the east the winds of war
Blew hot across the sand
While wings of doves caught fire,
And peace was forced to land.

From the east the winds of war
Blew cold across the plain
And; grounded doves lay dying
To never soar again

From the east the winds of war
Blew silent across the deep
Spores were scattered on the breeze
While freedom was asleep.

The west said, "We've the right to fight,
And have the will to kill."
While peace lay scorched and dead
And everything was still.

All cities gone, their towers; too
And no one left to care.
The peace we always hungered for
At last is everywhere.

A SIGN OF THE TIMES

(Quatrain)

Come play the pipe and beat the drum,
Sing it loud and sing it well.
The words are written by the people,
The melody is straight from hell.

From the far side of forever
To the now of present tense.
Come the cries of all the children
Searching for their innocence.

The smoke of dreams blow in the wind
And sets the children free.
We mourn… we weep…we bow our heads,
They are…They were…They'll never be.

234

DANCING FOR THE DEVIL
(Rhyming Quatrain...Historical Fiction)

The walls that ring the castle wide
To battlements they steeply rise.
With murder holes along each side,
that seem to sing with night wind's sighs.

Turrets on every corner stand
With winding; stony stair within.
I still can hear the footfalls land
Of many battle hardened men.

Strong bowmen at each murder hole,
Boiling pitch on ramparts high.
Men begging God to take their soul;
The screams of anguish as they die.

They scale the walls on spider's feet
Then swarm within the castle's halls.
Battering rams keeps up its beat
Until the tortured wood door falls.

The floors were slick with mortal blood,
The smell of death; the stench of fear.
The enemy tide becomes a flood.
My kinsmen dying far and near.

Battle noises from all around;
Clank of sword on metal shield.
Clanging armour and deadly sound
Of mace and pike that both sides wield..

My father lasts till near the end,
My brother's dead since early dawn.
Servants, neighbors, and there a friend;
All fallen to this Satan's spawn.

Blood flowing from both leg and arm,
My father fights in front of me.
He tried to shield me from all harm,
But they come on relentlessly.

The death blow lands with horrid thud,
His head is struck and rolls away.
His dying feet slide in his blood;
All over me that blood did spray.

DANCING FOR THE DEVIL
(continued)

And on his death, the fighting's done
With shouts of triumph ringing clear.
The women, chattel, they have won
And so begins our time of fear.

My mother murdered before my eyes;
The others used and then are killed.
Ripped from my arms, my sister cries;
With one quick blow her sobs are stilled.

Standing there, my heart is dead
For, I alone, am left to chance.
Into the hall then, I am led
And made to foreign music dance.

I spin alone to shouts and jeers,
Slipping in bloody pirouettes.
There is no feeling and no tears,
They'll see no anguish or regrets.

I was a maid until that day,
Too young to wed, or man to know.
And after ten upon me lay
I welcomed death's compelling blow.

That was back when *Rome* was strong
And to our isles it conquered then.
The arm of *Caesar* sure and long,
When war was waged by countless men.

And now I see the tourists walk
About the castle of my youth,
And hear the guides with practiced talk
But knowing not the awful truth.

I stroll these ramparts every night,
Seeing the faces that death has brought.
At last the tears do blind my sight
And wet the stones where kinsmen fought.

I'll guard this place till end of days
or throughout all eternity.
In bloody shroud my body stays
Until my *God* has set me free.

236

ARGOLYN
(Rhyming Couplet)

I dreamt that I was maiden fair
with garland flowers in my hair.

In silken dress of pearlish tints,
I crossed beneath the battlements.

To walk alone the heathered glen,
to meet my darling, Argolyn.

On his dark steed we flew on wings;
passed castles grand and stony rings.

We stopped beside a roaring strand,
'twas here he asked me for my hand.

So handfast, then, we didst bestow
our vows to God and all below.

To be as one for all our life,
husband to me and me to wife.

He left me at the castle gate
and rode away to meet his fate.

To fight with Scotland's beating heart,
for Scotland's freedom do his part.

On Stirling bridge is where he fell,
no maiden now of this I tell.

Handfast still, as handfast was then,
so goes the tale of Argolyn.

Authors Comments:
Historical fiction, handfasting was abolished in the early twentieth century.

Editorial Comments: by Yvonne Marie Crain, Senior Editor:

The September 11, 1297 *Stirling Bridge* battle, led by William Wallace between Scotland and England was a victory for Scotland. The bridge was barely large enough for two men and their horses to cross abreast. Although the losses were reported as few among the Scottish, the greatness of this battlement was that the Scots fought for their independence and won the first battle of the first war in Scotland.

COME WALK WITH ME AWHILE
(Quatrain ending with a rhyming couplet)

Come walk with me today awhile.
Perhaps I'll even make you smile.
Or maybe from your eyes will spring,
A simple tear of remembering.

You were my love since first we met
And still remain so even yet.
So, hold my hand and we will see
The lost beginnings of you and me.

While only children, we jumped ahead
Into our feathered marriage bed.
Through trials and joys, we made our way
And I've loved you more each single day.

As children come, our children went.
When did we start this slow descent?
On shoulders broad at times I've wept
While all our promises were kept.

I was your maiden ~ you my knight.
With comfort you assuage my fright.
I loved you then and love you still,
Know this; my heart, I always will.

On wings of love our time has flown.
Now soon we part for worlds unknown.
And, when my time on earth is through
my dying thought will be of you.

We'll meet once more…in heathered glen
Where we'll walk… awhile… again.

Author Comments:
After a serious illness and recovery, I wrote this for my husband.
It is framed and hanging in our bedroom.

ONLY THE WEAPONS CHANGE
(Rhymed Quatrain)

Wars began when the world was new
over the years, the weapons grew.
In the beginning, sticks and stones,
then clubs and spears they made from bones.

Then arrows came with sword and lance,
hacking and chopping in mortal dance.
Most combat, then, was hand to hand
to see which was the last to stand.

Cannons came with thunderous roars,
a chance to kill so many more.
War machines made by masterminds
with dead and injured of all kinds.

Then warplanes with their bombing run
anonymous to everyone.
No faces seen, their conscience free
to keep on killing mindlessly.

The bombs grew bigger to do more harm,
whole cities crouched in total alarm.
Then missiles fire from miles away
burning all that's in their way.

Then, the ultimate bombs begin
fighting battles that no one can win.
The world lies scattered with baking bones
as we come full circle to sticks and stones.

Author Comments: A bitter truth

THE CASTLE
(Poetic Prose)

We had searched for the most part of the day when I just happened to glimpse the far off turrets from our rental car's window, deep in the woods; with the backdrop of the rugged *bens* in the distance. I knew it was suppose to be in this area somewhere. And; here it was, forlorn and empty now.

The seeds of my being were sown here, in this fertile Scottish soil. Land of my forefathers...the kilt... the pipes... and the tartan. Ruined and neglected, the stones breaking away from the footsteps of ghosts who trod too hard. Here it was the place where my forebears lived and died...laughed and cried.

The feeling was beyond my reach. I had been here before in some bygone and forgotten time. I could almost smell the haunch roasting in the great fireplace while the skirl of the pipes floated down from the parapets.

The tallest turret was four flights in the air, a place where a princess maybe let down her hair.

I saw an ancient kinsman as he rode off to fight by the side of William the Wallace, Scotland's beating heart.

Both bonnie and braw,
King... for a day ~ or a moment,
Hero... still.

The stones whispered of lairds, first one and then another, being judge and jury, protector and collector.
And maidens fair.
All innocence or dancing naked neath a witch's moon?

Then, others that fell on *Culloden's Field* when one, not so bonnie, led them to bleed or starve or lose their heads. And, some to escape to the budding colonies in the west.

Hence, I come full circle, to find the roots, to hear the ghost's whispering; of this time I had forgot.

Till Now!

Author Comments:
This was my first visit to Buchanan Castle, the home of my forefathers. In Scotland

AFTER THE CRUSADES
(Poetic Prose, a work of fiction)

Inside the stony walls with murder holes just wide enough to see the bleakness of the gray and damp beyond, he sits upon his throne-like chair while petitioners drone on and on about one complaint or another.

His attention flags, as his mind wander and wonder about things past or yet to come. His eyes lower to the toughened scars that lace his hands and arms. He can picture the battle that brought them hence, but he cannot recall the pain of the sword slicing through skin, muscle and tendon. Pain so intense he thought he would never forget, and yet, the feeling is gone and cannot be recalled.

He can still hear the swords clanging as they met against sword or shield. And; the cries and moans of those fallen around him, both friend and foe alike. The smell of blood imprinted in his nostrils like cattle brands. Each remembered as if yesterday, and yet, the pain is gone. Remembered, but not recalled. The frenzied horses screaming, pierced by arrow, lance or sword. The ground was slick with mortal blood, a severed limb still twitching life. The screams of a dying man trying desperately to push his own intestines back inside a gaping, stinking hole, and yet, his pain not recalled with only these white and jagged traceries left to remembering.

He remembered the red-hot sword that cauterized his body wounds. He could even smell his own searing flesh, his screams echoing inside his ears. And after the wails and weeping of the women searching out their dead, did anyone ever win those contests of killing…the snuffing out of life…for the causes of church instead of men? How many had he lost while fighting for priestly quarrels, for land that would never belong to them? Did he lead them or deceive them? And, still they came for his advice; for his council or punishments or lack, thereof.

He would rest but he was too weary. Would sleep, but the screams inside his head ever awakened him. And, yet he could not recall the pain. With abject anguish, he did recall his son and the bolt from crossbow sunk deep inside his back, the wound itself not mortal. Instead, for weeks he languished as putrfaction poisons made him boil inside his own skin. Seventeen summers his child had seen; then gone just as autumn leaves fall from the trees.

For what?
For a mother weeping still?
His child…
His son…His own.

The pain of which he would ever recall, until he left this earthly plain… to wander the labyrinths of hell. And; still the pain from the scars he bore, he could not recall at all.

NOCTURNE
(Sonnet)

With flute and lyre the music calms the breast
of those who live inside this mortal coil.
To ease the pain that oft denies us rest
when day is spent and we no longer toil.

The strains that float upon the tender ear
in harmonies to take us far away.
to some enchanted place that knows no fear
where skies are ever blue and never gray.

And; sing we to the tune of sweetest sound
the rhapsodies that drift about the air.
We sway as all our cares become unbound
and close our eyes as music takes us there.

To sleep and dream until the end of night
While sun bids us come forth into the light.

THE GENTLEMAN
(Ottava Rima)

He was so very suave and debonair,

the gentleman who bowed his head to me

That rakish cap he wore upon his hair

with just the slightest bending of his knee.

One lifted brow to give him extra flair

and one small wink for only me to see.

Across the room I recognized the glance

Extend his arm, while asking me to dance.

THE GIFT OF MUSIC
(Quatrain)

For music is what helps me
climb the mountains of despair.
When my lost soul is trapped
and isn't worthy of repair.

The voices of the angels
come to pacify my mind.
With melodies so lovely
that euphoria I find.

I go beyond the fences
that imprison me within.
And; walk the outer limits
where my soul has never been.

There's symphony within me
that will bring me peaceful sleep.
Sweet morphia is given
with its promises to keep.

The crashing of crescendo
sends my soul into the air.
Flying like a winged bird
far beyond my prison's lair.

Beauty of the violins
and the strumming of guitar.
Open up the universe
while I soar from star to star.

Healing music brings me to
a serene and peaceful time.
Where despair is locked outside
with no mountains left to climb.

WORDS
(Sonnet)

There simply are no words that can express

the love I hold for you within my heart.

I promise…love…that I will not repress

a single tear of joy that you impart.

And, could I love you more than my own life?

I'd gladly give it up for you tenfold.

These bonds cannot be severed with a knife

nor ever in my simple words be told.

So take this hand in yours throughout our age

to hold at least forever and a day.

Just walk beside me through our final page

and know that I mean all the words I say.

You are the single heart that I adore.

Our next stop will be heaven to explore.

HE'S GONE AWAY

(Song Lyrics)

You toss and turn upon the bed
while movies play inside your head
then throw the covers off and pace
remembering his caring face.
You light your final cigarette
and then you struggle to forget
but all you feel is deep regret.

He's gone away
You call him on
the telephone
and all you get
is dial tone
telling you that
he's not home.
He's gone away.

On silent nights when sleep evades
the humming of the house pervades
and walking floors is all you do
while thoughts keep on pursuing you.
The glowing of your cigarette
can take your mind from him and yet
reminds you that you can't forget.

He's gone away
You're on your own
and you are left
so all alone.
He's gone away.
He's going stay.
He's gone away

THE SWANS OF AVIMORE

(Sonnet of fiction)

With long and graceful necks of snowy white

about the reedy water's edge they glide.

The pair at peace without the need of flight

they float sun dappled water side by side.

On banks of pond they make their nest with care

and hidden by the rushes all around

three eggs are lain while tending nest they share.

They sit and wait upon their precious mound.

But then a hunter comes with loaded gun

and fires it at the mother on her nest.

His aim is true; she had no place to run.

His mate now gone, the sire lays down in rest.

The pair no longer seen upon the shore

for now there are no swans at *Avimore*..

Editorial Comment: Yvonne Marie Crain, Senior Editor *Avimore* is located on the *Scotland Highlands*. Swans are within the family of birds that mate for life.

THE BLADE
(Quatrain)

He draws the blade across her skin,
much like cutting through soft butter,
dragging behind a line of red.
No final words from her did utter.

Sponging away the excess blood,
it must not drip onto the floor.
Counting each, no evidence leave
for who might find this dungeon's door.

Ever deeper the blade goes in
made razor sharp this flaying steel.
Cold air brushes his steady hand.
Unconscious victim cannot feel.

Slicing through veins to see the rush
of life blood's flow around the blade.
Moving slowly in harmony
to classical music being played.

He hums along unknowingly,
to him, a well remember tune.
Thinks to himself that haste can waste,
that he mustn't be done too soon.

Then, with his hands he spreads the wound
to see the pulsing life within.
And; smiles unknown, behind the mask
seeing the sins that lie therein.

He cuts them out with bloody ease,
offending parts that mock his sight.
He sets aside the sharpened steel,
satisfied with his work tonight.

When all is done, the lights go out
the place now filled with darkened gloom.
Behind his mask, he softly says,
"Take her to the recovery room."

Author Comments: Walking on the dark side...gotcha!

247

DEATH OF A UNICORN
(Fantasy Quatrain)

Among the reeds I found the silver horn,
with breaking heart; 'twas horn of unicorn.
And he lay dying somewhere midst the glens;
so, I began my search of glades and fens.

And; on my ear his mournful song of death,
I felt the wrenching sob that stole my breath.
Following his song to the place he lay
among the grass that smelled of new mown hay.

And; there he was, a shimmer in the sun
midst fairies, sprinkling dust that they had spun.
Midst elves, braiding flowers into his mane
while all were weeping crystal tears of rain.

A mighty dragon swooped to say goodbye
as diamond teardrops fell from out his eye.
I hid behind a tree, and watched it all
and, wept before this final curtain call.

Magic steed raised his head to look at me
and sighed as all before me ceased to be.
I held the horn… because I thought I must,
within my hand, the horn turns into dust.

JOYFUL RAIN

The rain was wistful teardrops from the gods,
on grand Olympus far from worldly eyes.
Queen Hera smiles at Zeus… and slowly nods
for happy tears are shed from heaven's skies.
The earth was sere, and needing gentle rain
with wells gone dry, and desert spreading fast.
Athena laughs and weeps without disdain,
while joyful mortals pray the rain will last.

Apollo dances on the cloudy floors
and Zeus produces lightning from his hand.
With skies alight, Apollo's thunder roars.
Oasis now is formed across the land.
So mortals lift their faces to the sky,
and bless the gods for teardrops that they cry.

MY MOTHER'S HANDS
(Prose)

Fingers, long and slender… with oval nails buffed to a high gloss by one of those gadgets you only see in antique shops these days. Always clean; no matter how hard she worked. Rarely still, shelling peas or stitching hems while talking on that old black rotary dial, or listening to Stella Dallas, or maybe Fibber McGee. Laughing every single time he opened that famous closet door.

Driving along in that old Studebaker, and spotting a horse with its hoof caught up in a barbed wire fence. Parking the car along side the road and freeing that huge animal with no more fear than a lion tamer at the 4th of July circus. I thought she was the bravest woman that I ever saw.

Peeling potatoes and not cutting herself even one time. Washing the dishes in one sink and rinsing them in another. Running the clothes through the wringer and always hanging them on the line to dry.

Wiping snotty noses with a real cotton handkerchief that had been ironed. Standing at the ironing board that came out of a little door in the wall while she ironed the sheets and my father's boxer shorts.

Rubbing my tummy in the middle of the night, as softly as hummingbird wings. Laying cool hands on a forehead hot with fever. Chasing nightmares away with a single touch.

Counting pennies for the Good Humor Man, during the dog days of summer. Spreading peanut butter and not once tearing the bread.

Stroking the cat every minute or two while she darned our socks with a burnt out light bulb. Clapping until her hands were bruised at my recitals even when I screwed up and played the wrong key. Taking my hand to cross the street or pushing a swing, "higher, mommie, higher."

Wiping the tears when I got hurt, even if it was only my feelings.

Now, those hands crossed upon a breathless chest, lay just so; to hide the bruises left by the needles that fed her near the end. Fingers still long and slender with oval nails buffed to a high gloss. Now, cold and stilled forever, these are my mother's hands.

Author Comments: A true account of a beautiful woman, my mother.

ASYLUM
(Skeltonic Verse)

The loony bin
is very quiet
here tonight.
I only hear
a whimper
down the hall.
Sometimes they fear
the dark of night
and crash their
heads upon
the padded wall,
especially when the moon
is full and round.
I often wonder
what goes on
inside their heads.
Are their thoughts
just like a
jumbled ball
of knotted threads?
A world of desperate dreams
or memories of
horrors unexplained,
that they are too ashamed
to share?
Sad and lost
within the litter
of their minds.
A cost
too steep for
them to pay?
And, me,
the keeper of the keys
that unlock
nothing more
than doors.
How very easy
it would be
to join the lunacy
and forget it all.

BURNT OFFERINGS
(Skeltonic Verse)

With eyes wide open,

she offered her heart

on friendships altar,

with her own life's blood

straining her fingers.

A burnt offering,

so freely given

as her sacrifice

to those she called friend.

Friendship lifted it

in its gnarly hands

and tossed it aside,

there to gasp and die

on the stone cold floor

of its icy temple.

When all was dead and still,

friendship realized

its terrible sins.

And weeps alone

because nobody wins.

Author Comments: To the death of friendships.

THE HIGHLAND FAIR
(Rhyming Couplets)

Come along with me, my love, to the fair...
All the king's ladies and gents will be there.

Knights and maidens will parade on the fields,
maidens with garlands and knights with their shields.

Mead made of honey in tankards we'll share
while the sun's golden rays dance in your hair.

We'll eat from the haunch and pies filled with mince
then we'll eat oatcakes with jams made of quince.

We'll watch the swordsmen practicing their skill,
jousting comes later with battles of wills.

Archers will send arrows into the sky,
while into the air the cabers will fly.

As nighttime arrives, the bonfires will glare
while sparks dance like fireflies up in the air.

Then tales of adventures told round the fire,
of witches and brews and of ghosties dire.

Of fire breathing dragons soaring in flight
and all of the things that go bump in the night.

The children will nod with dreams in their heads,
the cool summer grass for their little beds.

Come along with me, my love, to the fair...
All the king's ladies and gents will be there.

THE STRANGER
(Free style story in rhyme)

He came to town walking the railroad track,
hands in his pockets and a pack on his back.
He was mighty lean, but his clothes were clean.
Long hair tied back and wearing faded blue jeans.
The pack he toted couldn't have had much room,
maybe a change of clothes and some men's perfume.
Sneakers held together with silver duct tape,
carried a poncho like you'd carry a cape.
His blue eyes startled everybody he passed,
he held your gaze and didn't let go fast.
Seemed nothing about him to cause alarm,
though some of the ladies said he sure could charm.
Was very quiet spoken when he spoke at all,
mostly just listened, as I recall.
He walked into the diner, pulled up a stool;
asked Faye, the waitress, if the water was cool.
She poured him a glass and looked in those eyes,
"What can I getcha?" He ordered some fries.
She brought his plate and set it down
then said, "Well hon, what brings you to town?"
He looked up at her with a wry kind of smile,
"Well Fay," he said, "been on the road awhile."
Her name was on the pin that she wore
on her dress that was bought at the uniform store.
"Are you thinking' of settlin' down here?
It's a right nice town," she said in his ear.
"In the park is a trailer I know is for rent.
Don't cost very much cuz one side is all bent.
Belonged to *Old Gus* who upped and died,
Laid there a week before his body was pried
offen the floor of that rusty old bus.
Smells mostly gone since they cleaned up *Old Gus;*
Tell me your name and I'll put in a word."
He looked up at Faye while his coffee he stirred,
"My name is Billy, I'm *Old Gus'* son,
and the smell of my dad won't bother me none.
I just come from fightin' way over the sea,
tried so to hurry, but I've got this bum knee."
The diner fell silent, as all looked around,
the clock on the wall was the only sound.
"But; Billie, your dad said you died in that war."
"Yeah, that was me and I've traveled real far
to bury my dad out there in the loam,
and; I'll lay beside him when they bring me home."

253

THE TATTERED DRESS

(A story of fiction in quatrain)

Digging through the mansion's garbage
she came upon a tattered dress,
and drew it out so she could so she could feel
the softness that she could caress.

The color of the dress was pink,
like those wild roses in her dreams.
There was a stain across the front,
and... it was torn along the seams,

Two buttons gone from off the back,
simply rhinestones and made of glass,
and yet, to her were precious gems
which gave the dress that touch of class.

Though food had been her main concern,
the hunger she felt was gone.
She knew the dress would fit her frame
before she even tried it on.

She took it into her alley,
and held it like she had won a prize.
She stroked it with her grubby hands,
adored it so with rheumy eyes.

She had no mirror for to see;
how sweet the dress would look on her.
It mattered not for she would be,
so queenly gowned that hearts would stir.

THE TATTERED DRESS
(continued)

Inside the box, this was her home,
the rags she wore were put aside.
In only moments she was dressed,
no longer feeling need to hide.

She danced upon the city streets,
with full skirt swirling in the breeze.
She didn't feel the bitter cold,
nor did she notice breathless wheeze.

Next morning, found her lying there,
amongst the litter on the street.
In summer dress of perfect pink,
and smiling face so young and sweet.

Police asked the homeless man,
"Who was the young girl lying there."
"Her? Well, that's old crazy Annie,"
but, she weren't young, I do declare.

All of seventy, if a day,
she lived up yonder all alone."
Policeman shrugged and shook his head.
Now, *Potter's Field* is Annie's home

AFFAIRS OF THE HEART

By

Barbara Truncellito

Chi son ~ Che cosa faccio ~ E come vivo

Sono un poeta ~ Scrivo ~ Vivo!

Barbara Truncellito

Autobiography - Barbara Truncellito

Chi son? Sono un poeta. Che cosa faccio? Scrivo. E come vivo? Vivo
Who am I? I am a poet. What do I do? I write. How do I live? I live.

This excerpt from the great aria, Che Gelida Manina, in the Italian opera, *La Bohème*, by Giacomo Puccini, best describes how I view myself as a poet. As the essence of who I am, it is my companion in times of great celebration and my confidant during times of great trial.

I started writing as a child. However life took many other forms. I live in Manhattan, New York and on Long Beach Island (a barrier island off the coast of New Jersey). These are two very different venues but they symbolize the many aspects of my character and experiences. I have been a senior executive in retail management, Chair of the Board and Trustee of a project for homeless women and children (The York Street Project in Jersey City N.J.), and a political activist. In addition, I am Publisher and Editor of my own small press (Fragile Twilight Press). I have published four collections of poetry, *In Fragile Twilight*, *Beyond the Seventh Poinsettia*, *Moonflowers*, and *In Tribes of Running Rain*. I hold a BA in English and an MS in Management.

My first love is writing poetry. Colette Inez, author and poet, Associate Professor Columbia University the Writing Program New York, N.Y., has been my mentor and sister in poetry for over twenty years. Of my work, she has published the following comments: *I'm moved by the clarity and music of Barbara Truncellito's voice in these poems, how compassionately she faces the sorrows of the dispossessed, how calmly she meditates on histories of family losses and loves. Engaged with the natural world which she observes with confidence in its power to inspire and console, she also gives us a vision at once sensuous and delicate, earthy and spiritual that reverberates in memory.*

I recently wrote a novel which is in the process of its second revision. It's entitled *Lucy* and is about a homeless woman I met years ago in Manhattan while rushing off to Macy's to sell sweaters during the busy Christmas season. I was struck and held spellbound for a few minutes by the depth in her eyes. Covering nine decades of history, the novel intertwines the lives of two women; reflecting love, war, peace, and reconciliation. As I pondered all the eclectic parts of my personal history, I realize the thread that held it together was my mother, Sofina Truncellito.

Sofina Truncellito came to America as a small child from Italy While upholding all traditions from years of culture, she was able to become educated and as a result become well read and progressive in her approach towards her own life and those of her two daughters. She passed in September of 2007. She had the most dramatic impact on my life. No one will ever love me like that again. Sad as that sounds, how lucky am I to know this in my heart and to live the rest of my life with confidence and wisdom so aptly taught to me by this great lady.

I am most grateful to Dr. Harris "Cole" Vernick for his belief in me and my work. I would also like to thank Maxene Alexander for her editorial support working on the Bakers Dozen Vol. III. The world is a better place when individuals such as Dr Vernick will take time and energy to propose that a moment or two with a poem might bring about a more loving and peaceful world, one that is enriched with metaphor and possibility. This gift is from somewhere outside myself, from God.

Table of Contents

In Allegiance

One afternoon
when I was seventeen
I drank wine
in my mother's cellar
held my rubber ball
and Howdy Doody doll
from my first and second birthdays

Today I watch the sun
roll from east to west
yellow as high noon
burn the fog with heat red rays
I sit in cool breezes
remembering my youth
its nights of blue jazz
and throats with cultured pearls
how I dined on chocolate soufflés

Blinking at the first slits of spring
grazing in the soft beach sand
I stroke my left breast
with salt water to heal a scar
the closest thing to my heart

I remember a night
I wiped broken glass
and could recall the days
when my hand obeyed me
in the glare of florescent light
I whispered
for old movements
precise in their crusade
I wanted the sounds around me
to be new- a reward

tonight I wait for morning
for blinks at slits of spring
and with my left hand
in steady salutation to the sun
I play dolls with my daughter
handing her a rubber ball

To a Homeless Woman

That moth eaten fur coat becomes you
in morning light glancing
on the red of your lipstick
what regalia
to search for breakfast
in the trash

you pick up a mirror
leftover from someone's cosmetic bag
I look over and see my face, too
do we know one another
were you standing here
twenty years ago
did the wind blow too hard

it's the Christmas season
see the lights and manger
for you to adore
a few snow birds
hovering on naked branches
in chorus
signing in excelsis deo[11]

do you remember being a child
and Christmas breakfast served
hot cocoa and fruit cake
does the red on your lips
give you reason to smile
in the broken glass
will you be warm enough

Author Comments: Some years ago I was a senior executive at RH Macy Inc in New York City. In the month of December, I was absorbed with selling sweaters; yet this woman came into my view as I was hailing a taxi. Her eyes penetrated mine and she changed my life. I think she was an angel.

---

1   Excelsis deo may be translated as: God in the highest (or God in heaven).

Jerusalem

Parched roofs of Mount Zion
resting places for the wind
even grains of sand wait to move
as if stirred by God
the wind swallows sunlight
bellows out stars
balances night and moon

Let me tell you of snow
on the beach holding
marks of a sparrow
wind dances on sand dues
backdrop
of a sea connecting
the shore to itself

If you were human
I would sit beside you on a dune
we'd remember your life in Jerusalem
we'd give thanks
for walks to the beach in winter
snow on sand
you telling desert stories
I reading poems
while the wind stirs
in tracks left
       by a sparrow

The Mirror

Today I am eighty
eyes are two shades
of waning blue
I stand before a mirror
left hand
holds a walking cane
hip bone sore
arthritis
it runs in the family

I walk the ocean's edge
sun and wind
still my friends
delight in reminding me
of my children
talking to me
through their eyes
I remember watching them grow

I gather poems
momentous of travel
companions and records
for those who want to know more
after I'm gone
sun and wind read my last will
and testament to the sand
which will house my body
when the sprit rises

I stare into the mirror
"you don't scare me," I say

Author Comments: I wondered about ageing so I transported my self to the age of eighty. This is where I found my ageless self.

The Tale of Lillian Wheeler

We fly together
from Chicago to Memphis
I to share my poems
with strangers
you to share stories
with family and friends

Like a child
I rest my head on a pillow
listening to you
a share cropper
married at sixteen
your husband
self-taught
you collected his diploma
as well as your eleven children
in your black arms

More of the legend
oil wells inherited on land
in Louisiana
years as a beautician
coaxing a boy
to turn from drugs

"I'm ninety three," you say
your face free of caution
as you tell me
your nephew will be
the president of a university
we remember Dr. King
your hand in mine
a reminder
human touch leads people
to God who has no color

We touch down
the ground receives us
we embrace
I am filled with hope
as you say, "So, you see child,
I'm just too busy to die."

Affairs of the Heart
(Nessun Dorma[2])

Light flickers in quick turns
over the ocean
as in a ballet
yet waves bellow
from the same sea

I look for sunsets
from an old pink
whispering in secret
the sun floats over shadows
grayed with ashes
leftover from a summer fire

This may be an aria
Classic love song remembered
Tu pure, o princepessa
Nella tua fredda stanza
Guardi le stelle
Che fremono d'amore
E di speranza[3]

And you, too, princess
in your cold room
look at the stars
which tremble with love
and hope

The bleached pink is pale
against this twilight
and stars beckon
drift with us – for you
moonflowers bloom

---

2   Nessun Dorma (None Shall Sleep). From the final act of the Italian opera, *Turandot.* Some have called this the greatest tenor aria in operatic history. The story line concerns a Prince who has fallen in love with the beautiful yet unapproachable, Princess Turandot.

3   Translation (Aaron Green): *No one sleeps, no one sleeps .. Even you O Princess, in your cold room. Watch the stars, that tremble with love and with hope.*

The Desert

In the distance water quivers
from a soft wind
under a palm
leaves shade sand
left parched
by the sun

Images of those who also crossed
Moses and Jesus
Lawrence of Arabia
strands of wives
bonded in marriage
to an ancient sheik
each echoes a desert story

Facing the night chill
I am protected
from sun and storm
I wear a white cloak
and a sense of faith
I have not yet seen
the palm beckoning me
to tell my story

Will I get to where I'm going
does it exist
who will lead me there
how did I get here
am I sleeping

I stumble over a stone
the singing continues
until it reaches the place
where my heart waits for love

This day ends differently
the sun in obeisance
to my singing of the desert
directs palm leaves
to fan the twilight sky
into immortal colors
water trembling in my hands
made steady by a soft wind

I Call Her Ava

Her red dress and blue coat
glow next to her olive skin
gold hoop earrings guard
straight hair

I see her staring into the dark airfield
plane lights glare
through the window
her serene face still
a quiet moment
comparing companions
remembering them
toasting time away
like politicians
with no domain

I learn this
in dialogue with her
she is from Afghanistan
and is escaping the Taliban
who now rule the country
from the right
wing that hovers
over every woman
even a woman such as this
educated but with no rights
subject to stoning
death sentences for bearing an arm
in public

She has no name
no trace of her
in this moment
she does not exist
except for a red dress
shrouding an empty soul

Author Comments: I have signed many petitions protesting the mal-treatment of women around the world. However, it wasn't enough so I created a woman who was a refugee from Afghanistan who I meet at an airport. The name Ava just floated into my head so I went with it.

Ode to Isabella D'Oro

Your story lingers in Valsienne
town of my ancestors into a mountain
winding alleys and cobblestones sob
recalling you Isabella of gold
hair of sunlight
eyes from the sea
you lived in a castle
a lady waiting for the majesty of a lord
who would fulfill her destiny
instead you loved a commoner
the rush of his simple song
your lovemaking moans rising to cypresses
lauding over terracotta rooftops
background for an operatic ending
your brother put the scandal to sleep
with a knife to your throat

I mourn for you
your rightful place is in the sky
with Heloise and Mary Magdalene
the passion of saints will not be quieted
by men without souls
their version swallowed
by spirits of women
who return to tell their tales through a poet-
she can hear you calling
remember me as Isabella
who was not afraid to love

Author Comments: My paternal family's roots are in a small village in southern Italy called Valsienne. Translated, it means town overlooking a river. When I was a young woman I visited this town and heard this story.

The Fruit Man

At your fruit stand
you face the sun
on a jammed Manhattan side street

Umbrella blue and white shades you
in an oasis of colors
of Greek islands bleached and golden
apples red or green
bananas buckling in half moon circles
like the curves of a woman you crave

What are your dreams
as you stare towards clouds gathering
behind skyscrapers
is this the landscape of your fantasy
the isle of Corfu
sirens calling you to the sea

Coins are tossed
you escape under the blue and white umbrella
biting the red apple
kissing the curved woman
drowning in ecstatic lovemaking
oblivious to the tempo of the afternoon

Author Comments: I saw this man selling his fruit on 49th street and Madison Ave in New York City. I created his story on a clear spring day.

In the Wake of Katrina
For Betsy who we thought lost but was found

Orange and blue specks
visions of children building sand castles
ocean waves lush and wanton in September drawl
a last swim before winter
titillating kissing salt laced foam

I hear calls from the Gulf
drowning in fury
exhausted throats laced with thirst cry
come save me

I think of you lost
in Bay St Louis
tin roof played tunes for you to sleep
marshes covered the earth in winter

I conjure you
in windswept rolls of thunder
roaming looking for love
a tear drop your daily drink
I remember our college days when drink was plentiful
and fantasies of another year

Amazing grace how sweet the sound
you once were lost
now you are found
porcelain statue of Jesus remains
behind the cathedral in New Orleans
unmarked arms outstretched
Bourbon Street sings to Him among fallen willows
He sings to us as we sing for you

Come here a land of speckled children
wearing costumes orange and blue
dancing in summer autumn light
I will feed you golden apples to quench your thirst
sea winds soothe
dream of Bay St Louis
tin roof tapping
marshes warming
while sirens sing you to sleep

When Lilacs Return

Their moonrise scent duels the sun
with wooden sword carved from seasoned oak
my sprit rides the night

Craving last years' eclipse
love seems lost to me
a grave of exhausted prayers
I want to be held by the arms that first freed me

Poems call in my native tongue
moonlight warms cedar and pine
pale hues of sunrise
sea foam the color of my eyes
I am ready

Lighthouses burrowed into rock
casts a drawn shadow
eclipse behind me
I fall into lilac and dream
of one who may still love me

Lingering Dreams

(A Love Song)

Printed roses on the bedspread
faded and recalling
when you slept nestled in their bouquet
a wine glass coaxing you
to dream of me-
roads imagined and traveled
apart and near
faint whispers and a long breath
holding our memories

I gave you a rose at breakfast
you blew the petals open
and coveted its scent

my garden bloomed roses
in December snow
one remains in a perfume bottle
on my dresser
I still hold its red

faded roses in dewdrops at dawn
Venus and Neptune wake in twilight
stars intertwine like lace at midnight
recalling the delicate print of your touch.

Women, Etc.
(For Colette)

City bustling at midday
ruffling sounds
like my grandmother's skirts
cherries from a street vendor's cart
I imagine twisting their stems
wearing them as earrings
my mother did as a child
in Italy

In sunlight
golden as ripe melon
I lunch with you
an outdoor Turkish café
lavish with violet velvet cushions
white iris in glass vases
on white tablecloths
lulling caresses

I miss the women I love
whispering their secrets to me
in twilight sipping espresso
late day lessons

Sister poet also scarred
still standing
cries of a bustling city
are no match for language
gracing your crimson lips
a familiar and welcome melody
I am in awe of your infinite beauty
as you whisper secrets
into the ears of this child yearning
for her mother

Authors Comments: Colette Inez is my mentor and sister in poetry. She's my confidant and dearest friend. I would not be the poet I am today if it were not for her guidance, nurturing and love.

Under the Full Moon

July breezes caress my thigh
scent of lavender lingers
succulent tomatoes
from my garden
basil sweet and tender
sounds of Celtic music
drift among the pines
calling you to the sea

Secret love
infinite and regal
we toil in our garden

Haunting memories
I take to my breast
when the summer wind
kissing my thigh is gone
and it is winter again

July moon in twilight
our song
a single breath
dances along the ocean

Summer With Mother

A young boy offers me a starfish
I accept asking the sea
to grant a wish

Waves answer me with cold sea foam
I want to hold my mother's dignity
in the palm of my hand
the breadth of her life
threatened by age and illness
she smiles with grace

She is living with me this summer
seagulls and wind chimes wake us
whispers of rain lull us to sleep
the call from time stinted
as an intercession outside our universe

I make breakfast daily
speak against conservative politics
a simple kiss to her cheek remains on my lips
and I speak of choices made
I remember mother's words
when I doubted who I was

The boy runs the length of the beach
dropping the starfish at my feet
dew drops bead on my skin
tanned and laughing at the sun
as my mother greets another day.

Author Comments: I wrote this for my mother. A couple of years ago, there was a party celebrating the fifteenth year of my small press, Fragile Twilight Press. I realized it was the first time she heard me read before an audience. The smile on her face will remain with me all the days of my life.

Indian Summer

Hints of summer linger
where are you mother
among blooming roses
I cut one as you did for me
fog is rolling in

I see you in shadows from after life
pink flowers in your dress tell me it is you
I did everything to save you
touching my arm you dry my tears

Rolling waves send their scent
you chanted lyrics from the forties to them nightly
"the breeze and I are calling you tonight"
have you come in moonlight
I sleep in your nightgown
still fragrant from your perfume
can you hear me singing

Should I plant our garden again
you never tasted the tomatoes
deep red your favorite color
we listened to Italian arias
sipping espresso on the deck
in silence we spoke our native tongue
will I be warm in winter
when stones are cold
and winter fire spews sparks yellow as ochre
shall I wrap myself in your blanket
until the sun visits us in spring

I touch a photo of you in a gold frame
a young bride you seemed a queen
how did it appear in your final bed
is it you mother laughing as you play a prank
is this message to steady my hand

Lying on sand dunes fog lulls me to sleep
the silence of sandpipers allows me dreams
salt water heals, you said
I long to see you once more
a glimpse of sun appears through clouds
is it you mother
wrap me in your arms

Author Comments: I wrote this in the weeks following my mother's passing. It is raw with emotion
and filled with unmitigated grief. However, it helped me cross a threshold in the mourning process.

The Color Red

(In loving memory of my mother)

A rainbow dances
along walls of my house
where you lived
a sun-catcher its vessel
you in the color red
how it glowed
against your olive skin

As a child I remember asking
why are we washing and ironing
using our last pennies
giving it all to strangers
you replied because they are poor
someone once washed and ironed
a dress for me
it was red

Light lingers
I hear you telling me
look into this band of colors
catch a sunray
dance in its red
then give it away
blessings will be yours

Late August

Your long skirt covers your hips
wide from multiple births
sunflowers border the hem
the wind is brisk

You walk with seven children
as you did in Mexico
feet tingle, thirst, hunger
morning dew peers through holes in sandals
handmade by your husband

Summer green waning cast shadows
you catch litter
tossed from a red convertible
is this supper
wilted lettuce in a fajita
dried beans and rice a disguise
do your children believe in ocean waves

Sunrays pierce your skin
you drink left over rain
tread mud lifting the hem of your skirt
borders of sunflowers grasp at the wind

Author Comments: One afternoon I was driving the highway which links the mainland to the barrier island Long Beach Island in South Jersey. I observed a woman walking, possibly going home, possibly going to a second job. I wrote this for her.

Folk Angel

I speak to you
through verses of Kumbaya
by way of where have all the flowers gone
living in each other's presence
in dawn light poised for noon
in twilight fragile and yawning

Did you announce the birth of Christ
or provide oil to give light
winter solstice causes a pause
ancient hymns harmonize with peace prayers
I hear you singing

Angel, come to me in the night wind
sleeping in your arms I keep faith
with One who is greater than I

Author Comments: Angels live in the light of a child's smile or in a kiss from the wind. I continue to witness and wonder. May your heart be open to angels and may you know God's love.

Drops of Falling Rain
In the Voice of Mary Magdalene

I recall our days together
bread and wine a new gift
I dreamt another spring
careless in its design
of intimate wandering
I wanted to speak
you nodded an approval
it was you they wanted
late afternoon rain
who consoles me now
I wiped your tears
marks of sorrow
ancient rainbows rose over Jerusalem
wanton light and shadows
your last words
I entered into darkness with you
carrying herbs and ointments
to the cave where you lay
I anointed you kissing your hand
for the last time

Then, the dawn
you stood in a white robe
your eyes stark
my spirit filled with wondering
look at me, you said
not at the ground swollen from afterbirth
look at me and know
I live in late afternoon
among drops of falling rain

TAPESTRY OF LIFE

By

Joree Williams

I received a phone call offering me a merit-based publishing grant through *The Cole Foundation for the Arts.* This was a dream come true, publishing my thoughts with twelve other gifted poets. I had to pinch myself to make sure I was not asleep and dreaming.

I am taking this opportunity to thank you, Dr. Harris (Cole) Vernick, founder of *The Cole Foundation for the Arts, and Foundation Editor of The Baker's Dozen.* You remind me of the patrons of the arts throughout the ages, in Rome, Greece, Egypt, and throughout Europe, enabling artists to speak their within held thoughts.

Dr. Vernick has surrounded himself with caring; competent people: Maxene Alexander, Executive Editor ~ Vivienne Harding, Co-Editor and Art Director ~ Greg Graney, Graphic Artist ~ and all patrons of the arts.

Yvonne Marie Crain, Senior Editor is my mentor in this generous and gracious project. Her help, patience, and suggestions I have found invaluable.

Thank you all for giving poets a voice

Life is Neither Good nor Bad

It Just Is ~ Look for the Love

Joree Williams

POET'S PROFILE: JOREE WILLIAMS

By Yvonne Marie Crain, Senior Editor

Joree is what I call a lifetime survivor. She is married to her soul mate, Joseph Williams. They have two children, eight grandchildren, and two great-grandchildren. She has many friends; however, her best friend is her brother, Tony. They each bring a special joy and love into her life.

Joree graduated from college *Valedictorian, with highest honors*, and an officer of scholastic *Phi Theta Kappa Society*. Learning is one of Joree's greatest passions. She tutored students in college and after her college days, she volunteered in a program teaching adults to read. Unfortunately, this abruptly ended due to a stroke.

Joree, with a history of illnesses, including eight recent surgeries, a stroke, and breast cancer refuses to be defined by illness. Every action has a complete opposite re-action. She chooses the positives to help motivate a caring and loving life. Joree understands and is thankful that each illness has helped to enrich her life and bring her even closer to God.

Although Joree is a fairly newcomer to poetry, she writes with fervor as if it has been a cornerstone of her life for many years. Her poetic gift developed during a college writing class. Through all of the horrors she experienced as a child, she still knows that a heart graciously opened will be able to give and receive love. Many things inspire her poetic voice: Family, nature, anything that stimulates the natural and unnatural senses, and sometimes for the disenfranchised and abused to raise awareness.

Poetry is an integral part of Joree's psyche. She writes with the view that per chance a word or idea will touch someone's life and make a positive change. Joree writes with hopes that at the worst times of someone's life, they will know they are not alone in this world. She believes that poetry is prefaced by a belief that life unfurls as it must ~ all make choices to enjoy or not to enjoy what life offers. Joree, in her gifted way, expresses the key differences in the tough choices we make. Her literary future goal is to continue writing all that is within her heart…until her heart no longer speaks of life.

During college days, Joree wrote as a reporter and was honored by the *Society of Professional Journalist, the Inland Southern California Professional Chapter*. She received a plaque for writing the *Best News/ Feature Story* in a college paper. Joree was a recipient of *The California Literary Outstanding Volunteer of the Year 2003* for the service she provided teaching adults to read. Recently, Joree experienced the pleasure of having published a poetry book; entitled *My Poetic Thoughts*. The publishing house is well known by gifted authors of poetry, novels, and various forms of literature. Several books are in the works, one shall be entitled; *Poems Echo Through the Ages*. On a high note, Joree is delighted to return to her beloved volunteer program, teaching adults to read. She has found poetry is an outstanding means for teaching…meter, sound and sometimes rhyme is a way adults; joyfully, learn to read.

It has been my pleasure to tell you about Joree Williams. Now, I am proud to present to you, Joree Williams with her golden plume and poetic voice.

TABLE OF CONTENTS

CHAPTER ONE: Weavers Of Life

In His wisdom God weaves the strands of His tapestry of life. Many helpers has He, butterflies carry gossamer threads of beauty. Spouting porpoises tell us of the kinship and interconnectedness of all life. Whales sing their threads of songs, hoping we will one day understand. Loving spirits touch us with strings from their hearts. Many are the weavers, if we but notice.

Tapestry of Life

Have you ever noticed
how your life seems
to touch other's at the
most beneficial time?

How you can offer hope
love and understanding
based on your own past
or, be the recipient from someone else

How a stranger can smile
at you when you are
most down and it will
bring out the sun?

How friends are found
with the most love in
their hearts and spirits
to match your own?

Our lives impact one another
in the most amazing ways
every day that we live
it is all part of a plan

I call it the *Tapestry of Life*
each strand is woven with
perfection and love from the
Hands of the Almighty above!

He weaves His tapestry, pulling
this strand here and that
strand there to best benefit
His children; whom He loves

Author Comments: Each person is connected to all other living things in beautiful intangible ways.

What is Life to Me

To me life is a joy
Each day brings
New glimpses of beauty

Beauty of nature
Beauty of humanity
Joyously surrounds me

To me life is love
From a living planet
From celestial heavens

Exchanging Love
With fellow travelers,
Be they human or animal

To me life is a journey
A pilgrimage of self
A voyage of discovery

Of Universal love
Running thru time,
Tangible and true

To me life is a classroom
Experience the teacher
Learning lessons of the soul

The reward gained:
A soul of peace,
Serenity of self

To me life is a gift;
A covenant from above
Everlasting life
From a loving God

Author Comments: Life is joyous; each day a new lesson to be learned to expand my soul.

The Children's Secret

Between tall lofty snow capped jagged mountains,
Villages dot the deep misty valleys
A lane runs through the crisp; white, pure Countryside
Ending at a frozen deep lake of beautiful blue-green water
Trees with snow covered limbs hang to the ground
The children of the villages go there to ice-skate

On the smooth thick ice they race swiftly
To the middle of the enormous round lake
Unburdening themselves of their backpacks
They sit in the bright sun and brittle air
Waiting patiently for the gift to come
A fluttering of wings announces the arrival
The wait is over…the children are ready
To hear the birds of God sing them a melody

Healing Power of Music

In swishing grass of the savannah true
Humanity did sing before we spoke,
Used primal drum made in antiquity
With its heart beat thump-thumping rhythm sent man
On visionary journey searching for hope
In a trance music raised our consciousness
Power of music heals body and soul,
The music goes from ear to brain to heart
First fetus organ complete is the ear
Hospital drum circles raise white blood cells
Catatonic patients move their heads and dance
Alzheimer patients recognize themselves
To feel the music puts them in the now
They feel the music through their whole body
Responding as music touches their souls
God speaks to them through language of music
In all his many voices sending His love

The Song of Life

The song of life
Courses through my veins
Each note a chord of joy

Heart beating musical
The Cast:
Love for humanity,
Beauty of nature,
Wonderment of the Universe

All intertwined into
Beautiful lilting
Melody of life...
Symphony of love

Author Comments: Music is the voice of the soul

Being You

Do you wish for a brilliant formula
to make your life more comprehensible
Do you wish for a famous recipe
to make life pleasant and enjoyable
Do you wish for a renowned prescription
to make your life serene with harmony
Do you wish for a proven theory
to give your life contentment and balance
Do you wish for a magical charm
to make your life more bearably complete
Do you wish for a lifetime of guidelines
to make your life more satisfactory
The principle for living is simple,
be willing to be who you truly are

Author Comments: To be willing to be who you truly are is not always easy; but why deny your inner soul and heart. Remember, we all have lives that God has woven together. Every soul affects every other soul and keeps the tapestry intact. Being who you are does not include being a child molester or murderer – they have chosen to completely remove themselves from the tapestry altogether.

CHAPTER TWO: Lost Journey

Time imprints the mind in retrospect, mere wisps of memory and patchwork illusion. True time dwells in the corridor of the heart. Timeless is our redemption. Time is where we spend our regrets and where we will wait for tomorrow. What about today? Today is the day I worried about yesterday, and the dreams I have for tomorrow.

Come Walk with Me

Come walk with me
Along the edge of when

When stars were young
And wishes came true

When clouds played tag
In a sky of cerulean blue

When the sun smiled bright
Upon a world brand-new

When my child's eyes
Sang songs of trust

When my child's heart
Believed

When my child's soul
Loved

The edge of when
Before the horrors began

Come walk with me now
Along the edge of forever

Now that I have forgiveness
And love from above

Come walk with me
Along the edge of when-after

After hope had been sacrificed
Upon my unearned guilt

Author Comments: Do not judge with adult standards. Love and embrace; find peace in your life.

Little Girl Lost

She has a home
But feels all alone

All the abuse
She feels so used

Inside her mind
Twisted lines are forming

She sees them clearly
Fears them dearly

They make her mind
Place of strange signs

All omens yell danger
Her anger grows bigger

A rage and a wish
For the strength to punish

Her mind turns inward upon itself
A thing wrapped up on the shelf

To be deaf and feel safe
Hide she must in her mind – place

But she knows not
The key to get out

She sits alone on her little chair
Her tiny face strained by one tear

No one knows why she cries
Nor where she hides

Little Girl Lost

Author Comments: Little girls need to shed their unearned guilt to be set free - lost within. They do not know that the guilt and shame they carry belongs to the abuser. Give it back to him. But children do not question adults as adults know it all … Don't they?

Where is the Inner Child-Self

You Ask: Where is the child's laughter and joy?
I Reply: To control, he had to destroy.

You Ask: Where is the child's sense of self?
I Reply: Absorbed by his constant defilement.

You Ask: Where is the child's sense of wonder?
I Reply: Stolen through abuse and hunger.

You Ask: Where is the child's safety and security?
I Reply: Taken along with her purity.

You Ask: Why is the child so quiet, so still, so frail?
I Reply: He threw her away as too old the final betrayal.

You Ask: Why are there no smiles on that little face?
I Reply: She had to live her life in disgrace.

Power in Words

Unkind words cut like a sword

Leaving a wound that never heals

Said aloud in public

They can shame so badly

They will never be forgotten

Poisoning the mind and heart

CHAPTER THREE: New Day's Dawn

Into everyone's life rain will fall. Do we reject negative pessimism, or do we choose to live our lives with joy? Search for as much joy as possible. Contentment is determined by our choices.

Believe in Yourself

In yourself believe, it is a necessity
On your belief depends health, happiness, self esteem
Discover your intelligence and loving heart

You help others without question from your loving heart
Acknowledging assets not prideful but a necessity
You need realize your potential to gain self-esteem

Look inside find your wonderful self raise self-esteem
All who know you recognize your loving heart
Realizing who you truly are is a necessity

Belief in yourself is a necessity
To raise your self-esteem
And fill your empty heart.

Author Comments: Treat yourself as nicely as you treat your friends. If you do not believe in yourself, very few will believe in you; realize your potential; grow and shine.

Life Must Unfurl

When we can accept
Life must unfurl as it must
We find the wisdom
Of our true human spirit
We allow our soul to grow.

Author Comments: A lesson learned, our lives unfurl with a purpose so why pray for a better day or pray for a future of wealth or happiness. Instead, find something to be thankful for, if only the birds singing and the breeze in the trees, and send a thank you prayer upward.

Past Images

In my present day mind
Consume me

Scenes of yesterday
More vivid
Than today's reality

Pale Horse
Prowls the corridors
Totally in control

Death scenes
Worm dark
Tunnels to my soul

Acts of atonement
Unequal
To the debt

Lost in the past
A maze
Of remembering

Future of my present
Must it always
Be my past

A New Day's Dawn

Hopeless child in need of full absolution
Dreams of touching angel's wings can not happen
Faith found news benevolent new beginnings
Butterfly breaks free

Author Comments: This form was created by a woman named Sappos in 600 BC. Poetry with this form is called Sapphic. Make note of the date this woman survived, poetry has been around for many centuries.

If Hands Could Talk

We are the tools of Mankind
With us you can build
All you can conceive

We are the touch of man
The artery of his emotions
Humanities gift

All ideas of man, good and bad,
Are interpreted through us

All emotions, good and bad,
Are carried out by us

We are at Man's command
For better or worse
We have no choice!

ONLY MAN HAS A CHOICE

Author Comments: Change yourself, change the world.

Songs of Nature

I walk in the quiet starlight
Moonbeams dance in the comet's glow
Flickering fireflies blink goodnight
Morning dew sparkle bright hello
Bees buzzing garden below
Butterfly floats by on a breeze
Busy hummingbird humming low
Nature in her glory does please

Author Comments: My granddaughters are the flowers in my life. Nature can ease pain, give inspiration or just be beautiful to look at.

CHAPTER FOUR:
Starry Plains ~ My Brother Russ

Fate decreed her destiny, sparkling brilliant lights on the lane. Sun streaks through each iridescent icicle. Focused, a bright path to the door, fate decreed her destiny.

Starry Plains

Oh…How I've slipped the surly bonds of this earth
Oh…How I fly among royal stars of lavender silver
Sequence radiating in soft pastels are the starry plains
Bedecked with silvery white stars and old blue jeans
With jeweled crown upon my head
His light to forever guide me

Oh…How I surf on the singing solar wind
Oh…How I glide within the comet's tail
Beauteous kaleidoscope of rainbow colors rushing past
Dressed in flowing lavender robes and old tennis shoes
With a posy garland on my head and God's
Loving arms to uphold me

Author Comments: This poem was written in two parts. The first part by my Brother Russ, and the second part by me. Russ had cancer, he and I composed a few poems together; it meant so very much to him and me.

Death as a Door (Part I)

Be not afraid of death
It comes to us all
Fight it when it calls,
But if you lose your battle
Accept death with grace
For death is transitory;
An opening cosmic door
Into another existence
An unknown reality
Of undreamed possibilities
What a wonderful journey
Lies before us all!

Author Comments: My Brother Russ went to be with our Lord this afternoon. We left him yesterday thinking he was doing ok as he was released from the hospital. At the time of his death I was writing poems II and III. We were so very connected.

Death as a Door (Part II)

As you pass through that door
You will be welcomed by a
Light that is alive, welcoming,
Loving, aware; illuminating
Your soul

The Supreme Soul is God
Who will open His arms to you
He is the purest essence of all
He gave you a gift through
His covenant

Your soul is immortal, limitless,
Perpetual; the elemental, infinite,
Timeless spirit transcending all
Boundaries

Through His Grace and Love, you
Will begin living your true existence
Without pain or strife, Serenely
And peacefully content within and without

Death as a Door (Part III)

You have emerged from
This cocoon and your
Soul has taken wing

At the loss of you
My heart will break in two
And I will be overcome with
Loneliness for the sight of you

But I shall remember your life
Not your death; your laugh,
Your jokes, your hugs, your smile,
Your love; and I shall find comfort
In these memories of you

And when I see you bye and bye
Our souls shall fly together
Amongst lavender silver stars
Surf the singing solar wind
Glide within a comet's tail
Soar and play amongst the soft
Fluffy clouds; slide down the
Rainbows with glee, and chase
The orange ball sun

For after death comes our real life
A new and glorious adventure
With worlds to explore

HOPE
(The India Naani)

The greatest detriment in life
Is to be without hope
Our greatest asset
Is to have faith

Leap of Faith

How great the universe infinite vast
My life, a meaningless comparison
The core of life is the *Need to Believe*
Can I trust *God* will keep His *Covenant*?
All He asks in return was faith in Him
Unqualified; unconditional faith
Would He keep His promise of this free gift?
Promised salvation and life-after-death
A blessed union with my soul and *God*
The gift so great, the price so very small
Do I believe, is my faith true and pure
Can I trust *God* to give someone like me
So undeserving, and so unworthy
Can I receive from *God* this wondrous gift
No proof can there be of the *Covenant*
Man's evidence can never be the bridge
Between finite man and infinite *God*
Man cannot get to heaven through reason
My only hope is to throw doubt away
I need take absolute *Leap of Faith*
Say with all my heart: *Credo: I believe…*

Author Comments: SOREN Kierkegaard, a philosopher, wrote about his *Leap of Faith* being the only way he could find faith. He was a literal minded philosopher who went to church, but needed to have proof for his faith to be pure; his taking the *Leap of Faith* is that impressive. To me the *leap* is our ultimate reality

CHAPTER FIVE: Changing Seasons

A smile or a kind word may change a persons outlook on life or at the very least change his day; change just one corner of the world and it will spread outward. One of the gravest sins is to consciously hurt another. Our planet is where the people coming after us need to live; will the earth be livable?

African Sky

I love watching Africa's cloudscape
I once saw a buffalo shape in a cloud
Thunder clouds clap loud
Lightening strikes the landscape
Scaring the Great Ape
As the clouds drape the moon in a cape

One Star Alone

A curious young man had found
A book, wrinkled with age, tucked away
In the far corner of the library

One picture consumed his thoughts
Eating away at his peace of mind
Eroding the basic beliefs of his world

Shivering, he gazed at the photograph:
A couple stood on a hill holding hands,
With an older New York city sprawled below

Photograph, not an artist's rendition
Echoes over and over in his brain
Reverberating, as a doomsday refrain

For, above the couple was a sky at night
Lit up with thousands of twinkling lights
Radiant, as diamonds on a black velvet cloth

Slowly, he walked to the window
Looked up into the sky so black
One lonely star shyly winked back

Author Comments: Scientists say our universe is expanding so fast that one day there will be great spaces between stars.

Changing Seasons

Frost tinted trees
White washed sky
Cold yellow sun
Alabaster fantasy
Trees of chocolate brown
Budding leafs beautify
Golden sun and soft blue sky
Gentle breeze of airy hope
Red gold sun shimmers heat
Sky peacock blue sateen
Branches laden beryl green
Enchanting forest magical
Leafs of tangerine and plum
Flame kissed by scarlet sun
Slowly drop one by one
Forest gently sleeps again

Yosemite

Mossy green leaves
Tall lofty trees
Soft as silk grass

Mountains
Jagged with
Age

Out in the Cold

Barn framed by branches
Under attack, sleet covered
Artic cold, sparkling icy blue
Coated with winter's woes
Canopy of slate gray sky
Wind driven branches
Scratch at the barn
A plea to come in
Windows blink snowflakes
Doors tight against the cold

The Zaire
(A reverse Abecedarian)

Zebra strolls the banks of the Zaire
Youngling followed yearning
Xebec sails on trailing tones of xylophone
Warthog wears warts
Velvet monkey hanging on a vine
Undulating waves in unison
Tiger stretching muscles taut
Spider monkey chattering silliness
Rhinoceros charging rashly
Quadruple baby pups quarrel
Panther sleekly prowling
Orangutan wears orange
Night raven cries at night
Mountain gorilla gentle marvel
Lion sleeping by his lady
Kinetic leopard caught at the kill
Jaguar goes for the jugular
Invertebrates invading insects
Hyena yowls and howls
Giraffe on tree tops gnaws
Feral cats range free
Elephants meander elegantly
Darting chimps play daringly
Cheetah racing and craftily
Buffalo grazing on grass buffet
Antelope and ape co-exist in Africa

Author Comments: There are many ways to write an abecedarian poem. Commonly called an ABC poem.

The Star Nursery

Stars await birth in Star Nursery
Most new born stars grow to maturity
Gathering planets as their family
But, as in life, some burn too bright, too soon!
They go Nova sending out Gamma rays
Then shrink back to become empty black holes

Starlings

Animals have always communicated
But this ability is now more complicated
Chomsky's theory said man was best
Dumbfounded were those who put it to the test
Everyone thought man had the better brain
Flunking grammar, animals could not gain
Gentner's findings after a month of research
His results of birds have put them on a perch
Intriguing and startling news to all
Just makes their theories fall
Key to language skills is grammar
Learn it, you can and will go far
Many animals roar, sing, and grunt
None thought able to bear the brunt
Of recursive grammar except man
Perhaps we had a mind-ban
Quite true for long years round
Researchers now untrue have found
Starlings have shown cause.
They recognize a warbled clause
Up went our regard.
Victory to give was hard
Warbling Starlings were taught
Xanadu! They have caught
Young and old, we applaud
Zenith reached, a gift from God

Author Comments: Noam Chomsky's theory said recursive grammar was unique to humans and was the key to learning language; researcher Tim Gentner, of the University of San Diego proved starlings can differentiate between a regular birdsong and one with an inserted clause. This is a recursive grammar skill; what wondrous findings will come next?

CHAPTER SIX: The Butterfly Prayer

Too much loneliness is disease of the spirit; each person needs to care and love themselves. Show compassion to yourself as the three survival skills of Mankind are kindness, love and compassion. Begin, within...

The Butterfly Prayer

Deep in the forest
Stood a significant tree
On its branch
Was a cocoon
About to give
Life to innocence
Breaking free at last
Pure, guiltless, sin-free
Perfect in every way
Was the butterfly
As it flew away
With sunlight shimmering
Through its lovely
Delicate, intricate wings
I prayed, *Dear God,*
Have Mercy on my son, set him as free;
make him as innocent as the butterfly!

Author Comments: When we cease to breathe, it frees our souls to rise and seek God. I explored the depths of my being, searching for answers about my son; the possible motives; my failures as a mother, and I came to a crossroads: No one has the power to cause another's actions.

Aging

Rain splinters the ground
Clouds cover the sky
Darkness stays behind
Flowers broken in the wind
All lost to the journey

The Camp

The emaciated, prison-clad woman
sat trembling, holding the strange child
facing the smiling camp Commandant
What a pair they made!
She, filthy, smelly, uncombed…dazed
He, polished boots, uniformed, spotless,
every blond hair in place
Completely in command of all faculties

She, there at his invitation,
A way to relieve his boredom,
For on his lap sat her child

Surrounded by armed guards
He holds out to her a gun with only one bullet
Shoot the child or I will shoot yours

She sits dumb…She has seen too much cruelty
Smelt too many ash-filled days
Heard too many screams and cries for help

How can she kill a child…any child?
But what of her own wee-one?
She has sacrificed much to bring her babe…thus far?

He sits quietly smiling…really enjoying his new game
He must do this again but not so crudely next time
Refinements of technique need be considered

Dear God in Heaven, what am I to do…?
She screams in her mind

Author Comments: Prejudice of any kind is abhorrent to me; this poem is a warning of what is possible when prejudice is not opposed.

The Window

Every time we open our mouths
We open a window into our minds

Do we show that we are kind
Or that we are indifferent

Do our words show respect to others
Or only to others like ourselves

Do words of compassion flow to all
Or only to those we think deserving

Do we use harsh words to judge
Others for no authentic reason

When we speak to others, do we
Accept them for themselves

Do our minds understand that
Each of us is a work in progress

That none of us is perfect
And never will be

Here on this globe, we
Have the rare opportunity

To open our minds
To respect and dignity

By sharing our thoughts
Through our words

Shall we open the window
To let in kindness and love

Author Comments: The glummest faces are a facade for the unhappiest.

Last Wish

As my mind turns
Into mere wisps
As my soul
Prepares to go home

What will I wish
As I yearn
No more to roam
But to reach my goal

Will I be selfish
And wish to be missed
Optimistic, and hope
To see my loved ones

Or, altruistic, and think
Of what I leave behind
Wish for peace for all mankind
For the healing of Our Dear Earth

Or shall I give myself
To Our Lord trusting
Him to weave His tapestry
For the betterment of all

Author Comments: Death is our blessed opportunity to see our loved ones again and to walk in God's Garden of Love.

The Art Of

ECLECTICISM

by
Dr. Harris "Cole" Vernick
Founder of The Cole Foundation for the Arts

About the Author

I am a retired physician and have been writing poetry for approximately fifty-four years. I had started out with the rhyming poetry that was the style at that time and then as my interests changed, I became a fan and writer of romantic poetry. As my experiences and my life went through the usual transitions, I started to write free verse and then because of my work as a physician and a teacher of medical students and resident physicians, along with the realities of the career I had chosen, I started to write prose-poetry. I had to tolerate the comments that I was not writing poetry, but stories. I continued in this style and now see it as an accepted style of poetry by contemporary poets.

A number of years ago, I became interested in Haiku and other forms of Japanese poetry and started to write and of course experiment in this style. So as you see, my work is eclectic. One of my greatest joys has been to be sought out as a teacher of my various forms of poetry and see my students develop into far better poets in that particular style then this long time teacher.

Another great joy has been the Cole Foundation where I could join with my excellent editors, Maxene Alexander, executive editor and Yvonne Crain, senior editor. In the most altruistic manner I could ever expect, Maxene and Yvonne donated their time and talents to bring the three volumes of the Baker's Dozen to fruition. They have my eternal gratitude.

Carpe Diem ...

Ars Longa ~ Vita Brevis!

Dr. Harris "Cole" Vernick

INTRODUCTION

by
Maxene A. Alexander
(Executive Editor, The Baker's Dozen Trilogy)

The origin of the word eclecticism may be found within the practices of ancient philosophers who seeking new paradigms, drew from the best parts of beliefs held prior to the eras in which they lived. Out of such collected material they experimented with the choosing of the best of many theories, to form new ideas and new philosophies.

To say that one is an eclectic poet, may also be to say that one both understands and appreciates the best of many poetic forms and further experiments with them to construct a unique style of writing based upon a keen knowledge of that which came before. Harris "Cole" Vernick is one such eclectic poet and, as an art appreciator of over 50 years, is well skilled in the art of storytelling through poetic verse in such a manner so as to captivate the reader beyond technical exactitude – further gifting the reader with shared experiences through many perspectives and multi level understandings.

Personal poetic inclinations aside, Dr. Vernick is also a retired physician and philanthropist – as an art appreciator of many years, he is also well skilled in identifying and encouraging the talents of others. The Baker's Dozen trilogy is the completion of his life long dream to share the talents of many through merit-based scholarship publishing and in conclusion to this trilogy he humbly offers poetry which both reflects past poetic designs with a precise experimentation that forms new and novel approaches to the ancient art of poetry.

It is with great honor and deepest respect that I both introduce Dr. Vernick and serve as his editor for this collection of his poetry. Drawing from a wealth of experience this poet and mentor offers much to all regardless of status or station whether through humor, satire, or deeper ponderings. To experience the poetry of Dr. Vernick is to – experience a broader understanding of both poetry and, the many variations which give it life.

TABLE OF CONTENTS

FAMILY

LIFE'S COUPLETS

Bear me mother
So I can be your boy

Teach me all life
That I can grow with joy

Play with me father
So I can learn to compete

School me teacher
Make my mind complete

Compassion me family
So I can feel man's pain too

As I learn these lessons
I will show others what to do

Cry with me
For the world is in woe

Dry your tears
I have found the way to go

Sing with me
There is a woman in my sight

Love with me
She eases my warring fight

Give me the ring
She is to be my wife

Pray for us
A long and loving life

Share our blessings
A boy and a girl

Two beloved creations
Join us on life's whirl

She grows with me
As we are getting old

The truth I learn
Old years are not gold

The promise is kept
An old me the first to go

Just leaving memories darling
I loved you so

Reading from first column one and then into column two, reveals so many lifetimes within one – dedicated to both a loving mother and to an equally loving and devoted wife … offered here in standard rhyming couplets.

THE GREATEST POET EVER

In the history of all humanity,
Is only known by one person,
Who has studied him and
Intimately knows all his work.

HE WAS MY GRANDFATHER.

His greatest works came to him
In the nights, as he slept.
He would store them in his
Vast brain, locked away forever.

I remember watching him at work
Fast asleep, but working prolifically,
In that old feather bed that kept him
In the deepest sleep, nodding rhythmically.

When a particular stanza or line
Amused him or amazed him, he would
Smile. For many years, so perfect at work.
In rhythm, counting cadence, balancing, creating.

I could see his nodding through so many
Styles, experimenting until free style
Became his favorite. This was so
Observable as the nods became irregular.

YET, NOT A WORD WAS WRITTEN.

Poet to poet, I explained that his great
Works needed to be shared for all'
Especially for posterity, these, the very
greatest body of work. He nodded in sleep.

We set a day when he would start
To write. He nodded acquiescence.
Or we could have him dictate or because
Of sleep, mumble and I would write it out.

Every marvelous word, gifted by a muse
Would be made public. He nodded.
In the morning, I reminded him of our
Nighttime agreement. He grunted, I listened.

"Every word that can be said has already
Been said. Every word that can be written
Even our greatest creations, have already
Been written. I have nothing more to say."

My pen in its silence signaled me that
all those unique masterpieces would forever
be stored in his personal vault, because
Individually every word had been said before.

Watching him sleep but again, and
Nodding, I could see when he added another
Style or when he composed his free verse.
I could even tell when it was blank verse.

The world's greatest poet went to his grave
Unpublished, and unread. He never attended
A reading of his works and there is no collection/
HE WAS MY GRANDFATHER.

COMMENT: The title is the first line of the poem and must be read with the first stanza.

FALLING

Reaching up,
Trying to grasp
Those hands that
Held me so often.
The hands that
Had held my head
Above the water's
Surface.
There always when I
Counted on them
To guide me
And hold me through
Life's treadmill.
Now, I was falling.
I could not feel
Their feminine strength
That made me the man
I would become.
As I looked for them,
Above me, my vision
Lost them in the
Distance that became
More distant
As I fell further.
Until……….

WAITING

So nervously
Because she is my heart,
My life.

I watched as he moved
His well trained hands
Over her hurting
Abdomen, and prayed.
"Let her be well.
If you have to take one,
TAKE ME!"

This is the way it is
With a man who
Marries his heart.

REALITY

Wives become their mothers.
Husbands become whatever is aged,
Gray, bald, pot-bellied, disappointed.
For both, happiness slips down a generation.

Adaptation is their acceptance,
As dreams die, as they die.
Life is youthful only, old is old.
Weddings remind of what has gone.
Funerals speak of what will come.

HOUSE OF MEMORIES

The ancient home,
The crumbled masonry,
The rugs no longer laid smoothe,
Spoke of its elderly owner.

She was full headed white haired,
Obese as her age, sitting
In the lounge chair, edematous
Legs matching edematous body.

Her eyes were bright with
Expectation of the visit,
Possibly the last we would see her,
As ill life rushed by.

She amazed me with her
Memories. Stories gushed
Opening a vault of eighty-nine years
Witness of memories of numerous people.

We listened as she so
Hopefully went through all
Those years and we could see
That she wished she could have more.

She described the pains
She was bearing that
Wracked her every moment.
Then that time arrived.

Describing the heart surgery,
So complex that she knew
She could not survive, with
A ninety percent mortality in surgery.

But, one hundred if no surgery.
We were here as a part
Of the family to hear the decision
That she had carefully made.

"It is in God's hands.
I will not be torn apart."
Tears filled our eyes,
Knowing today it was over.

"I have a ring for you."
My wife glanced at it and
Told her that she would treasure it
Forever, and slid it on a finger.

On the way home, my wife told me
That she would miss her last aunt
She added that she loved this ring that
We had bought for the aunt's 60th birthday.

The house looked even older and shabbier
As we left. We knew that it was losing
The soul of the spirited woman
Who had lived there so many years.

REQUIEM FOR GRANDPARENTS

From my earliest,
I learned to love you both.
Behind those first young faces,
You were there.
Smiling, leaning over,
Looking
Over the shoulders of those first.
You, showing such love for me.
Patiently waiting, your turn
To hold me,
Again, and again.

But remember, I grow up,
As you grow older.

Wonderful sleepovers.
Cuddle time,
Each morning, so warm.
Musky smells of sleeping …
Perfume.
Yours, mine – mixing;
Just comfort.
Feeling good, feeling loved.
Arms squeezing me,
Pressing, turning, leaning.
My lips against smooth soft
To rough sandpapery.
Smells of bed, of warmth
Of sleep, of love,
Of you, and me.

But remember, I grew
So quickly;
As you aged.
I change each day, each hour,
Each minute and second.
Only in a small ay,
But I will never be
The same again.

But you change, too.
More rapidly, it seems.
From black to gray,

312

To white or bald.
From young to older
From older to old.
From vibrant, and vital, to …
Just too tired.
From so active,
To so inactive.
From player,
To observer.
Your love stays,
Always the same.
But I am growing,
Silently distant,
Watching.
Moving further away.

Those, still first,
For now,
Perhaps forever.

Then, new faces,
Younger, louder, running,
Talking, shouting.
Sharing all my feelings,
And smiles, and laughter, and thoughts
Excitement!
But I will remember,
Always,
Mostly the smells
And your love,
Just there, always.

I know that you want me.
But this cannot be,
You will have to stay
On the side,
With growing crowds
Of others joining my life.
Never first,
Maybe second now.
Later when SHE comes,
You may be third, fourth,
Or even … Oh, I don't know.

But you will be there,
In my heart, my mind
For whatever days we're allowed.

At times, For a very short while,
You were first,
A wonderful first.
When they went away,
They left me w ith you.
So short a time.
You remembered HIM
Of so long ago.
You made me HIM
You played THEM.
I was yours, you mine.
They returned,
It was over.
I will remember it always,
I did not want to leave you,
But I grow,
As you age.

School; new life begins,
And passes, quickly.
New sights, friends,
Learning, laughing,
Playing, competing
And growing.
Sports, studies, cars;
Freedom, breathing free.
New thrills, racing, speed, games
New Laughter.
Girls, girls, girls,
Kissing, holding, sighing,
Sometimes saddened,
Occasionally crying.
Only you really know,
And only you can understand.

I get older, bigger,
You, so much older,
Even smaller.

I need much more.
Running with runners,
For hours and hours.
Playing endlessly,
For days and days.
It measures unfairly,
To our shared, slow paced minutes.
But that is all you can give.

Still I need more.
Him and him, her and her,
And them.
But especially, HER
Isn't she so beautiful?
Just like you.
Today, still, to some degree,
At least, I see it.
But certainly in those pictures,
When you were so young,
But now HER,
To talk with, to dream with.
To fill my days,
And nights,
And thoughts.
To play with, to laugh with,
Share secrets and love,
And dreams.

I steal from the little time
That is so preciously yours,
Because I grow older
You much older.
And I need so much more

Was it only moments ago,
You filled so many of my needs?
My world has grown
Expanding so much
As yours shrinks,
Again and again.

It saddens me,
But I must breathe …
New fresh air.
And your future can only …
Stifle me.
But I will always be there.

Forgive me, For I must grow
And I will forgive
That you must age.
You have affected me so.

Look back!
I am both of you.
Remember, and you see,
That in me,
There is so much of you,
To live on,
To love,
To work,
To create new life.
A new me,
Another part of you.

Through me
You will never die.
Look at me!
See that I give you
Your dreams.
Through me,
Eternity forever.
For I am you,
As you were me.

Now I know my future.
You taught me
To love,
Unselfishly,
To live,
To enjoy.
But also to miss
And I shall miss you so.

REQUIEM FOR GRANDPARENTS

COMMENTARY

This is free verse, do not look for rhyme or meter, you will be disappointed. About a century ago, our best poets started to write in free verse. While I enjoy the rhymes, removing the pressure of rhyming allows the poet to write from their heart. This poem is about a boy and his grandparents growing chronologically, but unfortunately, aging also. If you were as fortunate as I to have loving grandparents, you will understand this poem. Read and re-read free verse slowly. There is much to digest. I apologize for the extensive length of my poem and my comment. The poem is worth reading. My grandparents, I do miss them so.

HOSTILE FEAR

Stop my child,
Carry not fear.
It is this very fear
That diminishes all you are,
All that you can be.

The ill that you fear so
Will be brought to you
Certainly.
Because the fear
Eats your strength.

Empty the hostility
From your mind,
Thoughts created by fear.
Hostility can only harm
And lead to your destruction.

Learn to look with glee.
Enjoy all the beauty you see.
All that is there and will be
Created as God's view,
To be gifted to you.

Carry not fear
Empty the hostility
Live life for the joy
Fulfill your destiny too
See the beauty in your sight.

NOT OF HER BLOOD

A stranger
Married to a close
But distant
Loving cousin.

Always thoughtful
Nice, easy talker.
Tentatively offered
Friendship accepted.

Always included,
Family familiar.
Intimacy shared,
Conversation meaningful.

Then once,
Benignly approached,
She struck clawed
Drawing mind blood.

Explanation proferred.
"You didn't know
she can be that way."
~~Careful~~

LIFE'S OBSERVATIONS

TELL ME

Has the earth aged
Since I was born?
Are there changes of note
Since that remote day?

Or is the passage of less
Then a century so
Insignificant to leave
No mark of its passing?

I notice the changes
In my mirror, in my eyes,
Yet in tomorrows, this
Will be of no note~nothing.

The stone I leave behind,
Marking my passing will
Diminish in memory until
Future decades will forget who I was.

Does immortality of soul buy
A few more years of recognition
Of this life and old
Cold remembrance stone?

I think not because I can
Remember three generations
Before, perhaps two after.
Yes, that is all that touched me

It is the non-existant present
And a little of my yesterdays,
And my tomorrows, a life so brief,
Yet added together as all that makes me.

THE BODYGUARD

watched her every move
discretely, from a discrete distance,
only venturing forth
when she beckoned.

he glanced away occasionally
then quickly picked up her red sweater
as she shopped and browsed,
unnoticed because of his skills.

he had mastered background camouflage
to an artful very natural state.
she never had to look for him.
only a single word or tilt head.

she relished the fact that
he was the most dangerous
man she had ever met.
she felt safety as a warm blanket.

the fact that he would give
his life for her was seductive.
his attacks at groups of men
to protect her made her breathless.

that was one of the things
about him when they first met.
she fell in love with him.
his pay was the reward of her.

LUCKY WOMEN

It suddenly dawned
on this tired mind
that while a woman
can think and dream
of romantic love, it is
soon diluted by the
stronger love of
her children, her parents
who suddenly become
miracles in her mind and
so many outside factors
that love of any
particular man is often
diminished in importance.
at the same time, most
men in love keep this
love for a woman
at the same level
unless decreased
by physical turnoffs
or life's misfortunes,
or transference to
another woman.
so a man in love
can love a woman
In a less diluted
purer, non-interrupted
perhaps higher way.
LUCKY WOMEN!

KILLERS
(occasionally the outlaw awakens)

the commonality was that
they were each mothers
two children apiece,
between two and four.

in a playground, they
befriended immediately.
everyday meetings and phone
calls. Emails and then love.

run away together, no
more demanding husbands.
but the children, that
was a problem, solvable.

drunk one night, they
came to a conclusion.
the children would always
interfere, poor fathers not an answer.

heaven was salvation.
all four, so beautiful. They
deserved a fast painless way
to heaven, to God's arms.

they would be angels,
so many people said they were.
a few doctor's visits
and they had enough pills.

they made magic
brownies. The kids
loved brownies.
these were special.

Outlaw poetry is not beautiful poetry. It is often tasteless, brings up topics we do not want to read about and in modern outlaw books consists of curse words, insults, defamation and a host of other insults to most of us. Do not want to read about or appreciate. Many of our best concrete poets write a bit of outlaw at times. It can be erotic, pornographic or just plain tasteless. In this particular poem, I allow you to write the end. In my mind, the mothers come back to reality at the right moment and throw away the brownies. It is up to you the reader to choose the ending.

LIGHTS OUT ON A GREAT DAY

Biology,
Love that word.
Fourteen
Years,
And everything so fine tuned.
Oh, what a great
Day.
Lord, thank you
For walking
Her
In front of me.
Oh, what a great
Day.
Look
At the way she
Moves that ass.
Thank you! Thank you! Thank you!

"Dude! You're looking at
my girl's ass?

LIGHTS OUT

THE LARGEST NUMBER
(Haibun)

In 1938,a nine year old boy conceived the idea of the largest number and for insurance, another much larger number. Both these numbers were so much larger then our concept of everything in the universe at that time. Thus the googol, a one followed by a hundred zeros and a googolplex, a 1 followed by a googol of zeros came into existence and were accepted by all of the mathematicians as much more number then could ever possibly be needed.

Now, seventy years later since this conception, the world has dramatically changed. We have explored the universe and expanded our ideas of our entirety dramatically. We have such powerful computers the ideas of such did not even exist seventy years ago, we have space ships, telescopes and the world wide web besides a massively expanded population. There is so much more particulate matter in our existence, so much more knowledge that the idea of a googol or a googolplex being the end all of all numbers that we may ever use should now be under challenge.

It is time that we expand the concept of the largest number. I propose that our new largest number grow each year to encompass and stay ahead of mankind's knowledge. Therefore I propose the only number that can stay ahead of our future because this number expands every year of our existence. It is an infinity number called the COLEPLEX. While based on the concept of a googolplex, it expands every year. The COLEPLEX for 2008 is a googolplex multiplied by one billion. For 2009, we will have a coleplex multiplied by one trillion. This is our infinity number because the COLEPLEX always stays ahead numerically of any possibility of increase in our knowledge, as long as there is intelligence in our universe.

> welcome new coleplex
> infinity's guarantee
> our newest number
>
> a number that never ends
> the Coleplex honors poets

Commentary: The Haibun is an ancient form of Japanese poetry that combines a prose part with a Haiku part. In this Haibun, I selected a Tanka as my Haiku. My first stanza is a senryu. While not a syllable counter, I did write a 5/7/5 7/7. Ask yourself a question. Why should the concept of the largest number not be a poetic concept?

TANKA AS WINTER BECOMES SPRING

winter oh winter
you have gone before you came
mild winter's beauty

the elderly so enjoyed
a little snow thrilled each child

march spring roars in wind
I smell the soothing warm breeze
green growth promised views

new life becomes my new joy
soon flower colors will paint

winter horror gone
I rejoice your disappear
spring and peace welcomed

this is God's season gifted
passed winters count time of lives

SLEEP ~~ I PRAY

Provacateur of my evening
Daydream of what will be.
Oh sleep, the unreliable.
The variable glue of my being.
Why do you behave so?

Tonight, perhaps a dream of
Dreams leaving me unconscious
To the world's taunts for an
Entire night, or will you be
As often you be, the teaser.

It is the teaser that I so fear.
There is must sleep, then jarred
Awake, the hours of thoughts
Till blessed fatigue wins, then
Cycled 'til awakening tired and ill.

You own me for eight hours of
Darkness, yet you control my life
Of tomorrows in all of its
Entirety, as the flip of a coin
Heads wonderful~~tails horror.

THE COUGH

The entire theater audience
Heard it. So loud, unmuffled,
A simple very deep cough
From a sick man without care enough
To cover his mouth, polluting the air.

What they did not see were the
Millions of infecting vapor molecules
Dispersed over the entire space of the
Theater, sucked into the air by the venting
Infecting everyone's air, poisoning lungs, throats.

The comedy play caused increased laughter,
Accompanied by the associated deeper breaths
That sucked the infectious vapors into
Everyone's nose, throat, sinuses and lungs.
None suspected the impending tragedy from comedy.

It started in two days. The first ten had
Simple sore throats, three sinusitis and two
Of the elderly developed a full pneumonia,
From which one died in the hospital. All
Because a man did not care to cover his mouth.

A murderer, yes, in a way, intentional,
Surely not, but just as deadly as a bullet
To the one elderly man who innocently died.
Such carelessness, even laziness.
An unmuffled cough can be deadly

A SEAT AT THE TABLE

was all he wanted for
years. Peyton was fourteen,
tired of sitting with the
kids. It was time to move.

one Friday night, his Ma
nodded and he sat at the
adult's table. Conversation
was simple. A yea or nay from him.

after supper, Ma gave him
his blue canvas jacket and pants
of the same color. Pa handed
him his old musket and raw lead ball.

"smooth them down Peyton, then
they'll go further then twenty feet.
Tomorrow you join the Maryland
Irregulars. You bring home honor."

he knew that honor meant
always protect the standard and he
would get that new medal, Medal of Honor,
and citizenship for the entire family.

he was fourteen and Shiloh was
tomorrow. He joined the march
after his name was recorded.
assigned as assistant standard bearer.

there was no training. He
ran and fired and stole
lead balls from the dead blue
or grey, brother, foe, friend.

when the standard fell, Peyton
picked up the flag and ran
straight at the startled grey
uniforms, who thought it was over.

the captain recorded the act
of bravery in his daily report.
Peyton lived most of the day,
But then died for eternity.

It wasn't a bullet, it wasn't
canon shrapnel, it was the same
type of raw lead that he smoothed
out for his very own musket

accurate at a little more then
twenty feet, a hand molded piece
of lead tore through whatever it
hit, totally mortal. Instant death.

the fourteen year old man,
who lived one day in battle
was sent home, torn body to be buried
Medal of Honor and citizenship for all.

Each war had its on definition for the ultimate in heroism. Originally thousands of Medals of Honor
were awarded in the Civil War for picking up the fallen standards.

I had written this poem as I watched the smoke in the air from my home, and the films (over and over) on the television. I was seeking answers. Why? Why? Why? I have rewritten this poem numerous times, and it is the most tearfully emotional work I have ever done. Shamefully, while New York is back, the towers are not. Shamefully the hatred and the threat of terrorism is worse than ever.

The Apocalypse From A Street Person's View – 9/11/01
To all the victims and their families

Startled, I awaken - surreal fantasy assaults my sleep shrouded eyes
What play is this?

Airplanes crashing those gleaming towers?
The majesty & power of America, exploding - afire?
I shake my head - My vision clears - I look again
It is gone .. It is all gone
Towers, no longer filing that space

Now a void, a cloud, torn gutted earth … twisted steel
Dust clouds exploding into the sky
of concrete, plaster, and stone
A cratered debris field **now** all that remains
from concrete & steel **built to last ages**
Gone, gone … all gone

Its once-proud war cry – I AM the US of A
No longer there, just a debris field
An ageless transplant of any city
Victim of endless wars, of any time
Of hatred and tumult and chaos
Of terror and terrorism, of thoughtless
Mindless, blinded … hate
Of tunnel-visioned people with hatred so great
They dance in the streets
As if their slaughter of innocents
Is **some** honorable victory

The cratered debris field of torn and gutted earth
The final resting place for, those too many, innocents

My tear-filled view, so horrible a vision
I plead in silent prayer – a prayer for the innocents
Please God, let them feel no pain – take them to heaven
Protect them from this horror
Keep them in everlasting peace and beauty

A world of dust envelops me, to blind my vision, and steal my breath
A last view brands my memory for eternity
Fire, heat, beyond belief – screams of pain assault my ears
It ends with a noise – what is it? An explosion? An earthquake?
Then a tower falls within itself

O silence, are you the voice of hell – or is it death that I hear?
The silence broken by a moan here, **and** over there
So few sounds from the thousands that should have been
A single muffled scream, there … there, only again, there
Oh God – Oh Lord – Oh Jesus – Oh Buddha – Oh Allah
Save me, help me – the pain …

Those men, faces I shall never see, rushing to save
The collapse extinguished their living
So sudden, alive … dead … Gone, gone, forever gone

These lives, stolen so young, or so old – but surely, too soon
You are the innocent victims of – Hate
All stand with me to mourn these thousands
Who will never, never rise again
To see the sun, to kiss the warmth of a child, a lover, a friend
Or see the ocean, a lake, the moon or the stars

But do not fear – the haters will pay a price, never imagined
Joy will turn to poison in their hearts
Mark this well you hate-filled people
What you see as victory – will burn your cause … forever
If you look beyond your hatred, you will see America as Phoenix
New York shall rise again – the towers greater for the world to see
Proud war cry, forever proclaimed
I AM the US of A – Don't ever again – tread on me

Now the final horror encompasses all my thought
Almost three thousand innocents – comprehend, I cannot
What have I/we done? What can I/we do?
Revenge, revenge, revenge, is all I think about
Against whom? Against who?

The unacceptable answer – attack them, and them
The unacceptable answer – kill, maim, destroy
But who and where?

The unacceptable answer – do nothing
Wait – but again, they will bomb and kill again
Eventually, they will kill themselves

The unacceptable answer – where is Harry Truman?

MAROONED

In a world of hate
I make my way
and accept my fate.

with wounds dealt not by choice
I seek the chalice,
a life to rejoice.

for no other knows this mind
whose joys and loves are there
only for me to find.

as I go through life
I age and weaken
by the burden of congenital strife.

'til near's so near the end
I carry no fear, only wondering
what's round that bend?

SHE / WHORE

Pushing a cart of all she owns,
She asked this friend loans.
A little money, make her way.
Help her survive another day.
Promising in morn by lifted skirt to pay.

He knew of never a paid return.
Her payment could be in a man's yearn,
But she had lived for years in dirt.
The stink of microbes would sure hurt.
There was no love in this old whore's skirt.

He'd rather see her live then die.
A five spot dropped before her eye.
She offered a look at what used to be.
But she had nothing left he wanted to see.
He said, "it's just a gift from me

SHOTGUN

Was what everyone called her,
Not to her face, of course. You've
Seen her standing next to countless
Presidents, forgettable in a Navy rain coat.

Shotgun gave that average look,
No makeup to speak of, wallpaper blend
But leather sling shoulder to right sleeve,
Held a sawed off 12 gauge shotgun.

Her 110 pounds of sinew and muscle
Made her the most dangerous woman
In the President's guard. Her expertise
With the shotgun made her the deadliest.

Once a month, she came to a secret
Range near my office. Repeated firing of the
Shotgun over two days caused muscle tears
And huge bruises and much pain. I was her Doc.

I started noticing her on television
Always searching the crowd and
Watching the President or First Lady.
She was always ready to give her life.

Her right arm always rigid by her side,
Swung in any direction that caught her
Attention. It amazed me that Shotgun
Knew her life was expendable.

I took care of her bruises every month
For her entire career. We never talked much,
I just did not have the clearance. I saw those little
Almost robotic muscles and fixed them.

Whenever I treated the damage
Of an abusive husband or boyfriend,
I would think of Shotgun and wish
I could send her around for a visit.

Warriors – To All the Veterans of War
(Haibun)

Two WWII Japanese Imperial Army soldiers were just found in the mountains of the Philippine Islands. Still armed, they were, respectively, eighty-five and eighty-seven years old. They were still fighting a war that they never knew had ended over sixty years ago. They stayed where their officer ordered them to remain until his return.

> sixty years of their lives
> and still at war and most dutiful
> totally disciplined
>
> to never know the touch of a woman
> to never know the warmth of a child

Water
(Classical Haiku)

> crystal clear water
> flows streaming blue-white beauty
> ~ wetness caresses

I Want To Think About It

A phrase I hear so often,
Especially now,
Recessionally speaking

No matter what the economy
The meaning is the same
In any retail store.

    NO! NADA! NEVER!
    Let me outta here now.

Watching A Woman

Putting on her socks,
Afterwards.

Is this more intimate,
More invasive
Then the act
Proceeding?

She is just a stranger,
Am I trespassing?
On her space,
Watching her
Put on her socks?

IN THE SHOE STORE!

A Most Important Walk

I watched the woman
With a determined stride,
Stretching long of reach,
Strong of stance, stable,
Making her way rapidly
Across the floor
As a swimmer against
The ocean's incoming tide.
I observed her important
Target, LADIES ROOM.

OH.

NAKED IN PARADISE

"no, it's a man."
"you're wrong, she's a woman."
"but the breasts are completely flat."
"her arms are raised over the chaise,
that flattens the breasts,
besides, her toenails are painted."
"oh, I guess you're right."

So now the poet was introduced
To naked in paradise at this resort.

The totally nude created another
Diagnostic quagmire.
Belly down, if you discounted hair,
You could only tell the difference
Among the younger sunbathers
The posteriors of the older ones
Adopted an identical look,
Regardless of gender.

Looking around the pool area,
There was definitely no sexiness
To all of this nakedness.

It is only romance or
Provacativeness that
Heats up the naked body.

Poor me, this is what
I had to put up with for
An entire week. I do have
To admit, I don't remember
What the beach looked like.

COMMENT: yes, I wore a bathing suit all week

THE BUFFET

Whale-like, but capable
Of rambling along on two feet,
They burst through the line
to sample everything first.

Then again and again
Until lunch added two or three
New pounds to their hulk,
Pounds not to be put to good use,

The added weight, the additional
Fat, minutely put more
Pressure on their hearts,
Squeezing, and shortening breath.

How many more buffets
Measured their remaining
Lives, until so suddenly, they
Could finally enjoy God's buffet.

Or the devil's continuous one.

For eternity

"HON"

"Yea, that's my name.
I noticed that you're
Also named Hon."
We all sat there
Stunned into disbelief
Sitting in the hot sun
On our escape vacation,
In the middle of an island
Flea market.

In the midst of thousands,
A familiar voice yells out
"Hon, I need forty dollars."
A dozen hands reach out
Each holding the money.
An unfamiliar woman pops
Out of the forest that
Grows pocketbooks and eats
Women and girls, looks at
The proffered money in
Mostly strange hands, grabs
One, gives him a kiss, yells
"thanks, Hon," and disappears
into that forest again.

Finally, mine appears with
Three enormous pocketbooks.
"Which two look best, Hon?"
women don't know that men
don't give a damn abou
pocketbooks or shoes.
It's "T and A" the whole way.
So I choose number one and three.
Whew, she also likes those two.
Thank you Lord!

A female voice booms
Out of the heavens,
"Your welcome, Hon."

POETIC MORBIDITY

"Poet. Why are you so morbid?
An expert on death and dying,
Depression and pain, sadness,
Loss, tears and tragedies, anger
Madness and illness? "

"Poet, why does love end
Always in your work?"

"It must be so dangerous
To be your lover, poet.
You know you will die,
Leave for another lover,
Cause eternal pain."

"Why should anyone
get involved with you
when they hear that morbid
phrase, I am a poet?"

"In my work and my life,
I am the observer, the witness
The viewer, the evesdropper."

"I write the truth, and so
much of life is tragic.
When you read my work
You read my observations
And only truth."

THE SMILES OF LITTLE FACES

An elderly man was asked
To say something about his memories.
"There were so many
Wonderful ones,
Tragic
Laugh makers
Tear jerkers.
There was a woman.
We shared life entirely,
But the one thing
I will take to my grave
Is the smiles of little faces.
That is my eternal memory.
It gave me such pleasure that I know it was God's plan."